SECOND SHIFT

SECOND SHIFT

THE INSIDE STORY OF THE
KEEP GM MOVEMENT

DAVID HOLLISTER • RAY TADGERSON
DAVID CLOSS • TOMAS HULT

Mc
Graw
Hill
Education

New York   Chicago   San Francisco   Athens   London   Madrid
Mexico City   Milan   New Delhi   Singapore   Sydney   Toronto

1 2 3 4 5 6 7 8 9   DOC   21 20 19 18 17 16

ISBN   978-1-259-64381-1
MHID   1-259-64381-6

e-ISBN   978-1-259-64382-8
e-MHID   1-259-64382-4

Library of Congress Cataloging-in-Publication Data

Names: Hollister, David
Title: Second shift : the inside story of the keep GM movement / David Hollister,
    Ray Tadgerson, David Closs and Tomas Hult.
Description: New York : McGraw-Hill, 2017. | Includes index.
Identifiers: LCCN 2016024410 (print) | LCCN 2016031926 (ebook) | ISBN
    9781259643811 (alk. paper) | ISBN 1259643816 | ISBN 9781259643828 () |
    ISBN 1259643824 ()
Subjects: LCSH: Industrial promotion—Michigan—Lansing. | Economic
    development—Michigan—Lansing. | General Motors Corporation. | Plant
    shutdowns—Michigan—Lansing. | Public-private sector cooperation—Michigan—
    Lansing. | Automobile industry and trade—Michigan—Lansing—Management.
Classification: LCC HC107.M53 I5335 2017 (print) | LCC HC107.M53 (ebook) |
    DDC 354.6/27—dc23
LC record available at https://lccn.loc.gov/2016024410

McGraw-Hill Education books are available at special quantity discounts to use
as premiums and sales promotions or for use in corporate training programs. To
contact a representative, visit the Contact Us pages at www.mhprofessional.com.

To Lansing's auto manufacturing workforce, and leaders from the UAW, GM, business, education, government, and the community, all of whom united to turn a decision to close plants into a successful campaign to convince GM to reinvest in mid-Michigan for decades to come.

CONTENTS

PREFACE

This book is the inside story of the "Lansing Works! Keep GM!" campaign and how a collaborative approach to solving complex problems turned a crisis into a gift that keeps on giving for Lansing, Michigan. It is also the codified description of the "Second Shift Model" solution for how communities around the world, companies residing in those communities, and business and policy leaders managing community relationships can move from crisis to collaboration in solving major problems. All insights, stories, and quotations are accurately depicted, as precisely as possible given historical accounts and writing flow, as the involved parties saw them in the context of the "Keep GM in Lansing" movement.

We believe that the "Lansing Works! Keep GM!" campaign provides a superb framework, learning experience, and comprehensive Second Shift Model for community engagement, commitment, and problem-solving mechanisms that can be used to tackle large-scale and complex crises and turn them into a collaborative win-win situation. Communities—small, medium, and large—depend on consistently having a viable infrastructure for economic development, and the Second Shift Model is presented in this book as a way to ensure that such dynamic success remains a constant even in the face of a potential transformational crisis.

The book's cover depicts the Otto E. Eckert Station power plant, adjacent to General Motors Lansing Grand River Assembly plant; the Olds Tower in downtown Lansing (now called Boji Tower); and the Lansing State Capitol building. The Grand River Assembly is one of GM's newest plants in North America. It was constructed in

1999 and is designed around GM's Global Manufacturing System, which focuses on maximum performance in safety, people systems, quality, customer responsiveness, cost, and environment. The historic 23-story Olds Tower, named after and built by automotive industrialist Ransom Eli Olds, is located at 124 Allegan Street in Lansing. On December 6, 2005, the building was included in the National Register of Historic Places. The Capitol takes us back to the Victorian era. Designed by Elijah E. Myers, one of the foremost architects of public buildings during the Gilded Age, the Lansing Capitol building contains over nine acres of hand-painted surfaces; it was dedicated to the citizens of Michigan in 1879.

We are very appreciative of the following 36 individuals who participated in lengthy interviews to capture the "Lansing Works! Keep GM!" campaign as accurately as possible and as completely as needed. Their commentaries served as the foundation for the content of this book. They are, including both of the lead authors of this book, in the order interviewed, Dave Hollister, Ray Tadgerson, Jim Zubkus, Joe Drolett, John Daher, Jack Davis, Mike Green, Bob Swanson, Ed Donovan, Steve Serkaian, Bill Adcock, Bruce McAtee, Randy Thayer, Jim Donaldson, Chris Holman, Paula Cunningham, Lou Anna K. Simon, Mark Hogan, Sean McAlinden, Janice Karcher, David Cole, George Fulton, Doug Rothwell, Virg Bernero, Bob Trezise, Tim Daman, Larry Meyer, Senator Debbie Stabenow, Governor John Engler, John Grettenburger Sr., Berl Schwartz, David Wiener, Alan Spitz, Joel Spitz, James Butler, and Bill Reed. These interviews were remarkably open, flexible, and in depth. The end result of the interviews is 807 pages of single-spaced notes, or some 330,506 words. The "data analysis" we did to capture the story in our book, while fascinating and accurate, scratches only the surface of the depth of these 36 interviews. The Second Shift Model, however, is based on a full analysis of the interviews, archival and current data, news stories, Mayor David Hollister's and Ray Tadgerson's materials and files, and the collective scientific input by the author team.

Many of the individuals mentioned are also featured in the film titled *Second Shift: From Crisis to Collaboration* (film.secondshift. org), which is a complement to our book (book.secondshift.org) and captures a documentary view of the "Lansing Works! Keep GM!"

story. We are grateful to the Michigan Institute of Contemporary Art for granting the license to build on and use the documentary film version of *Second Shift*, as approved by Glenna De Jong. We are also thankful to Terry Terry, founder and CEO, Tom Lietz, chief creative officer, and the team at MessageMakers located in Lansing's Old Town for facilitating various project details and for motivating us to write this book. Terry Terry served as executive producer and Tom Lietz served as producer and director of the *Second Shift* film that was created by MessageMakers.

Through the 807 pages of notes, thousands of advocates and supporters of General Motors in the Lansing area, and a large group of friends of the four authors in the community, we thank each and every one of you for creating a community of "Lansing Works!" In this context, we also sincerely thank Bob Swanson, finance director for Mayor David Hollister, for assisting us with fact checking across the interview notes and what went into the book.

From the perspective of Closs and Hult, as professors in the Eli Broad College of Business at Michigan State University, we are appreciative of the opportunity both to engage in a tremendously valuable dialogue with David Hollister and Ray Tadgerson on this project and to be part of capturing the uniqueness and the lessons of the "Lansing Works! Keep GM!" community development campaign. We thoroughly believe that integration of business and community development is vital to the success of the Lansing community (and all communities).

We also thank Knox Huston at McGraw-Hill Professional for spearheading this project, the second Hult and Closs business trade-book project in the last couple of years. McGraw-Hill Professional also published *Global Supply Chain Management* (2014), authored by Tomas Hult, David Closs, and David Frayer. Plus, the higher education division of McGraw-Hill is the publisher of textbooks by both Tomas Hult (*International Business* and *Global Business Today*) and David Closs (*Supply Chain Logistics Management*). Now, as then, Anne Hoekman is our go-to professional to catch our idiosyncrasies in writing style and copyediting.

Finally, General Motors has been in Lansing, Michigan, for more than 100 years—as discussed throughout our book—and strategically GM and Lansing have engaged in a great partnership built on knowledge, skills, trust, and the manufacture of high-quality auto-mobiles. More than 100 years also applies to the collective years the four authors of this book have been married to Christine Hollister, Dianne Tadgerson, Noel Closs, and Laurie Hult, respectively. We are grateful to General Motors for its commitment to Lansing and to our spouses for their commitment to us.

Lansing, Michigan
September 5, 2016
(Labor Day)

David Hollister
Ray Tadgerson
David Closs
Tomas Hult

CHAPTER 1

THE SECOND SHIFT MODEL

CHALLENGES AND OBSTACLES

S itting in his ninth-floor office in Lansing City Hall in 1994, newly elected Mayor David Hollister could look out his window and see two of the pillars that sustained the capital city's economy for generations: the majestic dome of the State Capitol and the smokestacks of the General Motors small car assembly plants. On the wall just to the right of the window hung three diplomas from Michigan State University, this representing the third pillar that had long provided stability and continuity to Mayor Hollister's Midwest auto manufacturing community.

Located in south central Michigan, some 90 miles northwest of Detroit, the City of Lansing enjoyed the economic benefits that accrue to a community from housing an automobile assembly opera-tion for more than 100 years. It was long understood that because of the complexity and logistics of manufacturing, there was about a 10-to-1 multiplier effect embedded in the Lansing automobile net-work, meaning that for every 1 auto worker employed on-site, 10 other jobs in the supplier, transportation, and service sectors were needed to complete the manufacturing process. For Lansing, this meant about 7,000 employees directly working for General Motors in the late 1990s, with some 20,000 jobs in Lansing connected to GM (e.g., suppliers) and with some 50,000 jobs around the state connected to GM's operations in Lansing.

Such a multiplier effect naturally means that mayors and com-munities compete vigorously to attract and retain these high-paying

Mayor David Hollister in his office at Lansing City Hall.
Hollister served as Lansing's mayor from 1994 to 2003.

jobs and the taxes and revenues they produce. Unfortunately, many Lansing citizens did not understand the full picture of the funda-mental transformation taking place as the 1990s drew to a close. Some even suggested that losing General Motors as a manufacturer in the community might not be that bad. The skills and knowledge in the region could then be used to produce other goods and services.

In some way, relatively newly elected mayor Hollister—tak-ing the oath of office on January 1, 1994, as Lansing's forty-fifth mayor—was not fully understanding of the impact of General Motors in the Lansing community either, although he and his team, of course, knew that GM was important. At the outset of his term, Mayor Hollister focused on building on Lansing's strengths and assets to become a world-class city. As did most in the community, he assumed that General Motors would always be the backbone of the local economy and the goal of world-class city recognition. After all, both his father and father-in-law had worked for GM for over 35 years and been successful in providing a middle-class lifestyle for their families.

It was easy to take GM for granted because of the 100-year history Lansing enjoyed with Oldsmobile and the excellent labor-management relations and the high-quality ratings the Lansing-produced cars received year after year. This attitude was true of newly elected mayor Hollister as he transitioned from the role of liberal, pro-labor activist and environmentally oriented lawmaker to chief executive officer of Michigan's fifth largest city and its state capital.

Hollister assumed that his major challenge as mayor would be to restore confidence in city hall, increase private investment, revitalize the central city, and grow the region. Little did he realize that it would require all his skills to create a new culture of collaboration and regional problem solving just to keep GM in the community. This ultimately became the Second Shift Model solution, to tackle "Lansing Works! Keep GM!"—far from the focus Hollister thought he would have during his first term in office.

Thankfully, the new mayor began developing a close relationship with Edward Donovan, the director of Municipal Government for General Motors, early in 1994. Donovan would regularly brief the mayor on the state of General Motors, its need to consolidate, downsize, reduce costs, become more efficient, and close older plants to stay competitive with international imports. This was an eye-opener, and the mayor became convinced that retaining GM would require a whole new way of thinking and acting if life as the community knew it was to continue.

Some two years later, in 1996, Hollister received what came to be called the "knock on the door" visit from Donovan. Donovan gave the mayor the good news that the Oldsmobile centennial would include a weeklong celebration bringing thousands of car enthusiasts to the region and that the new Alero would be built in the Lansing plant. But he also shared the bad news that after the Alero had run its course in 2004–2005, there were no products for the Lansing plants and it was GM's intent to close its Lansing operation.

Hollister and his leadership team immediately understood the dire consequences of such a decision for the Lansing area and knew that doing nothing was not an option. To convince GM to stay in Lansing required that Hollister rally regional leaders and develop a collaborative, strategic, and comprehensive plan for keeping GM. Party lines, old adversaries, and distant partners had to become close-knit strategic partners with a shared vision for the region. This sounded like an arduous task, and it was!

Before we go into the detailed framing of the Second Shift Model, we provide an overview of the evolution of the Lansing, Michigan, region from its development as a town in the middle of the forest to becoming the home and major production site of Oldsmobile, one of GM's major nameplates. We also talk about the challenges that the region faced when GM had to respond to the monumental changes in the global automobile market. Many of the communities with a similar reliance on the automobile industry did not have the vision or leadership to respond. In many cases, they still struggle today. The Lansing region did gather the leadership and develop that vision, and the result is high-tech production for a number of industries and a growing job market. The Lansing-based Second Shift Model is a model for all communities and organizations that are challenged by the rapidly changing, technological, and global twenty-first-century economy.

LANSING COMMUNITY

After Michigan became a state in 1837, the state constitution required that the capital be moved from Detroit to a safer and more central site within the state. During the War of 1812, Detroit had been captured by the British. There was also concern regarding the influence that the major population center in Detroit would have over the control of the rest of the state. Consequently, Lansing was designated as the state capital in 1847, albeit not as easily as writing that history down on paper! The Township of Lansing was only selected as the capital following frustrating negotiations with a number of the more developed communities around the state. Some of these analogous frustrations came to haunt the city again in the late 1990s with the potential GM shutdown in the community.

Lansing grew slowly in the early years but then began expanding rapidly with the founding of the Agricultural College of the State of Michigan in 1855 (now Michigan State University) and the establishment of the Olds Motor Vehicle Company in 1897. The college was the pioneering and original "land grant" college and was located in East Lansing, five miles east of the downtown and Capitol. Land grant colleges were established to provide regular citizens with the applied knowledge to support their careers in agriculture and manufacturing. There are now 76 land grant colleges and universities in the country, and Michigan State University served as the blueprint for the 75 that came after its 1855 founding.

The Lansing region grew with increased employment in its three primary sectors: (1) state government, (2) automotive assembly, and (3) higher education. By 1996, the employment base of the state government included approximately 64,000 direct jobs statewide, with a significant number being in Lansing. MSU's academic environment provided approximately 15,000 direct and indirect jobs and more than 50,000 students (with several thousand more students at Lansing Community College and other institutions of higher learning in the Lansing community).

The automotive assembly operations included original equipment manufacturing, primarily operated by General Motors, as well as other suppliers and logistics operators. In 1996–1997, General Motors operations had an impact on about 27,000 direct and indirect employees in the region (7,000 at the Lansing plants and 20,000 in the area who supported the plants). For many of these employees, GM was a lifetime employer with wages and benefits that established the middle class for the region. In many families, including Mayor Hollister's, multiple generations worked for GM, each increasing its toehold on the middle class.

As a result, Lansing attained its highest population of 131,414 in the 1970 census. The inclusion of the surrounding suburbs and bedroom communities brought the 1970 Standard Metropolitan Statistical Area (SMSA) population to 378,423. By 2000, the Lansing population had declined to 119,128, and many individuals had moved to the suburbs, with the SMSA population increasing to 447,734. While the region was growing, the population of Lansing itself had decreased by 10 percent in the 30 years since its high point. The City of Lansing covered over 36 square miles, while the SMSA covered much of four counties.

It is accurate to say that the Olds Motor Vehicle Company played a major role in the Lansing and mid-Michigan economy for much of the twentieth century. Olds was making automobiles in Lansing even before Ford began making cars in Detroit! The number of cars the company built grew from 600 cars in 1901 to 3,000 in 1903. Employment at the company grew from less than 1,000 in the early 1900s to more than 15,000 by the 1970s. With changes in GM's strategy and the decline in the demand for American-made automobiles, Oldsmobile's employment in Lansing dwindled to zero with the elimination of the Oldsmobile brand at the end of 2004. During that 100-year span, over half of the 35 million automobiles manufactured by Oldsmobile were built by workers from the Lansing region.

Olds hired employees who came from around the region as well as from around the eastern part of the United States. While many of the employees had mechanical experience from their previous manufacturing jobs, some were from farms in the region and had developed their experience by keeping the farm equipment operating. Many employees had also migrated from the South during World War II.

Due to this extended community involvement, Lansing was known as an Oldsmobile town—residents had the highest per capita Oldsmobile ownership in America, the local minor league Single-A baseball stadium completed in 1996 was named Oldsmobile Park, and many community buildings and sites were tied to the Olds name. The Lansing region clearly reflected the strong characteristics (skills, knowledge) of a manufacturing company town, but the region also had the unique strength that derived from being home of the state government and academic institutions, such as Michigan State University and Lansing Community College.

Lansing Car Assembly produced many of the Oldsmobile nameplates over the years. Some of the more recent nameplates include the Oldsmobile 88, 98, Cutlass, and Alero, along with short runs of the Pontiac Grand Am and Chevy Malibu. These cars were produced in a 180-acre assembly complex, some of the buildings dating back to the early 1900s. Like many Midwestern manufacturing complexes that were built in downtown areas, the Oldsmobile headquarters and the assembly plant were located, next to downtown Lansing, along the Grand River. Employee homes extended out beyond the downtown assembly plant for many miles. The plant, the city, and the community were entrenched and prospered.

In the 1960s and 1970s, all it took was a nameplate from one of the "Big Three" carmakers (General Motors, Ford, and Chrysler) to sell a car. With the growth of the middle class, the Big Three

Olds Motor Works, Lansing, Michigan, circa 1905
*(Detroit Publishing Co., available for use from the Library of
Congress, www.loc.gov/item/det1994017708/PP)*

sold over 12 million cars per year. During the 1960s and 1970s, Lansing Car Assembly had a capacity of over 2,000 cars per day in a two-shift operation. With the introduction of foreign cars into the United States in the late 1970s and 1980s, however, the domestic automobile industry began to be challenged by poor quality and increasing cost.

ECONOMIC DRIVERS

While the economic environment in the greater Lansing region included the three pillars of automotive manufacturing, state government, and educational institutions (most notably Michigan State University), a major factor was the relationship between the City of Lansing and General Motors Corporation.

In 1997, General Motors was the largest firm in the Fortune 500 and had revenues of more than $168 billion and profits of almost

$5 billion. GM had 16 percent of the world market and 31 percent of the North American market in 1997. General Motors was, at the time, an aggregation of six major car and truck lines (Buick, Cadillac, Chevrolet, Oldsmobile, and Pontiac, as well as GMC trucks), brands that had been acquired over the first 30 years of the twentieth century. Buick and Chevrolet had grown up in Flint, Michigan. Cadillac and Pontiac had grown up in Detroit and Pontiac, Michigan. The Oldsmobile headquarters and major production facilities began in Lansing and still remained there after 100 years.

Throughout the later part of the twentieth century, General Motors included not only the car assembly operations but also many of the so-called first-tier suppliers, including Delco Electronics, Delphi, and Saginaw Steering Gear. The corporate philosophy was that GM could maintain its intellectual property and economies of scale through the integration of the first-tier operations and assembly plants.

However, in many cases, each nameplate and model was built in a single plant, thus reducing the potential for production synergies and economies of scale. This resulted in limited exchange of expertise and reduced flexibility as demand for different car models evolved. The GM assembly plants included Arlington, Texas; Buick City (Flint, Michigan); Craft Assembly (Lansing, Michigan); Flint Truck (Flint, Michigan); Fort Wayne, Indiana; Lake Orion (Pontiac, Michigan); Lansing Car Assembly (Lansing, Michigan); and Lordstown, Ohio.

Over time, GM began to consolidate the products in each of these plants to move toward standardization and increased economies of scale. While the consolidation provided financial benefits, it also resulted in the car platforms for the different brands becoming more similar. For many consumers, it became difficult to tell the difference between a Buick Century, a Chevrolet Malibu, and an Oldsmobile Cutlass. This resulted in cannibalization of sales across product lines and a detraction in (at least) perceived quality across many of the GM brands.

So while the market accepted this commonality when the demand for automobiles was growing and there was not substantial competition for the Big Three, the slowdown in the demand for cars and the introduction of foreign competitors changed the entire environment. As noted by David Cole, former director of the Center for Automotive Research, Ann Arbor, Michigan: "In the 50s, we had three domestic auto manufacturers who ruled the roost. Volkswagen came in with the Bug or the Beetle, then a little later the Japanese arrived and gradually the market share of the domestics began to erode . . . and led to overcapacity and serious competitive problems because the new guys were building factories . . . Honda in Maryland and Toyota in Kentucky . . . they had relatively young workers, minimal cost for health care and retiree cost so the competitive position for GM began to deteriorate fairly significantly."

The result was too much capacity. The demand was also for cars that were differentiated and met increasing quality demands. As commented on by Sean McAlinden (vice president for Strategic Studies and chief economist for the Center for Automotive Research): "One of the things that Lansing got caught in was the idea that there is too much capacity. They were losing $1,000 per small vehicle. . . . The GM Board told management that every small car plant in the U.S. and Canada should immediately move to Mexico."

THE CHALLENGE

In 1994, Mayor Hollister met and developed an excellent working relationship with Ed Donovan (director of Government Relations for General Motors). In his 16 years working with local governments, Donovan interacted with officials on many issues that determine a manufacturing plant's success, such as water rates, zoning, labor-management relations, tax rates, environmental regulations, workforce training, infrastructure, law enforcement, and fire protection. Donovan explained that his job was "to ensure that all of these elements, whether it was the water rate issue, or it was property tax issues, or it was zoning issues, or all the things that happen over the life of a plant, could effectively be done and understood by all the parties because not everyone has the same perspective on how it gets done."

While complex, these issues could be addressed when General Motors was enjoying 40 percent market share. All of that began to change in the late 1970s and early 1980s as foreign imports, environmental regulations, technology demand for a higher-skilled workforce, and changes in consumer demands and expectations—combined with an international recession—forced GM to make significant changes. When Mayor Hollister first took office in January 1994, there were extensive discussions between Hollister and Donovan regarding the need for GM to work more closely with municipal governments than they had in the past due to the complexity of some of these issues. Donovan was skeptical. He knew of Hollister's liberal pro-labor voting record in the Michigan legislature, his strong labor support, and the Lansing business leader's decision not to support him in his run for mayor. As a formality, he made an appointment to brief the new mayor on GM's global position; the multiple economic, environmental, and market forces cutting into GM's market share; and the forces driving the need for efficiencies, innovation, consolidations, and downsizing.

Later, in 1996, Donovan made an unscheduled visit to the mayor's office, a visit that became known as the "knock on the door." Donovan informed Hollister of the pending decision to consolidate all the major engineering and management operations in Detroit, which would mean the loss of the Oldsmobile brand and headquarters from mid-Michigan. He cushioned the blow by unveiling the good news—that a Centennial Series of cars (Aurora, Intrigue, and Alero) would be launched and produced as part of the 100-year history of Oldsmobile and that the Alero would be manufactured in the Lansing plants.

Donovan also shared that a weeklong Oldsmobile hundredth birthday celebration would take place in August 1997 and bring thousands of vintage Oldsmobiles and 150,000 car enthusiasts to Lansing. He also confided that while not yet official nor public, GM had no further products for the aging Lansing plants, so production would conclude at the end of the Centennial Series cycle, expected to be no later than 2005.

Unlike any other U.S. mayor that Donovan had ever met with, Mayor Hollister responded that, "Not only will we make the Alero investment work, but we will put together a strategic approach to assure the long-term viability for a General Motors presence here, which includes making sure we have the supplier network and the economics that make GM's Lansing operation competitive in the global marketplace and keeps our manufacturing sector intact."

Donovan didn't think that the longevity plan would be possible because of the direction the corporation was heading but agreed to work with the new administration to facilitate the launch of the Alero. Donovan was impressed and commented that "after my first meeting with Hollister, [I noticed] two things about him that I saw infrequently around America: one he had a grasp of the totality of it all and second was that he had a win-win approach."

Donovan continued: "General Motors, like all automobile companies, was going through massive rethinking of how they had to compete in the marketplace. The ability to maintain a product portfolio that oftentimes went back to the turn of the century, meaning 1900, was under threat. There were all these different forces that were coming into play in Lansing. They were coming into all GM facilities, plus market share was being compressed . . . at one time well over 40 percent . . . and now down to 35 or 30 percent. There were plants [all over the country] that were built in 1900, 1915, and 1925 that had obsolete manufacturing capacity. Well in most cases, once the decision is made [to close a plant], it was irreversible." Hollister wanted to hear or agree with none of that.

GM plants that were actually closed during the mid-1990s included Baltimore, Maryland; Buick City in Flint, Michigan; Dayton/Vandalia, Ohio; Doraville, Georgia; Grand Rapids, Michigan; Janesville, Wisconsin; Linden, New Jersey; Livonia, Michigan; Mansfield, Ohio; Massena, New York; Moraine, Ohio; North Tarrytown, New York; Oklahoma City, Oklahoma; Pittsburgh, Pennsylvania; Pontiac, Michigan; Saginaw, Michigan; Shreveport, Louisiana; Trenton, New Jersey; Willow Run, Michigan; and Wilmington, Delaware. It should not have been a surprise that the Lansing plants were scheduled to be phased out as well.

Hollister reported that he was stunned by the announcement. The closure of the Lansing Car Assembly, without the building of a new plant, would take away over 7,000 direct jobs (people employed by GM), another 20,000 indirect jobs in the Lansing area (e.g., suppliers), and some 50,000 jobs in the rest of Michigan (various vendors to GM). He realized that this was a historic moment, and it was scary. In the entire history of General Motors, once the corporation announced a plant shutdown, it had never changed its mind, but Mayor Hollister made known his intent to form a blue ribbon committee to persuade GM to reverse its decision to leave.

At the time, the media buzz was not exactly positive. Initially, many media outlets, including the *Lansing State Journal*, Lansing's *City Pulse*, and local TV stations, were outright negative about the campaign to keep GM in Lansing. Thankfully, most, if not all, media came around. Though continued skepticism was expressed in a *Lansing State Journal* editorial on February 25, 1998, it reflected the general consensus: "There is little to lose by making a united pitch to General Motors to keep its car making operations here."

The launch of the Alero became a key part of a dynamic and evolving strategy to convince GM corporate officials in Detroit to continue to invest in the Lansing facilities even though they had privately decided to end all production after 2005. Complicating the task for Lansing community leaders was the illusion of normality created by the hype of the 100-year celebration of Oldsmobile and the announced Alero–Grand Am production in Lansing. Plus, the region's municipal and political leaders were just beginning to know, but not yet necessarily trust, the newly elected Lansing mayor.

The efforts were also scattered, not coordinated, and perhaps even had competing interests. For example, the Lansing Regional Chamber of Commerce was continuing its traditional retention efforts and had no specific plan to face the gathering storm (crisis). Fortunately, the Lansing mayor and Ed Donovan struck up a working relationship that was unusually trusting, one that allowed the mayor access to GM's most closely kept secrets. For example, Hollister knew long before it became public that corporate consolidation would compel the relocation of Oldsmobile management and engineering staff to Detroit, that the Oldsmobile nameplate and brand would be retired, and that there was no product for Lansing's aging facilities after 2005. But Mayor Hollister was not yet at liberty to share the confidential information publicly.

Hollister could, however, use the corporate knowledge he was building by actively engaging in the Alero launch to create strong personal and professional relationships that earned him an unofficial position on the General Motors–United Auto Workers problem-solving team. It was from this position that he learned that GM was considering a new plant somewhere in America, but surely not

Michigan, to test and implement a next-generation advanced manufacturing platform and facility. This new GM plant was intended to surpass its European and Asian competitors and usher in a new labor-management era.

So Hollister and his partners set out in the period between 1996 and 1997 to make sure the centennial launch of the Alero was the best ever. Looking back, 1997 was also the turning point as Mark Hogan (vice president of GM's Car Group North America, point person on the Alero launch, and corporate leader for GM's next-generation platform and facility) let it be known in an interview with the *Lansing State Journal* that there would be no GM product for Lansing after 2005. He also said, though, that mid-Michigan could be in the running for the next-generation facility even though such a facility being built in Lansing was highly unrealistic at the time. This was the first public acknowledgment of GM's intent to close existing Lansing plants and to shift production to a new facility. To understand how Lansing persevered through this turbulent period, one has to understand Lansing's history and DNA.

PULSE OF LANSING

At the state level, then governor John Engler reflected: "Well, I think the announcement came obviously as not a complete surprise because the company [GM] was going through a lot of challenges. I think when any announcement comes like that, it impacts a community significantly. I mean General Motors, Oldsmobile, had been a part of Lansing almost from the beginning. You had Michigan State University out in the East, Oldsmobile downtown, and then state government. Those three legs of the stool represent the Lansing economy in large part. Well, as a governor you want to see your state growing. You would like to see the entire state growing. So a loss whether it's a decision to close a plant as one auto company did in Willow Run, or to move the headquarters out of the state, or even when two companies consolidate and somebody ends up disappearing, all of that matters."

Debbie Stabenow, U.S. senator from Michigan who also previously served as U.S. representative for Michigan's Eighth District which includes Lansing, echoed Governor Engler's sentiments: "I was horrified, I think along with everyone else, when I first heard about GM pulling out of Lansing. I grew up in a General Motors family. Oldsmobile had always been a part of my life, and when we found out what was going to happen, I was really afraid and worried about my community, and what was going to happen to Lansing." Clearly both Republicans and Democrats understood and appreciated the value of having a stronghold of GM production in Lansing.

When then provost and now president Lou Anna K. Simon of Michigan State University heard the news, she reflected: "So when you feel like you are making enormous progress on what people say they want to have occur, then all of a sudden the rug seems to be pulled out from under you, I think everyone was shocked. . . . Well, I think if you look at this community, GM is an important part of it."

Sanjay Gupta, the Eli & Edythe L. Broad Dean of the Broad College of Business at Michigan State University, agreed with President Simon's sentiments and said that "continuous collaboration between MSU's Broad College of Business, General Motors, and the greater Lansing community has become a way of life and part of our community's fabric, and we are actively working to ensure that there are no more rugs being pulled out from underneath us. The climate in the community is now one of win-win, also a testament to the work done while David Hollister was Lansing's mayor."

Steve Serkaian, Mayor Hollister's communications director, reflected on his initial thoughts: "It was kind of a story a lot of folks didn't pay attention to. Here you had General Motors with a 100-year presence in Lansing. All of a sudden there was the amorphous news story in the *Lansing State Journal* that signaled that General Motors didn't have a new product for its assembly operation in Lansing. I initially thought it was nothing more than a negotiating tactic for GM's negotiations with UAW. But later I learned it was something a lot more, a lot more serious. When Hollister communicated that to me and his cabinet, I just kind of sat there. I didn't really know what to make of it."

It was clear that the announcement had caught politicians and residents of the Lansing region and the rest of the state by surprise. The region had been used to having GM assembly operations provide the Lansing region with a strong economic base, and it now looked like that foundation was crumbling. One hundred years, since 1901, and now possibly gone forever! In some way, those 100 years created a certain resolve in Mayor Hollister. While prior to his election he had envisioned Lansing as a "world-class city" and the surrounding region as a world-class environment, his focus now turned to keeping GM, and—perhaps unlike many politicians—he would initiate a collaborative effort to convince GM to stay. The early challenge to accomplish this feat was to get the region to work together.

Robert L. Trezise, Jr., then executive director of the Lansing Economic Development Corporation (and now CEO of the Lansing Economic Area Partnership), still remembers the day. He recalls: "I had actually worked for Delta Township and I still remember very distinctly being in my office and receiving a call in the afternoon from the *Lansing State Journal*. They said they were going to be running a major article tomorrow morning and it is going to discuss the total closure of the GM plants, plural. Again, recall that there was a lot of historic tension between the townships, cities, and the State of Michigan. I mean real tension, they really didn't like one another."

John Daher, the Lansing Township supervisor at that time (a charter township surrounding the City of Lansing), reflected that "back in the 70s, 80s, and 90s, many of these communities were somewhat isolationist. They were kind of independent silos just taking care of themselves, not too concerned about what was happening to their neighboring communities. . . . There was a lot of contention among the political jurisdictions. East Lansing was interested in taking whatever land they could, and Lansing was interested in taking whatever land they could, and that's the reason why we had a supervisor that quit in the middle of his term. Another supervisor was defeated. A third supervisor was recalled because there was concern that she was just too close to Lansing and she was interested in pursuing some of the same interest that we're pursuing today, regionalism."

Early on, due to all the region's fractional bases and interests, it was clear that any "Keep GM" solution would have to be collaborative and transformational. The conflict between the individual communities, the firms, and the unions would not help. There was a need for a significant culture change in the community. MSU president Simon said that "the campaign model works if you're organized, persistent, and have a great product to sell, but what we've done is to move beyond a campaign into a culture change for the community." Along those lines, Mike Green (president of United Auto Workers Local 652) noted: "Historically, people don't like change. Nobody does. You get in a comfort zone, and you don't really want to change from that. Well, if you're going to be building cars in the United States, you need to get on board. . . . When you empower people to do something and you give them the tools to do it, they are hungry to do it . . . and they did a great job of it."

To achieve such a collaborative, transformational culture change, there was need for an organized effort between the state and regional politicians, economic developers, private-sector firms, labor unions, educators, and the region's residents.

THE ENVIRONMENT

Lansing's Mayor

David Hollister attended Lakeview High School in Battle Creek, Michigan, where he was interested in politics, football, and journalism. He graduated from Lakeview in 1960. Hollister then attended Kellogg Community College, earning an associate's degree, and Michigan State University, earning bachelor's and master's degrees in history and government. He was awarded an honorary doctorate from Michigan State University in 1997 for his civic leadership in the Lansing community. He has served at the local, regional, and state government levels since 1968, with his first public office being on the Ingham County Commission.

In 1974, Hollister was elected to the Michigan House of Representatives, where he served until 1993. He served on the powerful appropriations committee and chaired the social services appropriations subcommittee for over a decade. Hollister sponsored and was instrumental in passing significant legislation in such areas as open meetings, right to die, hospice, adoption reform, mandatory seat belts, clean water, Blue Cross Blue Shield reform, and anti-redlining and neighborhood improvement. To achieve these accomplishments, Hollister created task forces and coalitions of stakeholders who were instrumental in helping to nurture the development of the legislation and advocating for passage.

His role as Lansing's mayor began in January 1994. Hollister was elected in 1993 and reelected in 1997 and 2001. Throughout his career, Dave understood the importance of simplifying complex ideas to facilitate understanding. *Vision, plan, partners,* and *perseverance* (VP3) was one of those formulas that he claimed guided his several personal career choices, but he also applied it to communities as they sought to undertake a significant change or meet a specific challenge. As a new mayor in 1994, Hollister quickly embraced and articulated VP3 as an organizing principle for his new administration. In his first inaugural speech he called on citizens of the greater Lansing region to join him in embracing the vision that Lansing could become a world-class city. Thereafter every major initiative was measured, evaluated, and marketed on its role in achieving this goal.

In this framework, once vision is articulated, understood, and accepted, a plan is needed to achieve the goal or vision. Hollister had a clear perspective on this. First, the plan needs to be relatively simple and easy to understand and has to be clearly aligned with vision. With the vision and plan in place, assembling a broader set of key strategic partners to share in the endeavor begins. Assembling the most diverse, inclusive, comprehensive set of stakeholders is the most critical task of a leader. This group of stakeholders functions as the problem solvers, the advisors, the reality checkers, and the advocates for the vision and the plan. Second, all segments of the community need to be part of a well-operating collaborative coalition, and the broad cross section of stakeholders in the strategy group needs to function in a transparent manner to develop trust and mutual respect, always seeking win-win solutions. Third, constant two-way communication needs to be established and maintained within the group and externally, with a constant reminder of the vision and plan.

Even with a clear and accepted goal, a well-developed and understood plan, and a coalition of committed partners, there will still be setbacks and failures, so perseverance is a critical part of the formula. In a complex technological, international economy, the community will be constantly challenged, but if the community has a vision, a well-understood plan, engaged and empowered partners, and the willingness to work to find win-win solutions and persistently problem-solve, the community will be successful. "Win-win solutions" was a mantra of Hollister's. This governing philosophy was evident from the beginning of his first term and throughout his three terms as mayor. Many people contend that the relationships Hollister built prior to the "Lansing Works! Keep GM!" campaign were critical to his success in bringing diverse groups together at a time of potential economic crisis in 1997.

City Seal and the Vision

When Hollister took office, nothing captured the sense of malaise and lack of vision and stagnation more than Lansing's city seal. The seal featured a pioneer cutting down a dead tree. What? So one of Hollister's first initiatives was to assemble a diverse Image Task Force made up of regional public relations firms and media executives and charge the members of the task force to come up with a modern logo that captured a sense of vitality and renewal.

An Image Summit was held in April 1994. In August that year, the city unveiled a new logo, a multimedia image campaign, and a media blitz totaling $1 million in free advertising. The Lansing City Council would subsequently adopt the popular new logo as the city's official seal.

Hollister focused on this symbolic initiative because he felt that the region needed a fresh start, a unifying vision, and a sense of action and coming together. While the focus groups liked the idea of Lansing being a world-class city, there was an overwhelming consensus that it was not there yet. But the new logo and yearlong media campaign provided hope and encouragement that "we are making it happen!"

Seal of the City of Lansing, Michigan

CATA Transportation Center

A symbol of the ineptitude of Lansing was the decades-long effort to upgrade the Capital Area Transportation Authority (CATA). While each year for a decade the legislature had appropriated and set aside funding for a new Lansing facility, the city administration, CATA officials, and the Lansing City Council could never agree on a location. So each year the funding would lapse and return to the state. This sounds somewhat amazing but was emblematic of some of the root problems demonstrating lack of collaboration and weak decision making in the region at the time.

Hollister saw the CATA situation as an important project, both substantively and symbolically. Playing off his 19-plus years in the legislature and 16 years on the Michigan House of Representatives Appropriations Committee, he went before his former colleagues and asked for one final year of funding, pledging that if there was no action on locating a downtown facility in that budget cycle, the city would forgo the state grant and let the funds lapse and be redirected to a more deserving and better coordinated community—a gutsy move that paid off.

Armed with this agreement from the legislature, the Lansing City Planning Department brought the stakeholders together, agreed on a location, secured the land, awarded the project to a local developer, and monitored the project so it came in on time and under budget. Local press coverage was extensive, as this was seen as an early test of the administration's management skills. And now several years later, it appeared as a logical, easy, and needed upgrade to the CATA system. But history has a way of repeating itself.

Minor League Baseball and Insurance

The CATA media coverage caught the attention of Tom Dickson, executive vice president with the Chicago-based Leo Burnett advertising firm (one of the largest advertising agencies in the country). Dickson had as one of his main responsibilities the Oldsmobile account.

Tom and his wife, Sherri (profiled in *Women Entrepreneurs Only*, a book featuring 12 prominent female entrepreneurs in the United States), were co-owners of the Springfield Sultans, a Single-A minor league baseball team associated with the Kansas City Royals. The Midwest League had undertaken a multiyear effort to upgrade its operations, facilities, and marketing. The Dicksons were looking to relocate the team after officials in Springfield, Illinois, turned down a proposal to provide economic incentives to upgrade its aging and outdated stadium. The couple was forced to look for a new home for the team or forfeit the team's standing in the Midwest League.

Due to his ties to Oldsmobile marketing, Tom Dickson was a frequent visitor to Lansing. He was also aware of the Lansing City Council's interest in minor league baseball. The City Council had even created a blue ribbon committee in August 1993 to investigate the feasibility of a minor league baseball team operating in the city. While the members of the council-sponsored group identified strong community interest, they didn't have a team owner or a developer committed to the project, so the idea went dormant until Dickson made an appointment with the new mayor to explore his interest in minor league baseball.

Hollister welcomed Tom's interest in Lansing but was reluctant to convert one of its premier parks or one of its four golf courses into a baseball facility. He was, however, interested in cleaning up the "sin strip" that besmirched the entryway to the State Capitol building. Additionally, Hollister believed a low-cost, family-oriented venue was essential to bringing people downtown and moving closer to becoming a world-class city. The Dicksons and Hollister shook hands and agreed to a "creative partnership" that would involve acquiring the land; designing, building, and financing a stadium; naming and marketing the team—and doing it in 18 months so the Dicksons wouldn't be forced to operate the Sultans a second year in a community it was abandoning.

The announcement that minor league baseball was coming to town created quite a stir. The critics claimed it was doomed to fail because the new stadium was to be built downtown and nobody would go to a night game in an area where the crime rate was high and there was inadequate parking and no restaurants or bars within walking distance. Hollister responded by focusing on the vision of a world-class city. He assembled a group of local bankers who developed a unique financing mechanism that allowed them to partner with the city and have the stadium paid off in 15 years.

Hollister also retained Ray Tadgerson, president and CEO of Capital Consultants (now C2AE), to head up a team of 10 subconsultants to complete a six-week-long feasibility study to determine whether a stadium could be built and supported by the region. The city then retained Tadgerson to oversee the "fast-track" design and construction of the new ballpark. Hollister also negotiated a project labor agreement with the developer and building trades that the city would use only unionized companies on the project. The unionized workers, in return, would guarantee no strikes and a commitment that the stadium would be built and ready to play in by April 3, 1996 (one year to the date of the groundbreaking). Additionally, the unions pledged a five cent per hour per worker contribution to support the mayor's school improvement efforts.

Mayor David Hollister engaging with Lansing-area citizens at Oldsmobile Park, home of the Lansing Lugnuts, a Class A minor league baseball team (the ballpark is now called Cooley Law School Stadium). Hollister together with John Engler, Debbie Stabenow, Carl Levin, and Ray Tadgerson threw out the first pitch at the ballpark's grand opening.

Building on the Dickson–Leo Burnett Oldsmobile marketing relationship, Hollister offered John Rock, general manager of
Oldsmobile, the option of naming the stadium. While Rock couldn't
personally sign off on the $1.5 million request without approval from
GM headquarters in Detroit, he was able to commit $100,000 a year
for 15 years as part of his marketing and public relations budget so
that a revenue stream could be added to the financing package.

Drawing in the local community early, Hollister and Dickson
also agreed on a public "name the team" contest to reinforce the idea
of maximum citizen engagement. Dickson had spent professional
time on the Disney account, and the family entertainment approach
had been incorporated into drawings and a marketing plan for the
mascot, the merchandise, the paraphernalia, and the whole minor
league experience. Community commitment and involvement early
on, they thought, would be a key to success.

The initial response to the public announcement of the team's
name was stunned disbelief because the word "lugnut" carried a negative connotation in various sectors of the auto industry. Hollister's
office received 125 calls the morning that the *Lansing State Journal*
ran the story, and all were negative. However, within hours of the
noontime announcement, every piece of Lugnuts merchandise had
sold out! As the project continued and the first season progressed,
Hollister and Dickson took satisfaction in seeing the team set the
minor league record for attendance and merchandise sold, hosting
the all-star game, and winning the Midwest League Championship
in 1997. After two decades, the Lugnuts continue to be the best-
selling minor league merchandise brand.

The successful completion of the minor league baseball stadium
on time and on budget, the creative financing by local banks, the
collaboration with General Motors in naming the stadium, the sell-
out crowds, and the spin-off development of restaurants created a
sense that Lansing was capable of managing a complex, transformational challenge. While the mayor and his team were scrambling
to create a regional plan and strategy to preserve Lansing's historic
automobile manufacturing sector, though, a new threat presented
itself to an emerging insurance and finance sector.

The Lansing-based Jackson National Life Insurance Company
was considering relocating to Denver or California. Jackson National

Life was growing exponentially and had outgrown its facility in south Lansing. Then CEO and president Bob Saltzman lived in California and flew back and forth on weekends. He liked Lansing, the workforce, its work ethic, and the quality of life, but circumstances were pointing to an exit from Lansing. A traditional Lansing Regional Chamber of Commerce–led retention effort was not going to keep Jackson National Life in town. Fortunately, the Lansing mayor's finance director, Bob Swanson, was well versed in incentive packages and the intricacies of tax-sharing agreements, having spent years in state government, most recently as staff director of the Michigan House of Representatives Taxation Committee.

Bob Swanson brought the issue to the mayor's attention and got his approval to explore ways to keep Jackson National Life in Lansing. Swanson was aware of recently enacted legislation designed to aid urban cities in attracting and retaining businesses. Unfortunately this legislation had never been tested. After conferring with Saltzman and getting an understanding of his management style and approach, the mayor's team went on a search for a new location and found the perfect fit in Alaiedon Township. Located seven miles east of Lansing on Interstate 96, the available land was large enough to accommodate Jackson National Life's massive new headquarters building, and the wooded lot and river provided a quiet, natural environment for employees to exercise and relax.

Alaiedon Township, however, was determined to keep its rural heritage and was fearful that any new business would change its character by opening the township to strip mall development. Using their legislative experience, Hollister and Swanson designed a Public Act 425 tax-sharing agreement that effectively made the Jackson National Life property part of Lansing for income and property tax purposes, granted a 100 percent abatement of personal property taxes on computers and other equipment, and shared the tax revenue with the township. Most importantly, Lansing would provide sewer, water, and electric service to the Jackson National Life property. Such utility services would not be available to the remainder of the township, thereby preserving its rural nature. It was a win for the township, a win for Jackson National Life, and a win for Lansing.

This win-win approach was key to the economic development initiatives undertaken by Lansing under the watch of Mayor Hollister.

Governor John Engler; Marvin Lott, Alaiedon Township supervisor; Bob
Saltzman (then CEO, Jackson National Life Insurance Company); and
Mayor David Hollister sealing the deal to locate the headquarters of Jackson
National in Alaiedon Township but with a Lansing address and support.
Saltzman says below the picture, "We got it done! Thanks for your help!"

But it did not come without a fight. Alaiedon Township's hearing
on the plan brought out a hostile, standing-room-only crowd that
jeered and booed both Saltzman and the mayor. Ultimately, the
township board voted to proceed with the agreement, which also
resulted in the board's being subject to a recall election. All the challenged officials, however, survived the recall, and the project went on
to surpass all expectations. In subsequent years, as Jackson National
Life continued to grow and expand at the site, the business was so
well integrated into the fabric of the community that no opposition
was expressed. This experience with a 425 agreement and the personal property tax exemption would prove a critical precedent for the
"Lansing Works! Keep GM!" campaign.

Alero Launch

Hollister enjoyed the confidence of local labor leaders and appreciated the invitation by Art Baker (shop chair of the United Auto
Workers) to sit in on UAW Local 652 strategy sessions, plotting ways
to make the launch of GM's Alero a platform for persuading GM
corporate leaders in Detroit to keep investing in mid-Michigan after
the Centennial Series of cars ran its course. Lansing labor leaders
had a reputation for being flexible, innovative, and entrepreneurial, so it wasn't surprising that Jim Zubkus, the plant manager for
GM's main assembly plant and the Fisher Body plant in Lansing,
was also brought into the strategy sessions. Baker and Zubkus were
determined to make this the best launch ever and early on made
two decisions that would determine the fate of auto manufacturing
in mid-Michigan.

The first decision was made by Jim Zubkus to launch the Alero
on the second shift and send a message to the corporate headquarters
in Detroit that Lansing's GM operations had enough confidence in
the workforce that operations management would entrust the second
team to successfully reengineer the production and make the process
as efficient and quality oriented as any of the import competitors.
This approach was unorthodox—no one launches new car models
on the second shift! GM's corporate leaders were also skeptical about
a second shift launch. The second shift, after all, is typically where
only essential personnel are working and a bulk of the engineers and
other skilled employees are not. Zubkus prevailed, and the launch
was ultimately hailed as the most successful in GM's history.

The second decision was to submit to the Lansing City Council
and the State of Michigan a middle option concerning emission
controls and the all-important tax abatement package needed for
the Alero production. While the least expensive option would technically abate odors and pollutants, it would put Hollister and his
100 percent pro-environment voting record in the legislature in an
awkward position. Choosing option two would demonstrate sen-
sitivity to neighborhood concerns, and it would also save millions
from option three; those savings would go a long way toward a successful launch, truly a win-win approach that Mayor Hollister had
made a staple of his administration.

However, a small group of Lansing's Westside residents were unsatisfied with the middle (compromise) approach and began organizing a vocal opposition to any tax break to GM until the odor problem was solved. They began lobbying Lansing City Council members and also reached out to state environmental groups to oppose further GM expansion in the region, citing odor and health-related problems. Hollister responded by assigning his deputy mayor, David Wiener, the task of assembling a broad-based neighborhood health advisory task force in 2000–2001 to address the issues being raised. The task force included officials from the County Health Department, the State Department of Environmental Quality, the State Health Department, the Lansing School District, environmental groups, GM's environmental engineers, neighborhood representatives, and various city departments.

The health advisory task force identified and prioritized the major concerns and began a data collecting process. GM agreed to set a weather station at a local high school and assigned environmental engineers to work with school staff to incorporate weather, weather patterns, and environmental monitoring into the school's science curriculum. A community website and hotline were created to provide direct input into the data collection and problem-solving process. An odor training session was conducted so neighborhood volunteers could be directly engaged and regular "odor patrols" conducted. Within a year, a scientific study concluded that the emissions posed no threat to the neighborhood, and multiple groups signed a consent decree allowing the air quality permit to go forward.

While the odor controversy was being proactively addressed by engaging the neighborhood in serious community problem solving, some on the Lansing City Council chose to use the issue as a lever to attempt to get more concessions out of General Motors and to raise issues and create roadblocks in a way that positioned themselves as the guardians of virtue against the "evil" corporation. Their obstructionist rhetoric and antidevelopment behavior manifested itself in a 5-to-3 split decision on a critical council resolution needed to secure a tax abatement. Had one more councilperson voted no, the GM investment in mid-Michigan would have ended when the Centennial Series terminated production in 2005. That close call convinced the mayor to create a coalition with the United

Auto Workers and the Lansing Regional Chamber of Commerce to recruit candidates to replace the incumbent council naysayers in the 1997 election. Such a joint effort had never been undertaken, as local labor and the Lansing chamber had always been adversaries. Hollister won an easy reelection challenge and swept in the council slate that he, labor, and the chamber endorsed.

On a number of dimensions, 1997 was turning out to be a critical year. The early collaborative relationship between the United Auto Workers and General Motors' management to make the Alero launch the most successful ever had caught the attention of top management in Detroit. Mark Hogan, vice president of GM's Car Group in North America, let it be known that mid-Michigan was being considered as a possible location for its newly designed manufacturing operation. Hollister seized on the opportunity and the relationship being developed to formalize the process by creating the Blue Ribbon Committee to Keep GM. He announced the creation of the initiative in his 1998 State of the City Address. Figure 1.1 is the proclamation that established the Blue Ribbon Committee. The Appendix includes the "Lansing Works! Keep GM!" press release from October 8, 1998: "Unprecedented regional agreement focuses on retaining General Motors in Lansing area—forty regional partners endorse resolution."

School Improvement

The important link between the health of the City of Lansing and the quality of the schools became crystal clear when Mayor Hollister was discussing General Motors' decision to invest $600 million to manufacture the Alero in Lansing's antiquated auto plants. GM executives were very clear and precise: Lansing's competitive advantage was its skilled, reliable, productive, and hardworking labor force. In productivity and product quality, the Lansing workers are second to none and have always promoted good labor-management relations. This stamp of approval for Lansing's GM manufacturing was also reinforced and publicly communicated as recently as January 26, 2016, in a keynote by Mark Reuss, GM's executive vice president of Global Product Development, to some 500 attendees of the Lansing Economic Club.

DAVID C. HOLLISTER, MAYOR

We're Making it Happen!

Proclamation

WHEREAS: In the Winter of 1998, over thirty community members were asked to serve on the Mayor's Blue Ribbon Committee to Retain General Motors; and

WHEREAS: Committee members included elected officials from the region, representatives from the Lansing Regional Chamber of Commerce, the UAW, local schools, Michigan State University, Lansing Community College, the Michigan Economic Development Corporation, the Lansing Economic Development Corporation, City of Lansing Department Directors and staff, small and large business owners, neighborhood organizations, and the faith community; and

WHEREAS: The Steering Committee was chaired by Jack Davis, and included Lansing Mayor David Hollister, the Lansing Chamber of Commerce, Delta Township Supervisor Joe Drolette, with Ray Tadgerson of Capital Consultants serving as the Project Director; and

WHEREAS: Early activities of the Blue Ribbon Committee included an extensive public relations campaign, featuring easily-recognizable billboards and bumper stickers and a comprehensive presentation to General Motors which highlighted the Lansing Region as a site for replacement plants; and

WHEREAS: The committee members dedicated much time and effort to the campaign to retain General Motors, with the Steering Committee and some sub-committees meeting weekly (or more frequently) as issues arose, the Public Relations Committee developed a working relationship with local media, ensuring that information was provided in a timely, yet sensitive manner; and

WHEREAS: A resolution, developed by Steve Webster, VP for Governmental Affairs at Michigan State University, was signed by 40 regional governmental leaders, expressing their united goal of attracting and making successful a General Motors plant through regional partnerships and cooperation; and

WHEREAS: The Keep GM Committee and its leaders developed good working relations with the team at GM and GM Executives responsible for making decisions, developing a level of confidence and trust between and among the key players in the process; and

WHEREAS: The partnership and good working relationship between the Committee, the UAW, and General Motors was successful due to the efforts of Committee Chair, Jack Davis, UAW Local 652 President, Ralph Shepard, and GM's Lansing Car Assembly Plant Manager, Amy Farmer, as well as many the other dedicated individuals involved in the process; so now

THEREFORE, I, DAVID C. HOLLISTER, Mayor of the City of Lansing, by the power vested in me, do hereby recognize and honor the Blue Ribbon Committee to Retain General Motors and thank those involved for their hard work and dedication, which has proved successful twice over, with General Motors' decision to locate two of their new plants in the Lansing Region. I ask all Lansing residents to join me in congratulating the committee upon the receipt of the South Lansing Business Association's Outstanding Achievement Award.

Given under my hand and seal this twenty-eighth day of March in the Year of our Lord, two thousand one.

_____

DAVID C. HOLLISTER, MAYOR

Figure 1.1   Proclamation to Establish the Blue Ribbon Committee to Retain General Motors

But at the time, Hollister was stunned when the GM executives pointed out that one-half of Lansing's current production workers would be eligible to retire in the next 10 years. They asked, "Mayor, how are the Lansing schools doing in creating the workforce of the future? What are the standards of excellence? How do we measure up against other districts, the state averages and our foreign competition?" Mayor Hollister had no immediate answers. But he was immediately concerned, since he knew Lansing students were performing below the state averages in math, reading, and science and were also experiencing unacceptably high truancy and dropout rates. Hollister also knew that this labor pool issue was something of concern to every businessperson he encountered, not just General Motors executives, and the issue had to be solved.

As a result, Mayor Hollister asked Peter McPherson, then president of Michigan State University, to lead a 16-member blue ribbon committee of key community leaders in developing a comprehensive strategy for school improvement. Subsequently Hollister appointed the Commission on Lansing Schools Success (CLASS) to follow up on the many recommendations of the committee.

It was critical to the GM effort that major employers and businesspeople embrace the school improvement goals and also provide intense and sustained pressure on the schools to improve. The Lansing Regional Chamber of Commerce agreed to be the focal point of the initiative and to house its day-to-day operations. Within days, an office was established, a telephone hotline (319-KIDS) was operationalized, and General Motors, the Lansing Regional Chamber of Commerce, Michigan State University, Lansing Community College, and the City of Lansing joined together and contributed more than $500,000 in resources to the education endeavor.

Over the next four years, 58 initiatives were undertaken by CLASS. General Motors embraced and helped guide the community effort on education by assigning its director of finance in Lansing, Glenn Kirk, to chair CLASS. GM also assigned Jim Menapace, on loan, as executive director during its initial year. And GM did so much more: it financed the phase-in of the Galaxy science and math curriculum in all elementary schools, had 16 engineers tutor daily at J. W. Sexton High School in Lansing, assisted teachers to integrate air-quality and odor issues into the high school science curriculum, and established the Lansing Area Manufacturing Partnership—a unique experiential learning curriculum taught jointly by General Motors and United Auto Workers staff. With such high-level buy-in by General Motors, Michigan State University, Lansing Community College, and the City of Lansing, the school improvement initiative took hold in the entire greater Lansing community. At its peak, CLASS had 1,100 volunteers tutoring high-risk third graders in an effort to raise their reading comprehension skills.

When General Motors announced that the Alero launch was the most successful ever and awarded local management a $25,000 grant to celebrate its achievement, the collective leadership team of General Motors and the United Auto Workers decided against a party but instead had a plantwide drawing with the winner receiving a scholarship for any family member to the college of his or her choice. This decision reinforced the "Lansing Works!" message that Lansing was sending to GM Corporate in Detroit: Lansing had a very skilled, knowledgeable, and high-quality workforce, and everyone was teaming up and working together to solve its many challenges.

FRAMING THE SECOND SHIFT MODEL

A successful collaboration across all layers and networks in the greater Lansing community required a solution framework based on Mayor Hollister's vision and the available (and potentially available) resources for the "Lansing Works! Keep GM!" campaign. A six-dimensional framework we call the "Second Shift Model" was constructed to drive the solution. While the core dimensions of the Second Shift Model are not unique per se, they do provide an integrated and elaborate direction and structure for organizing a project with complex political and economic considerations. The six-dimensional framework that makes up the Second Shift Model is captured in Figure 1.2 and includes identifying, partnering, building, solving, celebrating, and persevering.

Identifying captures the idea of naming the challenge and its potential impact. *Partnering* refers to developing meaningful relationships. *Building* denotes constructing the strategy as you go. *Solving* captures the engagement in constant problem solving.

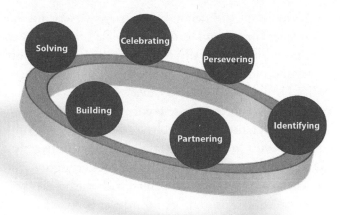

Figure 1.2   The Second Shift Model

Celebrating is the marking of successful milestones. And *persevering* denotes adapting and enduring to get the tasks done. Each dimension is briefly described in this chapter, with a more comprehensive discussion in Chapters 2 through 7 and with practical guidelines and implementation mechanisms discussed in Chapter 8.

Identifying: Name the Challenge and Its Impact

The first issue that Hollister's team faced, which is usually the first step in the process, was to identify the challenge and quantify its (potential) impact. While the obvious challenge was the need to try to change GM's decisions regarding plant closures in Lansing, even though GM virtually never changes strategic decisions like these, the larger challenge was to change the regional culture regarding collaboration.

The cities and townships in the region generally had the attitude that unless the solution involved a production facility in their locale, they were not interested in being involved. Even further, some of the cities and townships were willing to challenge the initiatives of other locales to try to win the business. This allowed companies to play off the offerings of different locations without either side understanding the total regional impact.

Many of the politicians and citizens viewed the major consideration regarding plant location to be local taxes. However, the larger consideration is typically the direct and indirect job impact. The direct and indirect impact of these jobs does not stop at the municipality borders since workers live and shop throughout the region based on their lifestyle preferences. At this point, GM had about 27,000 direct and indirect jobs in the Lansing region (plus an additional 50,000 jobs in Michigan that were indirectly connected to GM's plants in Lansing). Of these jobs, roughly 7,000 employees worked at the Lansing GM plants, with the others typically working for so-called first-, second-, or third-tier suppliers (as well as GM service providers). The implications of such a job loss and its economic impact would be significant and devastating to the region.

Partnering: Develop Meaningful Relationships

The second dimension of the Second Shift Model entails developing meaningful strategic partnerships with community leaders and representatives. Mayor Hollister requested Ray Tadgerson, an experienced consulting engineer (who, as noted earlier, had worked with the mayor on the ballpark project), to work with him to lead the collaborative efforts. As Michigan State University's current president, Lou Anna K. Simon, suggested, "Lansing, Michigan, needed to do some economic gardening, and Ray was needed as the gardener."

Jack Davis, a prominent Lansing attorney and former chair of the Lansing Regional Chamber of Commerce, described a meeting with Mayor Hollister, Ray Tadgerson, and Mel Kent (former president and CEO of the Lansing Regional Chamber of Commerce). During the meeting, Hollister made it clear that he wanted a widespread regional effort to retain GM in town. Though John Rock (general manager of Oldsmobile) let it be known that there was no planned production for the Oldsmobile facilities after the year 2005, Hollister indicated that he would like to involve the Lansing chamber for business support, Michigan State University for conceptual and analytical support, and the Michigan Economic Development Corporation for state government collaboration.

MSU president Simon, who was provost at the time, characterized the role of the university as a neutral broker, particularly when there are a number of governmental units involved. Steve Webster, vice president for Government Affairs at Michigan State University, made a substantial contribution by getting 40 units of government to sign a pledge to set aside differences and unite to make retention of GM a priority for the region. These community entities also agreed to cooperate in finding mutually beneficial solutions. With Michigan State University getting behind the initiative and viewing retention of GM as a regional priority, the university was able to leverage its assets and relationships to get others to join and participate in the "Lansing Works! Keep GM!" campaign.

The team of Hollister, Tadgerson, Davis, and Webster began learning as much as it could about the GM organization and decision making. Hollister went as far as to develop a handwritten organizational chart of GM executives, including, importantly, their roles in plant strategy decisions. The issues related to plant location are very complex, involving cost, regulatory, marketing, labor, and governmental considerations. It was necessary to organize an inclusive team of regional leaders to effectively capture all potential tangents in this effort. Hollister requested that Ray Tadgerson provide a framework for designing and organizing a blue ribbon committee that could be effective in keeping GM. This committee had representatives from both the public and private sector and involved both regional and statewide representatives. At its peak, more than 50 of the region's key citizens and leaders in business, labor, education, and local and state government participated on the Blue Ribbon Committee to Retain GM.

Tim Daman, the current president and CEO of the Lansing Regional Chamber of Commerce, characterized the partnering that Mayor Hollister structured as "a public/private partnership model which was the reason for the success. When you look at that and you have labor and the business community and your local elected officials and your community leaders all at the table, all working for the same goal; that to me is what drove the success of the program. I do believe that was a model that could have been franchised nationally as how to effectively retain businesses." While the members of the Blue Ribbon Committee to Retain GM came with many different perspectives—political, economic development, education, business, labor, and community development—they all came with the understanding that failure to keep GM would have dire consequences for the region. Their goal was to make partnering and collaboration work.

Building: Construct Your Strategy as You Go

The third dimension was to build a strategy "on the go," as the members of the Blue Ribbon Committee learned how to work together as a team and develop a synergistic strategy. Hollister's experience as a business and community leader had taught him to always learn what you can from others. Proactive problem solving requires that the team learn what it can do and then move ahead with the solution. As it turned out, the mayor of Toledo, Ohio (about 100 miles southeast of Lansing), had faced a very similar challenge when Chrysler announced that it was moving its Jeep plant 50 miles outside of the city. In creating a "building platform," the Lansing mayor and 14 Lansing business, labor, and community leaders took a road trip to Toledo on January 13, 1998, to develop insight and review the lessons learned by Toledo. The *Lansing State Journal* and all four local Lansing TV stations also sent staff to cover the trip.

One of the key lessons from the Toledo trip was learning how to communicate with officials at GM in a language that they understood. Rather than using "government" or "political speak" language, it was important that the Blue Ribbon Committee involve staff who could communicate in business operations and engineering. Communication and inclusiveness became the foundation of the Second Shift Model. Communication was also critical to both GM and the community.

In the case of General Motors, it was necessary to clearly and directly communicate to GM that GM was very important to the community. In the case of the Lansing community, it was necessary to clearly communicate why GM was important to the community and the region. This meant that the Blue Ribbon Committee had to reach out to the entire Lansing community—to business, to labor, to elected officials, and to the education community.

Hollister told the Lansing community, "Listen, whatever differences we have, business, labor, politics, you've got to set it aside and unite. And let's get the job done to tell General Motors we want them to stay." Hollister added that "today's managers are not kings . . . they're coaches. They understand that businesses are incredibly complex organizations and decisions require consideration of a wide range of variables. Governmental and political leaders can't know everything. So the Blue Ribbon Committee's task is to build a team led by a coach that was, early on, a model of how you really operate in this increasingly sophisticated, complex, hard, and cold world that we are in."

As Hollister organized the Blue Ribbon Committee into sub-committees and synthesized the information from the different perspectives, inclusivity began to pay off as the different perspectives began to coalesce. The politicians, unions, and community began to understand the challenges faced by General Motors. Similarly, GM began to understand the advantages that the Lansing region and the multitalented and flexible workforce brought to GM in terms of skills, knowledge, productivity, and quality.

Solving: Engage in Constant Problem Solving

Like many Midwest cities during the decades before the dawn of the twenty-first century, Lansing was declining. Downtown retail stores were closing or moving to the suburbs, and restaurants either closed or were open only for lunch. While State of Michigan office and related industry office workers as well as Cooley Law School students were visible on the downtown streets during the day, the streets were mostly quiet at night. However, the success of Hollister's baseball vision of "If you build it, they will come" provided some credibility regarding his vision for GM. So while there were still many skeptics, Mayor Hollister had a track record of bringing his vision to reality.

During the scouting visit to Toledo, Mayor Hollister asked Toledo's Mayor Finkbeiner, "What would you recommend?" Mayor Finkbeiner said, "Hire an engineer."

Walking out to the bus to go back to Lansing, Mayor Hollister said to Ray Tadgerson, "Can you do this?" Ray said, "Absolutely," but all the way back to Lansing, Ray kept asking himself, "What did I just do?" The more he thought about it, though, and reflected on the plan that they had used for the baseball stadium, he figured they could develop a plan with a similar organization team—which is exactly what they did.

Speed was, of course, of the essence. Mayor Hollister asked for a plan within 10 days. The plan was to include a number of organizational requirements. The first was that there must be a champion who was influential, recognized as a leader, and able to articulate a vision or goal. Second, the Blue Ribbon Committee had to include team members that were strong and diverse and were committed to win-win solutions. Third, the committee had to develop a strategic plan that went directly to the desired goal.

Although the plan included a number of cross-organizational requirements, a critical component was a champion or point person who could take responsibility and accountability for solving the daily issues that were encountered when dealing with GM. Mayor Hollister established a "single-entry, single-exit" policy to address all issues needing resolution. The single-entry, single-exit policy also meant that all issues were to be directed to the mayor's office and the only official communication would emanate from the mayor's office. If either GM or the community representatives felt that a topic needed to be secret, the mayor's office worked with the organizations and media to keep it secret. Otherwise the policy was to make the discussions transparent to the media and the community. The policy regarding transparency turned out to be, singularly, the most important thing. It was collaborative. It was designed to be a win-win. That's the approach the mayor and the committee took to solve a multitude of complex problems.

When the Blue Ribbon Committee met with General Motors and began to dialogue and then negotiate, GM knew that the mayor's team was representative, accountable, and proactive. So GM almost immediately had the confidence that the mayor's team would do what it said it was going to do. The idea was always that when GM brought a problem to the Blue Ribbon Committee, it would solve the problem and turn it around within a couple of weeks or no later than 30 days.

Mark Hogan, GM vice president, reflected that "there are a myriad of old things that needed to be done, to first of all demolish the old plant, get the permits and all the other associated things that need to happen with the multimillion square foot facility. And all those efforts, whether it was from permitting to tax abatement . . . the support of the Lansing team was incredible and made our job we had at GM a lot easier. I mean there was absolutely no obstacle." Hogan continued to characterize the Lansing team by saying: "There was a can-do attitude among everybody. It was one of the most incredible displays of partnership between various constituencies that I've seen from a business standpoint. It really is a model to this day of how to work together."

Celebrating: Mark Successful Milestones

Mayor Hollister and the Blue Ribbon Committee knew that the road to success would be long and difficult. The steps and complexities were almost endless, including organizing the team, designing collaborative solutions, and working with GM to implement an approach that could satisfy both GM and the community; all of this was going to be very demanding. However, it was important for the team to celebrate initial milestones and the road to success. Such celebrations helped morale and confidence. The celebrations were somewhat ad hoc, which worked well in conjunction with the "constructing of the strategy as you go" approach that the Lansing team had to adopt.

The celebrations reflected both specific events and overall changes in the environment. Some of the specific events included the demolition of the old GM plants, the start of construction for the new plants, the assignment of the model line for the production in the new plants, and the first Cadillac rolling down the line. These were obvious achievements that were visible and reported in the media.

The less obvious causes for celebration, but actually more important for the central Michigan economy, were the dramatic changes in the types of jobs being developed in the region. Michigan's governor John Engler reflected that "the result was a long process which turned what was going to be disaster into a tremendous opportunity to pay dividends for Lansing certainly well into the twenty-first century." Without the collaboration of the Blue Ribbon Committee with people representing government, private sector, labor, and education, the Lansing region would have continued its way down many separate paths, many paths that would have only provided a short-term solution of jobs since many of those industries no longer exist.

President Lou Anna K. Simon of Michigan State University reflected: "Not only did we keep what we had; we've grown the production capacity. I think we couldn't probably contemplate at that point in time the way technology would affect the number of jobs. So you have to look at success I think in terms of production capacity and the desire for GM to continue to reinvest in the production capacity in this community, and to value the workers and the quality of work done in Lansing. In that sense, it was an enormous success."

Regarding the dramatic change in the regional job market, Bob Trezise, who, as mentioned earlier, is the former director of the Lansing Economic Development Corporation and now CEO of the Lansing Economic Area Partnership, commented: "We've had huge growth in high-tech companies. It's really hard to imagine all of that happening now, without the original retain GM effort. I think it kept place in a community, and within the remarkable rebirth of a community we've had all kinds of new industry emerge. Why? Because we're a great community. Because we still have Michigan State University and the Capitol, and because we are a functioning healthy tax-based community, good education system, not a lot of crime, and actually pretty decent infrastructure. Why all those things? Because we saved GM. Because without GM we would have a completely collapsed community. So, it is the gift that keeps on giving."

In order to retain GM, employees in the region were forced to evolve from the assembly-line worker of the twentieth century, typically a high school graduate, to the high-tech manufacturing worker of the twenty-first century. This also allowed the region to maintain its U.S. competitiveness through the use of information technology. Throughout, it was important to celebrate the evolution that Simon and Trezise capture and the numerous little win-win scenarios that led to the huge win-win in GM reversing course and staying in Lansing.

Persevering: Adapt and Endure

A core feature of the Second Shift Model integrates the notion that since customers and competitors as well as the labor market and technological advances seemingly always change, the necessity of adapting and enduring to whatever may come has to be part of the fabric ingrained in the success formula. There were daily twists and turns, potholes, and even a few U-turns that the Blue Ribbon Committee had to face. Mayor Hollister reflected on this: "It fell apart several times. You just suck it up, regroup, get your team together, complete an analysis of what's going on, and you move forward. If you have a vision, and if you have a plan, the biggest issue is perseverance, just not getting confused with winning or losing. If you have supportive partners, you can overcome any setback and you will persevere over time. What you will find is the friendships and partnerships you develop will carry you through the tough times."

Ed Donovan, former director of Governmental Relations for GM, probably offered the greatest reason for an environmental celebration. While many of the communities that were homes to automotive assembly plants could not take up the challenge to change, the Lansing region did through strong leadership and collaborative efforts. Donovan noted: "So, I suggest to anybody in America, here's your answer to finding that magic look to these problems. Is it easy? No, it's not easy. I think I met Mayor Hollister around January or February of 1994 and I had little hope for where this was going, but look where we are. I've really become convinced after my experience that one of the things this process has taught me, the Blue Ribbon panel and the success of the two new plants and the next 50 years of having a vibrant middle class here, because of the jobs and supply of jobs, is the fact that it wasn't a race to the bottom."

WHY THE SECOND SHIFT MODEL?

The six-dimensional framework we call the Second Shift Model was constructed to drive the solution to complex community problems involving multiple stakeholders with oftentimes multiple goals. Some would see the outcome of such an approach as "being on the same page," "having the same vision," "driving toward the same goal," and so on.

As we stated earlier, while the core dimensions of the Second Shift Model are not unique per se, they do provide an integrated and elaborate direction and structure for organizing a project with complex political and economic considerations.

Again, as a summary of the six dimensions (see Figure 1.2): *Identifying* captures the idea of naming the challenge and its potential impact. *Partnering* refers to developing meaningful relationships. *Building* denotes constructing the strategy as you go. *Solving* captures the engagement in constant problem solving. *Celebrating* is the marking of successful milestones. *Persevering* denotes adapting and enduring to get the tasks done.

Integrating these six dimensions into the Second Shift Model has two core definitional properties that capture the Lansing community engagement experience, the car industry, and the "Lansing Works!" mentality. Specifically:

- Second Shift plays off the decision made by Jim Zubkus to launch the Alero on the second shift and send a message to the corporate headquarters in Detroit that Lansing's GM operations executives had enough confidence in the workforce that they would entrust the second team to successfully reengineer the production and make the process as efficient and quality oriented as any of the import competitors. "Lansing Works!"
- Second Shift plays off the sociology-based notion describing the labor performed at home on top of the paid labor that employees perform in the formal sector outside the home. The "Lansing Works! Keep GM!" captures the sentiment of Lansing as a "home" community, with everyone pitching in at "home" and at normal paid-for work to retain GM in the community. For us, it is a way to think about the collective efforts of the region's leaders in business, labor, education, and local and state government and the emotional involvement of almost every greater Lansing (and Michigan) citizen in the "Keep GM" campaign.

Having framed the solution for what was needed in the "Lansing Works! Keep GM!" campaign, in Chapters 2 through 7 we delve into each of the Second Shift Model's six dimensions of identifying, partnering, building, solving, celebrating, and persevering. Finally, Chapter 8 brings the case study story full circle by providing guidelines and implementation mechanisms.

CHAPTER 2

IDENTIFYING

NAME THE CHALLENGE AND ITS IMPACT

The first step in addressing a challenge is to identify the scope of the challenge. The broad picture of the challenge facing the Lansing mayor and Lansing's community leaders was how to convince General Motors to stay in the Lansing region after 2005 in light of the GM Board of Directors' decision to close aging, inefficient manufacturing plants around the country. Lansing had the oldest plant in the portfolio of General Motors' manufacturing facilities, and the city was ripe to strategically have GM shut down its car production given that GM closed a number of plants in the 1990s.

As discussed in Chapter 1, GM plants that were closed during the mid-1990s included Baltimore, Maryland; Buick City in Flint, Michigan; Dayton/Vandalia, Ohio; Doraville, Georgia; Grand Rapids, Michigan; Janesville, Wisconsin; Linden, New Jersey; Livonia, Michigan; Mansfield, Ohio; Massena, New York; Moraine, Ohio; Oklahoma City, Oklahoma; Pittsburgh, Pennsylvania; Pontiac, Michigan; Saginaw, Michigan; Shreveport, Louisiana; North Tarrytown, New York; Trenton, New Jersey; Willow Run, Michigan; and Wilmington, Delaware. It should not have been a surprise that the Lansing plants were scheduled to be phased out as well.

Carefully delineating the challenge facing Lansing is not the same as Mayor Hollister receiving the "knock on the door" visit from Ed Donovan (director of Municipal Government for General Motors) in 1996. Much more was involved with identifying and communicating the challenge. Figure 2.1 illustrates the Second

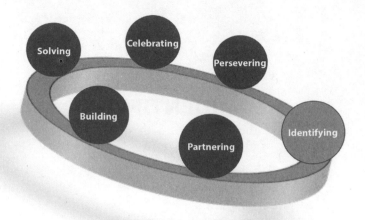

Figure 2.1   The Second Shift Model—identifying

Shift Model, highlighting the "identifying" component discussed in Chapter 2. Remember, Donovan also told the mayor the good news that the Oldsmobile centennial would include a week's celebration, attracting thousands of car enthusiasts to the area, and that the Lansing plant would build the new Alero. Within this context, Donovan revealed the bad news that, after production of the Alero had ceased in 2004–2005, GM was going to close the Lansing operation. Basically, the Lansing community received a lot of mixed messages from General Motors.

The fact that production of GM products would stop after the 2004–2005 period, almost 10 years after the 1996 meeting, likely would not bring urgency or a do-it-now attitude from the Lansing City Council, nor create any form of resolve for action among the region's myriad of key citizens and leaders in business, labor, education, and local and state government. People from these groups ultimately became part of the Blue Ribbon Committee that Mayor Hollister set up, and Hollister desperately had to figure out a way to engage them sooner rather than later. For the public, a critical incident that turned out to be an eye-opener was a study by George Fulton and Donald Grimes, both professors at the University of Michigan (with Fulton being director of U of M's Institute of Labor and Industrial Relations). The data illustrated clearly that the outlook for Lansing was dire in regard to its infrastructure, finances, and quality of life if GM shut down (more on that later in this chapter).

The portfolio of constituency groups, regional context, and metrics included: the corporation (GM), state policy (tax relief and support), regional conflict (among the many townships and neighboring communities), public sentiment (was Hollister believable in his reporting, and even so, did the public think it would matter if GM left?), and quantification of the impact of a potential GM shutdown. The mix of constituency groups, regional context, and metrics made the naming of the challenge and its impact unusually difficult, given the multiple layers of complexity, stakeholders, and even timing (e.g., elected officials seldom think almost a decade out in the business future).

IDENTIFYING NARRATIVE

Auto manufacturing was in mid-Michigan's DNA, Lansing having been the headquarters for Oldsmobile since 1901. The general public and perhaps even the most insightful auto experts took it for granted that General Motors would always be present in the community because of the highly skilled, dependable, and management-friendly workforce that had continuously produced high-quality, award-winning products. As it turned out, Lansing had to resell itself and make GM focus again on the skills, knowledge, and high quality of the Lansing workforce as a mechanism to reverse GM's course of action.

The bottom line was that Lansing had come to take GM's presence in the community for granted. But everyone knows that "you can never take what you have for granted, particularly in this very complex global marketplace where you're not the center of corporate decision making. . . . You have to continue to show value for what you're doing," as Lou Anna K. Simon, president of Michigan State University, said.

Showing value, coupled with constantly identifying potential problem areas, should be part of every corporation's strategy, and by the same token, part of every community's strategy. Unfortunately, our political system is such that many politicians who are community leaders and are elected to service roles are short-term oriented in mindset (e.g., when is the next election, and how can I get reelected?). This mindset strongly influences critical thinking about identifying potential challenges facing the community. In the case of GM in 1996, even when the problem was identified, the fact of the closings taking effect sometime after the last Oldsmobile Alero was produced in the 2004–2005 period did not create strategic or political urgency on the part of many.

However, Mayor David Hollister, Ray Tadgerson, and several other key individuals jump-started the identification and solution process. Effectively, the meeting Hollister had with Jim Donaldson, Michigan Economic Development Corporation's vice president of Michigan Business Development, was the critical incident that ultimately led to the creation of the Blue Ribbon Committee to Retain GM and the Quick Response Team and set the stage for the blueprint of the Second Shift Model.

Hollister's team exemplified much of what President Simon also said: "You can't just wait for something bad to happen, in order for the community to mobilize and continue to both promote what you have and the quality of the workforce that you have, at the same time looking for new opportunities. People thought we won, so we relaxed, and now in this world, you can't do that. You've got to continue that kind of structure and that kind of regional focus on creating new things and keeping what you have."

The "we won" mindset of Lansing was in stark contrast to the reality facing the community. In Hollister's words, there was not a "win-win" scenario here. "We won" did not include General Motors. In fact, GM had come to believe that Lansing was just another manufacturing community with outdated facilities that could no longer justify the investment needed to make the company competitive.

The identification of the challenge soon to face the Lansing community was masked by General Motors, perhaps not intentionally but still effectively, and that hurt Mayor Hollister's voice on the matter to his constituencies. Specifically, the GM masking strategy, direct or indirect, correlated with the 1997 Oldsmobile centennial celebration and the announcement of the launch of the Alero in 1998. These two celebratory events de facto masked the reality that General Motors was being forced by multiple environmental factors to downsize, consolidate, and close outdated facilities.

The "Lansing Works! Keep GM!" logo that served as the
symbol for the movement's communications

While the mayor and his team were informed in 1996 that there
was no product for Lansing's aging facilities after 2005, that information was confidential and not to be made public. So organizing
a successful regional effort had to be in stealth mode for some time,
and then that effort had to kick into gear rapidly, strategically, and
with force as soon as Mayor Hollister felt that he could go public
with the news of a GM shutdown in town. He did so very soon after
learning of the plant closure decision.

As soon as the GM shutdown decision was made public, Mayor
Hollister and his leadership team's Second Shift Model was put into
motion. It was created strategically "on the go" but with a core focus
on continuously identifying challenges, partnering with strategic
community players, building strategic vehicles, problem solving via
a quick response team structure, and persevering by adapting and
enduring to whatever came the team's way.

In between all these challenges, the mayor also saw fit to celebrate
successful milestones to build morale, motivation, passion, and commitment to the end goal of his win-win vision—"Lansing Works! Keep
GM!" This campaign very clearly spelled out the win-win. Lansing
gets tremendous benefits from General Motors, and GM receives tremendous benefits from the high-quality, skilled Lansing workforce.

REFLECTIONS ON IDENTIFYING

David Hollister

While I lacked the traditional executive experience that would war-
rant the confidence and trust of regional partners, I felt confident

that my 19-plus years of coalition building, collaborating, and seeking win-win solutions in the Michigan legislature provided the framework and model to overcome turf battles, personalities, and petty politics.

My task was to create and communicate a vision and a plan, bring the diverse partners to the table, create a problem-solving mechanism, and commit to win-win outcomes. It wasn't easy and it wasn't fast, but over the next several years the model delivered a renewed commitment by GM to keep and expand its auto manufacturing plants in Lansing and the tri-county area.

Ray Tadgerson

When I first heard about the GM announcement, my reaction was one that paralleled the business community, and it was complete disbelief and one of impending doom. I also heard about the successful Toledo campaign to save Jeep. I immediately wrote a letter to Mayor Hollister and suggested Lansing may want to consider such a campaign. The letter as written was not with totally altruistic intentions. My firm, Capital Consultants (now C2AE), had been doing a considerable amount of engineering work, as consultants, for the local GM plants; and we certainly did not want to see them leave.

Also I knew GM leaving would devastate the region and cost many thousand employees their livelihood. The mayor responded by inviting me to take a reconnaissance trip to Toledo with his leadership team. That trip and our report to the mayor led to a daylong trip to Toledo by the Blue Ribbon Committee. I believe Dave felt a level of confidence in me and my firm due to an already established relationship with the mayor via his appointment of me and my firm to oversee the study, design, and construction of the Oldsmobile Park baseball stadium in downtown Lansing.

MAJOR CHALLENGES AND OBSTACLES TO IDENTIFYING

In completing the step of identifying, we found seven major challenges and obstacles:

1. GM was ceasing operations in Lansing by 2005 due to facility age and cost of operations. The greater Lansing community and the region had never faced a major problem like this. General Motors had been a presence in town for more than 100 years.
2. Mayor David Hollister and the Lansing Regional Chamber of Commerce disagreed on how to approach GM and address the problem. It was a lengthy process to get the chamber on board to pursue the plan of "Lansing Works! Keep GM!"
3. The surrounding townships were historically at odds with the capital city of Lansing, and if GM decided to build locally, the townships would likely want a new plant to be built in their community. A shared vision for the region across neighboring communities did not exist.
4. The "Toledo Loves Jeep" campaign worked for Toledo, Ohio, but Lansing faced a totally different set of challenges. Lansing would need to create a new strategic plan that not only specifically addressed the city's issues but also involved its neighboring townships, and thus it would need to build a strategic, common-vision partnership where minimal collaboration had been present previously.
5. Mark Hogan, vice president of GM's Car Group North America, stated that he and General Motors did not want a public campaign like "Toledo Loves Jeep" and wanted no politicians involved. Both issues were a challenge to overcome—Lansing would involve politicians (with Mayor David Hollister as the champion) and would mount a full-court press in a "Lansing Works! Keep GM!" campaign. Hogan ultimately came around and became a strong supporter of the "Keep GM in Lansing" movement.
6. The Lansing mayor had an internal advisory group that met nearly every Monday morning for over 2½ years to strategize how the city should handle the various challenges as they emerged. The group included Dennis Sykes, Bob Swanson, and Ray Tadgerson on a regular basis. Others who attended periodically were Patty Cook, Jim Smierka, and Steve Serkaian. This Monday morning team spun into two critically important groups: the Blue Ribbon Committee and the Quick Response Team. The former had more than 50 community leaders at

its peak, and the latter served as the "executive team" for the movement.

7. The members of the Lansing City Council were divided on whether to try to keep GM in the city. They were also sharply divided on whether to provide incentives and tax abatements. The differences were summed up with the "wine and quiche" versus "beer and bowling" comments from the council members.

FIVE COMPONENTS OF IDENTIFYING

Successfully identifying and addressing the upcoming challenges required regional leaders to (1) understand the corporation (General Motors), (2) know state policy, (3) understand regional conflict, (4) recognize public perceptions, and (5) be able to quantify the impact economically if General Motors went ahead and shut down operations in Lansing (Figure 2.2). We review each of these entities and elements that presented a challenge (and an opportunity to showcase Lansing's skills and knowledge) for the Lansing mayor, Quick Response Team, Blue Ribbon Committee, and overall greater Lansing community.

Understand the Corporation

Ransom Eli (RE) Olds was one of the founders of the automobile industry. It is clear that Oldsmobile would not have existed without Olds's leadership and entrepreneurial spirit, and it is likely that General Motors would not have existed either. Oldsmobile, or Olds

Identifying
(Name the Challenge and Its Impact)

1. Corporation
2. State Policy
3. Regional Conflict
4. Public Sentiment
5. Quantify the Impact

Figure 2.2   The Second Shift Model—components of identifying

Motor Works as it was first called, started in Lansing in 1897 and then moved to Detroit in 1901. After Olds built his first factory in Detroit, it burned to the ground in 1901 before any Olds automobiles were ever produced.

Before RE Olds could rebuild the plant, a group of city leaders from Lansing approached him with an offer to give him the old fairgrounds as the site to rebuild his plant. In 1901, Olds moved his Olds Motor Works to Lansing. Subsequently, GM bought Olds Motor Works in 1908. The fairgrounds site, which was at the south end of the city, was still the site of General Motors' Lansing Car Assembly until it closed on May 6, 2005. At that time, the Lansing plant was the longest-operating car factory in the country. The site is now home to GM's state-of-the-art Lansing Grand River Assembly plant.

Throughout the twentieth century and particularly in the last two decades, GM pretty much dominated the economic decision making of the Lansing region. Employees of Oldsmobile and much of its supply base worked and lived in the Lansing region and had important roles in state and local politics. Oldsmobile executives and management participated and led many of the community economic and charitable organizations. In 1996, there were 7,000 General Motors plant employees at the Lansing plants and another 20,000 people working with GM suppliers in the Lansing area (plus an additional 50,000 people working in various supplier and services positions in Michigan supporting the GM Lansing plants). In the last two decades of the twentieth century, GM focused the Lansing Car Assembly plant on the small car lines being marketed by Oldsmobile, Pontiac, and Chevrolet. The last Oldsmobile (an Alero sedan) rolled off the line at about 10 a.m. on April 27, 2004, at the Lansing Car Assembly plant, and the plant was officially closed down on May 6, 2005.

One rule that is absolutely fundamental in manufacturing is that if a plant has capacity, it needs to use it. Capacity utilization is critical for profitable operations in a manufacturing environment. So if you are operating on one shift in a plant, you are in deep trouble (even the title of our book would suggest as much!). At one point in 1992, every GM North American assembly plant was operating at less than one shift. With such low utilization of its production facilities, GM was losing $1,000 on each of its small cars sold.

Since the Lansing Car Assembly's goal was 300,000 cars per year, or 1,200 per day, the projected total loss was $300 million. Community leaders did not know the exact figures, but they knew that GM's operational losses were significant at the time. These leaders wondered what GM was going to do to fix the problem and when the company was going to do it. That level of loss could not continue forever, obviously. Sean McAlinden, vice president for Strategic Studies and chief economist at the Center for Automotive Research, believed that "the GM Board would soon tell the GM management to close every small car plant in the U.S. and move production immediately to Mexico. The result would be that the very old plants in Lansing and their associated stamping plant would certainly be shut down and not replaced."

GM's perspective was that it needed to remove production capacity and that the first place to focus on was the older plants. This did not bode well for Lansing! But it was not clear that the GM executives in Detroit fully understood the situation, other than the fact that the Lansing plants were old, and that made them vulnerable. As a matter of fact, GM's plant on the south side of Lansing was some 100 years old. It was the only plant in General Motors that still had wooden floors, theoretically a fire hazard. The Lansing Car Assembly plant was also the only facility that was still hauling car bodies from the north side of town by truck to the south side to be assembled at a cost of some $20 million per year.

Foreign competition, falling market share, increased regulation, overcapacity, and the recession converged to force the GM Board of Directors to make significant changes. It seemed obvious and logical to close the Lansing plant. What was not obvious was the unique DNA that distinguished the region—its workforce and its community leadership. This was ultimately to become the win-win scenario that Mayor David Hollister so desperately was seeking, but not without a lot of agony and hard work.

Mike Green, president of UAW Local 652, characterized the feeling of many in Lansing: "What you have to look at is it wasn't just us. There were many people facing the fact that they had no product scheduled for the future. It used to be, 'Okay, what's coming next? What are they going to build now?' In the past, we have built just about everything in Lansing, including most of the

Oldsmobiles, the big Oldsmobile 88s and 98s, and the Cutlasses. We built the Pontiac Grand Am. We built a gazillion of those cars, and they look at you one day and say, 'There's nothing slated to come here.' Well, that'll stop you in your tracks! Historically, people don't like change. Nobody does. You get in a comfort zone, and you don't really want to change from that. Well, if you're going to be building cars in the United States, you need to get on board and do some of those things, which, like I said, the membership got on board. . . . When you empower people to do something and you give them the tools to do it, they're hungry to do it, and they do a great job at it."

Any GM closing would come with an enormous cost and financial setback for the region. Bob Swanson, finance director of the City of Lansing, reflected that GM was the largest employer in the city by far, and the city's finances were really tied to how well local GM operations did. For example, GM has a large physical presence in the city, which contributed significantly to property tax revenue. The management and production employees who worked in the assembly operations also paid City of Lansing income taxes.

GM's property and employee income taxes had been critical to the region's financial stability. However, the age and relative inefficiency of the plants made them a primary target for closure. In order to move forward, it was essential to understand the true impact. While the direct impact could be the 7,000 GM jobs, the multiplier impact could be 10 times that for the entire region (Lansing and the rest of Michigan). The most significant consideration was the fact that in the entire history of General Motors, it had never changed its decision on a plant closure. Mayor Hollister and Lansing faced a tough challenge!

Know State Policy

The GM-related challenge for the state of Michigan was to try to understand the trade-offs and implications of the potential closure of an assembly plant. While many states have developed initiatives to attract automotive assembly operations, Michigan already had many assembly plants in many communities around the state. In effect, Michigan had not planned to attract assembly plants or even thought about the need to have a plan to keep them. It was simply taken for granted.

In other states, the governors and state legislatures would use tax incentives to attract the automobile manufacturers to the state. In the Michigan situation, the assembly plants were already present, and state law allowed incentives only when a net increase in jobs would occur. Even if GM decided to stay and reinvest in the Lansing area, there would be fewer jobs due to increased use of technology in the plants. Michigan's Republican governor John Engler illustrated the complexity of the situation, saying, "The City and GM had to approach this differently." They had to make an argument that said that "the premise of this in the past was net new jobs. Now we were going to have to emphasize retention so it was 'net from zero,' because zero is what you're going to have if everything went away. And we are in a global economic competition today, and virtually every other nation has tools."

In addition to the challenge of job-attracting legislation, there was also political tension in the 1990s when John Engler was elected governor of Michigan and David Hollister was elected mayor of Lansing. They had both served as Michigan legislators in the 1980s, Engler as a conservative Republican and Hollister as a liberal Democrat. Now they were both in executive positions in state politics and had to work together to keep jobs in Michigan. However, they had very different perspectives regarding the use of state or city retention funding and tax abatements. In general, Engler did not believe that such initiatives were necessary, and he was concerned that other regions around the state would question why they could not get state funding to attract industry as well.

Mayor Hollister summarized the challenge when he said: "We had to change the tax abatement law because previous to this, you could only get state tax credits for a manufacturing facility if you were adding jobs. We went into this knowing that even with this new plant, there would have to be fewer workers because of technology. They were moving so quickly toward technology. So, we were really groundbreaking for the new economy."

The shift toward more manufacturing technology changed the job profile in many states. Not only are there fewer jobs due to increased technology, but the nature of the jobs requires substantially more technical skills. The challenge for Michigan, as for many other states, is to recognize how technology will impact both the number and profile of manufacturing jobs.

Understand Regional Conflict

In the case of the Lansing region, there has been a 50- to 60-year history of tension between Lansing and its surrounding townships. Lansing is the state capital, surrounded by a number of relatively small but feisty townships. These townships were often competitive on many issues, resulting in many regional conflicts.

While the impact of manufacturing jobs extends beyond localities due to the suburban communities and the multiplier impact of suppliers and support industries, there is still significant competition among communities to attract major assembly plants. Michigan has very strong township laws that restrict the ability of cities to annex township property. This allows townships, which typically have more land to offer potential manufacturers, to attract firms to locate within their boundaries as an alternative to locating in cities, which often have higher income and property taxes.

Paula Cunningham, then president of Lansing Community College (and now executive director of the Michigan AARP), offered a very good overview of the regional conflicts: "There were many ups and downs. Just like everything, politics get in the way, what the unions wanted, what management wanted, what Delta Township wanted, what Lansing Township wanted. And [when] you sit at the table, when you get inside it's like you see the sausage getting made. You think, oh, this is never going to happen, but there was always that common denominator, that common goal of General Motors will leave if we don't get our act together. And that was the unifying force for us, that we had to figure it out, a way to work through whatever the issues were. And, that's what I saw happen, week after week after week, that we would leave really angry with one another or something, and then the next week we would come back to the table again, or the next day."

There were some 130 local taxing units in the tri-county region (Clinton, Eaton, and Ingham Counties) that needed to work together to develop a synergistic strategy to retain GM. Joe Drolett, former supervisor of the Delta Township Board, offered a perspective that was common with the township board members: "I believe [in] working together. There were some other factions at the time when I got in there [the Township Board] that people had a fear of working with Lansing because Lansing was the big boy, and we were the little guys out there at the time."

The scenario highlighted by Drolett was not unusual, and in fact, more complexities existed in the tri-county region. For example, there also were some cases where individuals were working with both the City of Lansing and some of the townships. In other cases, some of the townships had not been very collaborative. John Daher, Lansing Township supervisor, characterized some of these relationships by saying: "The fact that I was working with Lansing and Delta Township made a lot of people feel that we weren't doing the right thing. But I felt that we were. Back in the 70s, 80s, and 90s, a lot of communities were somewhat isolated. They were kind of independent silos just taking care of themselves, not too concerned about what was happening to their communities."

The examples by Cunningham, Drolett, and Daher illustrate some of the sentiments in the region. Basically, in this complex regional tri-county environment, of which Lansing is the central and largest city, the challenge was to bring the regional political and business communities together. This included the community leaders, chambers of commerce, business leaders, and representatives of key stakeholder groups.

While it may have been obvious that keeping GM should be good for all tri-county entities, Mayor Hollister had to take concrete action to first mount a campaign to rally the region in support of keeping GM. So he decided he would turn to the Lansing Regional Chamber of Commerce for initial support. Hollister, Jack Davis, and Ray Tadgerson had a meeting with Mel Kent (then president and CEO of the Lansing Regional Chamber of Commerce) to determine his concerns regarding the approach to keep GM.

Kent's concerns focused on what the other people involved with the Lansing chamber would think about a collaboration with Mayor Hollister, because he was one of the most prominent Democrats in the state. After a while, the team worked out an organizational chart that identified relationships and responsibilities so that the political and business communities could understand the team, have a place on it, and be supportive of a shared vision for the "Keep GM" campaign. Given Mayor Hollister's political propensities, it was very important to make sure that there was a real coordinated effort here and that the initiative was not simply promoting labor.

Recognize Public Sentiment

While there were significant challenges posed by GM's announced shutdown in Lansing, the state of Michigan, and the regional political and economic organizations, one of the most significant challenges was created by the breadth of the regional citizens' perceptions. In many cases, there was not a good understanding regarding the contributions of GM to the community and region.

People really did not understand that losing 7,000 GM jobs also had an indirect effect on some 20,000 additional jobs in Lansing and about 50,000 more jobs in the rest of the state. This 10-to-1 multiplier effect of the GM jobs in the city was difficult to grasp, explain, and quantify. But more telling, people did not believe the storyline. To some, the potential of losing GM seemingly had no direct effect on them. Naturally, such thinking is flawed since beyond the 10-to-1 multiplier effect, the region's infrastructure (e.g., housing, education, products to buy, and things to do) is directly connected to the financial impact that General Motors had and has in the region.

As such, in the community, vastly different perspectives existed regarding GM's future plant closure. Some had concerns that the "Keep GM" movement did not reflect enough objectivity regarding what GM means to the community. While GM was a corporation that had been loyal to its communities in the past, it was still a business, and it could leave at any time. There were some individuals during the "Keep GM" movement who said, "You know we're not willing to give everything to GM to keep them." There were also a few Lansing City Council members who were not entirely behind the "Keep GM" movement. Two of the members saw GM as a big corporation that was going to do what was in its best interest and felt that the council should stand up to GM at times even at the risk of the company's leaving the city.

Others had a different viewpoint but were still rather skeptical. Specifically, there were some people who didn't feel that GM would actually pull out, while there were others who thought that GM might pull out if it felt that the Lansing region did not appreciate the company enough. The situation became public quite early, as three of the Lansing City Council members were quoted in the *Lansing State Journal* saying: "If GM leaves us with no production, it's not a big deal. We'll become a wine-drinking community like Ann Arbor instead of a beer and bowling community like we have been."

Thankfully, there were others on the Lansing City Council who tried to take a more positive perspective. In 1997, Larry Meyer, one of the newly elected council members with a pro-business perspective, noted: "You know the City Council doesn't have a lot of power. It really doesn't. The mayor is there and is the head of government, but what the Lansing City Council can do is they can be irritants. They can cause a fuss. They can cause a dust-up. They can be mean spirited. They can have all kinds of things happening. We just can't do that. We just said, Okay, what do we have to do to be positive? What do we have to do to get this done for the betterment of the region?"

Even when people were supportive, the task of working to keep GM was not straightforward. For example, John Rock, general manager of Oldsmobile, was involved with the Lansing Regional Chamber of Commerce. Rock let the Lansing chamber know directly that there would not be any further production in Lansing after the Oldsmobile line ended. Jack Davis, chair of the Lansing chamber, asked Rock, "What do we do about it, because I'm not at Oldsmobile and General Motors?" While Rock was supportive of creating an initiative to keep GM, he would have had trouble leading the effort because General Motors headquarters would not want him to undercut whatever its plans were. And keep in mind that John Rock was a blunt-talking GM executive who wanted to save Oldsmobile in Lansing in perpetuity if he could.

Just as U.S. presidents get a more favorable review the longer they have been removed from office (with some exceptions of course), many of those involved in the "Lansing Works! Keep GM!" campaign have very fond memories about getting together, developing a great relationship, and achieving a positive outcome. However, many people forget that there was tremendous tension internally—but to their credit, the players kept it internal. This tension exemplified itself in many suspicions, deep suspicions that one party was speaking on behalf of the region while it was really secretly trying to work on its own behalf.

Bob Trezise (then executive director of the Lansing Economic Development Corporation and current CEO of the Lansing Economic Area Partnership) commented on the tension among the community partners: "The truth of it was it was tension filled where one side didn't trust the other side. There was yelling. There were private sector folks involved that kept things on an even keel like Ray Tadgerson from C2AE, Jack Davis from Loomis Law firm, and John Rock from Oldsmobile. I think it would be a big mistake for people to assume in this model that it was 'kumbaya' from the very beginning. It was not. In fact throughout the entire process there was a lot of tension. I think people should not be tricked into thinking, 'Boy, how do those guys be so in love all the time?' We weren't; we were just normal people, but had a very abnormal process that kept people in check and really worked, internally, kept things internal. To the public, to the outside like GM, it really did look like we were all in love."

These stories from Larry Meyer, John Rock, and Bob Trezise illustrate the range of public sentiment. Some people thought a GM plant closure would have serious implications for the region, and some people thought that a closure would allow the community to become more upscale. This range of perceptions meant that the leadership team needed to take credible steps to quantify the impact of a plant closure in the region. Clearly, emotions and sentiments could not be driving the "Lansing Works! Keep GM!" campaign; quantifying the impact so that everyone could understand, beyond their own self-interests, was paramount to get buy-in from the greater Lansing and tri-county communities.

Quantify the Impact

Mayor David Hollister and Ray Tadgerson realized how important it would be to quantify the number of direct and indirect jobs that would be lost as a result of the closure. Although Mayor Hollister had publicly talked about 15,000 direct jobs and 6 times that (90,000) in indirect jobs, some in the community questioned these numbers. Some suggested that Hollister's number reflected a "sky is falling" mentality and questioned whether GM would actually leave and, if so, whether the job impact would be that significant. Research history and available data—which we have reported on throughout Chapter 1 and this chapter—show that the actual numbers turned out to be very close to what Hollister had estimated. Specifically, data indicate that there were roughly 7,000 GM jobs at the Lansing plants, but these 7,000 jobs also had an indirect effect on some 20,000 additional jobs in Lansing (e.g., suppliers, services, logistics) and about 50,000 more jobs in the rest of the state (e.g., suppliers, services, logistics). This 10-to-1 multiplier effect of the GM jobs in the city was difficult to grasp, explain, and quantify.

To move forward and develop broad support, the leadership team needed to find an expert who could complete a credible quantitative analysis of the state and local economic impact that would enlighten the Lansing City Council, the community, and all the other regional constituents. University of Michigan professors George Fulton (director of the Research Seminar in Quantitative Economics and director of the Center for Labor Market Research) and his colleague Donald Grimes were contracted to complete the analysis.

Fulton, in particular, had significant experience at the University of Michigan's Research Seminar in Quantitative Economics. His institute is one of the premier economic forecasting organizations in the country. Building on the REMI database, Fulton and Grimes used an economic model to predict what would happen if the Lansing plants closed and nothing else happened. The first part of the study focused mainly on the value of the existing plant to Lansing and what would be lost if the plant was closed and basically no other activity occurred.

Later on, there was a discussion of actually attracting a new plant with state-of-the-art technology to Lansing, which developed into the idea of attracting two assembly plants and a stamping plant to Lansing. With the support of Fulton and Grimes's analysis, the leadership team began communicating the implications to both the constituents and the community regarding how much the current plant was worth and what a new plant could be worth. At the time, the study found the Lansing region would lose 15,000 direct and indirect GM jobs.

Beyond that, Michigan would lose at least 40,000 jobs. The numbers were pretty staggering in terms of the negative implications of GM's decision. As a result of the analysis and its publication, many people who had not really noticed before suddenly became concerned. "That was a real eye-opening experience for them to hear the numbers and to hear it from somebody who had nothing to gain in Lansing," said city finance director Bob Swanson. "So the expert told the story and told it very well."

Fulton and Grimes's analysis concluded that "the most compelling thing was that if they were able to build two assembly plants and the stamping plant, even while losing the existing plant, our estimates of the impact were that there was a present value of $10.8 billion of personal income from 1999 to 2020 for the Lansing region, and $38.6 billion for Michigan as a whole. Now as you can imagine these are very significant numbers."

❖

IDENTIFYING SUMMARY

For the Blue Ribbon Committee and the mayor's leadership team to move forward, it was vital to identify the key constituents and determine their perspective. This allowed the team to develop a synergistic approach to meet the various challenges.

Unfortunately, General Motors' small car production facilities were operating significantly below capacity, and it was critical that GM shut down some of its plants to reduce fixed costs. Since the Lansing Car Assembly plant was the oldest plant by far in GM's arsenal of plants worldwide, it was squarely on the chopping block for closure.

Despite the State of Michigan having a history of being collaborative with automakers, the concept of using state funding to retain jobs came with all kinds of implications that Governor Engler was not initially excited about. An investment to retain a reduced number of jobs in Lansing would open the state up for similar investments for many more communities around the state.

While the Lansing Car Assembly plant was located in the City of Lansing, there were many other cities and townships in the region that benefited significantly from GM operations. In some ways, the region's political entities appeared to collaborate, but in reality there was substantial suspicion and distrust. Basically, the City of Lansing, it was perceived, was out to develop a solution that would optimize its financial base while taking resources from other communities.

In the case of the local populace, there was a wide range of perspectives. There were some who recognized the regional impact of the loss of the plant, others who didn't take the possibility seriously, and yet others who thought GM's departure would be better for the community. It was clear that there was no consensus in the community, and this presented an initial challenge for Mayor Hollister's team. The community really needed to be on the same page and have most of its citizens buy into a shared vision for the "Lansing Works! Keep GM!" campaign. Thankfully, the Fulton-Grimes report provided the ammunition to develop the required consensus.

CHAPTER 3

PARTNERING

DEVELOP MEANINGFUL RELATIONSHIPS

Historically, once the top-level leaders at General Motors decided to close a plant, they did not change their minds, and there was little anyone in the affected communities could do. GM generally deliberated, carefully evaluated, and nurtured any strategic idea internally and under nondisclosure agreement confidentiality until the company was ready to publicly unveil the decision. In many respects, this is still the operating model for impactful strategic decisions at GM.

Reversing a strategic decision of one of the world's largest corporations was a monumental challenge, particularly since the greater Lansing region had no history of or mechanism for regional problem solving. Instead, what the region had—as many regions around the country can relate to—was a relatively large number of community organizations, multiple leaders tackling various areas of the community, and a number of business leaders with oftentimes differing viewpoints of where to head next in the community.

The greater Lansing region (and really mid-Michigan) was at risk of losing one of its major employers unless people could set aside old grudges and turf issues and embrace new ways of doing business. The region's leaders in business, labor, education, and local and state government, as well as citizens at large, needed to come together and let GM know how vitally important it was to the region and why continuing to do business there was in GM's best interest. This was more than reaching out to GM in a coherent way; this entailed strategically "selling" GM on the notion that its decision was wrong for logical and compelling business reasons. No one wants to lose a large employer like GM, but why its decision was strategically the wrong one for the company had to be the position—and very compelling justification had to follow.

With a starting point of a disconnected collection of regional leaders in business, labor, education, and local and state government along with concerned citizens, the collaborative task of developing meaningful relationships and strategically partnering across "party lines" became a must. Without such unity, why would GM believe it should, or even care to, engage in a dialogue with the greater Lansing community about potentially reversing a strategic decision that had been carefully evaluated? As such, to engage GM in a meaningful partnership would require extraordinary leadership, commitment to the goal of keeping GM in Lansing, a detailed plan of action, and strong cooperation and collaboration. Figure 3.1 illustrates the Second Shift Model, highlighting the "partnering" component discussed in Chapter 3.

PARTNERING NARRATIVE

The region's general response to the news that GM planned to close its existing manufacturing facilities was complete disbelief along

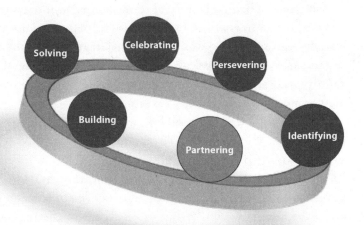

Figure 3.1 The Second Shift Model—partnering

with an "oh well" attitude that nothing could be done. Some perceived that this was a ploy by GM to gain more financial support from the community or perhaps concessions from the United Auto Workers union and that GM would not walk away from Lansing after having been in the city for some 100 years. Many felt that it would be a waste of time, money, and effort to try to change GM's decision. This meant changing mindsets and convincing everyone that this was a fight worth fighting.

Moving in uncharted territory, the Lansing mayor set out to learn more about how Toledo, Ohio, had organized its campaign to reverse Chrysler's decision to move its Jeep production out of the city. David Hollister sent a reconnaissance team made up of Bob Swanson (City Finance director), Dennis Sykes (Planning and Neighborhood director), Patty Cook (City Economic Development director), and Ray Tadgerson (CEO of Capital Consultants) to Toledo to investigate the "Toledo Loves Jeep" campaign. Mayor Hollister then made a personal visit to Toledo along with a delegation of diverse stakeholders, including key city and state administrators; city council members; chamber of commerce, labor, and education leaders; businesspeople; and the media—all of whom came away with a better understanding of the challenge that had confronted Toledo and what was in store for the Lansing community.

The Toledo trip was also a bonding experience in that the Lansing team clearly saw that the mayor was determined to take the lead. And most importantly, Hollister was also incredibly focused on developing meaningful partnerships across the landscape of diverse opinions and interests in the Lansing community. Diversity is good when it leads to a better outcome; diversity is bad when the outcome each diverse constituency wants is different! The Lansing community would have a chance to save GM in the local area only if it were driving in the same direction in a unified cross-community organized partnership involving all key players.

This could not be an exclusive team, and this could not involve team members who did not buy in to the ultimate outcome—keeping GM in the Lansing community. It sounds easy, perhaps, but behind the scenes some community members also saw this as an opportunity to get more GM activity in their local area. Such fractionalization in focus on outcomes had to be squashed, and the core focus had to remain on developing meaningful relationships that ultimately led to the strategic decision for GM to remain in Lansing.

Another key takeaway from the Toledo scouting trip was the need for a coordinated regional effort led by an engineer. The strategic leadership at GM "spoke engineering," not politics, so to engage in a stay-in-Lansing dialogue with the GM executives, the people on the Lansing team needed to make the GM folks feel comfortable by "speaking their language"; as well, the Lansing team needed to be able to better understand the viewpoints of General Motors and its decision to move. Consequently, Hollister asked Ray Tadgerson to join and become a key member of the Lansing team.

Tadgerson was the engineer who had been hired by Lansing to guide the building of Oldsmobile Park. He was now the core person tasked with putting together a comprehensive and strategic plan to keep GM. Within two weeks, Ray Tadgerson presented his recommendations to Mayor Hollister to create a blue ribbon committee to keep GM that would help formulate strategies for moving forward via a "Lansing Works! Keep GM!" campaign. Hollister and his team embraced the plan and began the challenging task of developing meaningful partnerships by selecting and engaging potential regional partners. They ventured into this relationship-building territory fully aware that the vice president of GM's Car Group North America, Mark Hogan, had clearly stated he wanted no such public Toledo-like campaign. So one of the first steps taken by the mayor could ultimately backfire, making outcomes even worse than the decision that had already been made by GM of leaving the community.

Now, given these highly political, highly public activities, for strategic reasons it was important to first gain the support of the Lansing Regional Chamber of Commerce. The chamber had endorsed the mayor's opponent in the 1993 election and did not want a relatively liberal politician interfering with its own effort to retain GM, its largest member. The reaching out that had to be done to the Lansing chamber was a microcosm that spelled out the path to developing meaningful relationships with other partners in the greater Lansing region. Building a partnership between the Lansing Regional Chamber and the mayor was instrumentalin developing other meaningful relationships that could uniformly work and also be viewed by other community members as working across the political bridge.

Unwaveringly, Mayor Hollister was not about to be a passive observer as GM made the painful decisions to downsize, consolidate, and close facilities. At the invitation of the UAW and GM management in the fall of 1997, Hollister had already become involved in the planning and implementation of the launch of GM's new car model Alero and had developed reliable networks that allowed him to monitor the pulse of the corporation. While the Lansing chamber approved of the mayor's recent economic development successes—the new Capital Area Transportation Center, a new minor league baseball stadium, and an agreement that convinced Jackson National Life Insurance Company to keep its world headquarters in Lansing (technically located in Alaiedon Township via a PA 425 agreement, or the Intergovernmental Conditional Transfer of Property by Contract Act, which practically meant that Jackson National has a Lansing address)—the Lansing chamber and the Lansing mayor were on a collision course regarding how to keep GM and who would take the lead. The Lansing chamber wanted to proceed by following GM's request to keep the conversation very low key and not engage in a public campaign. But why? GM was already gone, with that mentality!

Complicating matters was the opinion of some Lansing City Council members that they would rather see GM leave than offer it any more tax breaks. While the local UAW leaders were more amenable to meeting with the mayor due to his longstanding support for labor, they were worried that such an effort would compromise their pending negotiations with the corporation in a number of areas. They were willing to talk with an informal agreement to "not share what was said in the room."

The mayor overcame the Lansing chamber's objections by asking the chairperson of the Lansing Regional Chamber's Board of Directors, Jack Davis, to cochair the Blue Ribbon Committee to Retain GM and serve as its spokesperson and public face. Hollister followed up by inviting Peter McPherson, then president of Michigan State University, to cochair the effort, thereby committing academic expertise to the endeavor. Michigan State University is the major university in town, and the university has a multibillion dollar economic impact annually in the region. The Davis-McPherson team leadership seemed like a perfect and powerful start to developing meaningful relationships in this endeavor.

Additionally, potential competitors—Delta Township supervisor Joe Drolett and Lansing Township supervisor John Daher—were invited to be part of the leadership team, as were area legislators, Lansing City Council members, and labor, education, and neighborhood leaders. The group would grow to include more than 50 influential and highly active community leaders, but the bulk of the work was facilitated by a smaller leadership group, the Quick Response Team. In a show of ultimate commitment, and in response to the potentially dire outcome of having GM leave town after some 100 years, the Quick Response Team met weekly for 2½ years and then sporadically for the next 5 years. These were not meetings of lots of joy, reminiscing about a job well done, and quick fixes. The Quick Response Team performed an admirable task along with Mayor Hollister to hold the community together in a strategic partnership to save GM.

At the core, partnering focused on developing meaningful relationships involving a broad cross section of the region's influential leaders in business, labor, education, and local and state government, as well as citizens. By assembling this diverse, inclusive, transparent problem-solving group representing all elements of the community, the mayor evolved the reluctant partners into trusted allies committed to resolving every issue confronting the region as it fought to retain GM.

REFLECTIONS ON PARTNERING

David Hollister

Choosing whom to partner with in your personal and public life is one of the most important tasks of a community leader. I do not believe in the "self-made" person, as there are mentors, peers, and sought-out partners who contribute to one's life and successes. I always seek out the most talented people when I hire staff, choose advisors, or make appointments.

Importantly, for this group of talented professionals, I try to establish clearly defined goals and then empower those individuals to accomplish them. Synergistic goals, or at least shared goals among the group, ultimately get accomplished via empowerment, communications, and trust as critical components to any partnerships.

In this instance the goal was a world-class city, and to achieve that, we had to retain GM in Lansing. Yes, Lansing is the state capital of Michigan, but Lansing needed to keep GM. And we also thought GM needed Lansing; this became a passion and a vision.

The Blue Ribbon Committee, with all its disparate members and conflicting interests, was focused on the goal of keeping GM. Members participated because it was understood that all members would be heard and solutions would be "win-win." Keep in mind that some neighboring communities saw GM's move away from Lansing as a potential long-term opportunity for their community! Ultimately, Lansing and our team were successful because the "participants" came to believe in and trust the process. Our team evolved into "problem-solving partners," and our partnership became very meaningful to all involved.

Ray Tadgerson

After the daylong meeting with Mayor Finkbeiner in Toledo, Ohio, Lansing's mayor, David Hollister, was told that the best thing he could do would be to hire an engineer to run his campaign. Perhaps because of my engineering background, I thought this was a great idea!

So when the Lansing mayor asked if I could do this, I said, "Absolutely!" Then on the way back to Lansing, I started having second thoughts. But taking a moment to think about it in the bus going back to Lansing, I reflected on how Hollister asked the same thing about the baseball stadium and how I had responded back then. Thankfully the stadium project was just a few years earlier and still fresh in my mind and also in the community's mind. Maybe this was possible after all—we could build meaningful relationships to save GM.

So I thought I would do the same thing I did for the stadium and put together a strategic team. As the new mayor's "hired gun," I became a participant in Dave Hollister's inner circle, having meetings nearly every Monday morning with his team to discuss strategies on how to proceed for the week (and months) ahead.

Our first major objective was to determine whom to recruit to assist with gaining support for a campaign. This chapter is titled "Partnering: Develop Meaningful Relationships" for a reason.

Recruiting, gaining support, and basically being accepted across the political and community spectrums presented a daunting challenge. The starting point to tackle the challenge was to meet with influential leaders in the community and explain what the mayor would like to accomplish and how. But this could not be a wish list from just the mayor; it had to be done in such a way that it appeared both to have the strong support of the mayor and to be a shared community vision at the same time—not an easy task.

Getting the opportunity to meet with Mark Hogan, vice president of GM's Car Group North America, and with the Lansing chamber leadership, the local UAW leadership, and of course the Lansing City Council was the highest of priorities at this beginning stage. As we discussed in the opening sections of this chapter, Hogan was clear that he wanted no public campaign similar to the "Toledo Loves Jeep" campaign. Plus, the Lansing chamber wanted to lead the effort and wanted to work quietly with GM. Several Lansing council members also pushed back and stated that if GM wanted more tax relief, they would not support it. So it began with weeks of meetings to convince the community to join the mayor in his efforts. A shared meaning of the end goal of having GM stay in the community was a key to ultimate success.

At this time, in the early stages of the campaign to keep GM in Lansing, the mayor also asked me to create a strategic plan and wanted it back in 10 days. With the help of the mayor's leadership team (Bob Swanson, Dennis Sykes, and Patty Cook), we identified all the constituencies who needed to be contacted and recruited to help with the campaign. I wrote a strategic plan, which the mayor and the Lansing chamber approved. We also established an organizational chart noting how all the constituencies would be addressed.

MAJOR CHALLENGES AND OBSTACLES FOR PARTNERING

We identified eight challenges and obstacles we needed to confront:

1. Moving into uncharted territory, Mayor David Hollister formed the "Blue Ribbon Committee to Retain GM," made up of

notable leaders from the greater Lansing region. Many of these influential individuals had longstanding conflicting ideas and thoughts about how to address a number of issues in the community, including the looming future of GM leaving Lansing. The mayor also retained an engineer, Ray Tadgerson, to manage and direct the effort of getting everyone in agreement regarding GM's existence in the community. Hollister and Tadgerson had previously worked together on what was then called Oldsmobile Park (and now is called the Cooley Law School Stadium).

2. The Blue Ribbon Committee, initially with 28 members, grew to more than 50 people and ultimately proved to be largely unwieldy in terms of orchestrating meetings and responses to new challenges as they arose almost on a daily basis. As such, an executive team of six leaders was formed, called the Quick Response Team (QRT), but with the consequence that some Blue Ribbon Committee members felt left out. This did not help the idea of developing meaningful relationships, but it was a necessity to adopt a quick response mentality when tactically needed. Strategically, the Blue Ribbon Committee was still at the core, but the feeling of being left out created a major challenge and obstacle. Overall, though, the QRT was to respond to GM's questions and concerns quickly and thoroughly to ensure the communications lines were maintained.

3. A campaign slogan—"Lansing Works! Keep GM!"—was created and designed to have a twofold purpose: to communicate with the community and to send a message to GM. The effort included billboards, bumper stickers, a jingle, a video ad, and even license plates. Many in the community thought it was over the top and too expensive. Plus, of course, Mark Hogan had already sent a clear message that he wanted no public campaign similar to the "Toledo Loves Jeep" campaign. Lansing's challenge was to make the issue public and get community involvement while not alienating GM even more.

4. Raising money for the all-out effort to retain GM was a monumental challenge. It was estimated that Lansing needed "hundreds of thousands of dollars" for the total campaign effort, with obviously no certainty in the outcome to be achieved. At the conclusion, the fund-raising campaign brought in more than

$250,000 from local organizations and the private sector along with some contributions from the local government.

5. Having a dialogue with General Motors and the United Auto Workers was a challenge in that both were concerned that the conversations among the parties would be leaked to the public or played out in public forums. What large companies say publicly becomes the rule, or the truth, and what large and influential unions such as the UAW say becomes the talking points and strategy for members. This could have been a public relations nightmare in the making!

6. The relations between the local Lansing-based UAW and GM were known to be among the best in the country (to this day GM stands by its saying that the Lansing GM plants have among the best and most qualified workers in the company and also in the auto industry). However, the beginning of the "Keep GM" campaign also aligned with employee contract time, and GM was looking for some concessions in the new contract to become more competitive with Asian- and European-manufactured vehicles, namely fewer jobs by virtue of robotics and highly efficient plant operations. GM also wanted a two-tier wage structure and, importantly, a certain set of work rules. Without going into the technical details of these issues, these were highly contentious concessions, as viewed by the UAW, and remained in the background of the "Keep GM" campaign efforts.

7. Meetings with local UAW union leaders at the time—Art Baker, Tiny Sherwood, and Ralph Shepard—were often held behind closed doors with the understanding that whatever was said could not be shared outside that room. This level of trust was remarkable and much appreciated by everyone involved. Keep in mind that there were diverse and often conflicting interests at play. So the deal was that if anything was to be shared, it would require a conversation with the involved leaders first.

8. Michigan State University, through the efforts of President M. Peter McPherson and Vice President (for Governmental Affairs) Steve Webster, convinced 40 governmental units to sign a resolution pledging support to the "Lansing Works! Keep GM!" campaign and effort (see the Appendix). As the large, established

higher education leader in the community and one of the top universities in the world, Michigan State University could adopt a broker role in getting governmental characters on all sides of an issue and both sides of the aisle to the table and to a resolution agreement. This was vital at the governmental level for the campaign.

SEVEN COMPONENTS OF PARTNERING

Developing meaningful relationships and partnering on the basis of shared goals with the region's leaders in business, labor, education, and local and state government, as well as citizens at large (especially those with stakeholder connections to GM), entailed seven components. These included (1) reach across boundaries, (2) seek out champions, leaders, and expertise, (3) practice inclusiveness, (4) build trust and mutual respect, (5) share common goals and vision, (6) keep disputes private, and (7) provide hope and courage (Figure 3.2). The partners in the meaningful relationships that were established in this effort came through on these—clearly and with great passion.

Here we look at the seven partnering components, infusing them with a wealth of quotes and stories from community leaders who care, who have partnered regularly since this time, and who believe in Lansing.

Reach Across Boundaries

Reaching across boundaries symbolized a lot of agony along with diverse or even competing goals. This was the starting point for

Partnering
(Develop Meaningful Relationships)

1. Reach Across Boundaries
2. Seek Out Champions, Leaders, and Expertise
3. Practice Inclusiveness
4. Build Trust and Mutual Respect
5. Share Common Goals and Vision
6. Keep Disputes Private
7. Provide Hope and Courage

Figure 3.2 The Second Shift Model—components of partnering

partnering with community leaders and developing meaningful relationships—being on the same page, as the cliché would depict it. But this was no depiction of clichés; this was reality.

Mayor Hollister had a clear vision in mind of how to reach across boundaries and even called it a model for community behavior. He said, "The key elements of the model are to be regional and inclusive—so we don't leave people out, even people we don't agree with; collaborative; consensual; win-win; data driven; and most importantly of all, keep disputes private."

To accomplish this Hollister model of reaching across boundaries, Chris Holman (CEO, Michigan Business Network) stated the implications succinctly and appropriately—at least as they were at the beginning of reaching across the boundaries—when he said: "Well, first of all you had a lot of silos, because for a long time the greater Lansing area was kind of fractionalized. There were townships, cities, and there were counties; there were all kinds of municipalities existent who were oftentimes competitive with each other on many issues, or fought with each other on many issues."

Paula Cunningham, executive director of the Michigan AARP, echoed Holman's sentiment: "There were many ups and downs. Just like everything, politics gets in the way—what the unions wanted, what management wanted, what the Delta Township wanted, and what the Lansing Township wanted." Cunningham continued: "And [when] you sit at the table, when you get inside it's like you see the sausage getting made. Oh, this is never going to happen, but there was always that common denominator, that common goal of General Motors will leave if we don't get our act together." According to Cunningham, this was "the unifying force for us that we had to figure it out, a way to work through whatever the issues were. . . . And that's what I saw happen, week after week after week, that we would leave really angry with one another or something, and then the next week we would come back to the table again, or even the next day."

"Dave Hollister decided to get real active on orchestrating a campaign, and he wanted to bring about a community and a regional effort," said Jack Davis, a prominent Lansing attorney and former chair of the Lansing Regional Chamber. This is the same Jack Davis who needed to be part of the campaign to get the chamber on board. According to Davis, Mayor Hollister "decided he would turn to the chamber for business support." Davis continued, "We had a meeting and Mel Kent [then the chamber president] had issues, but Ray Tadgerson talked to Mel about his issues and they worked them out."

A transparent and important point for Jack Davis was the organization that Mayor Hollister and Ray Tadgerson developed. Basically, as Jack Davis highlighted this: "After a while, I saw the chart, a semi organizational chart, and Mel was comfortable. Mel had issues, probably thinking of other people involved with Lansing Chamber, what they would be concerned about because Dave Hollister was one of the most prominent Democrats in the state of Michigan, so I wanted to make sure that we had a real coordinated effort here and not something that was being promoted on behalf of labor." Davis's sentiment carries tremendous weight but also captures the fractionalization of community thoughts that had to be overcome in successfully reaching across the boundaries in the community.

The trip to Toledo, Ohio, was instrumental in laying the groundwork, and perhaps also in providing the blueprint, for the "reaching-across-boundaries perspective." Steve Serkaian, Mayor Hollister's communications director, illustrated this when he discussed the trip: "Hollister came back from the trip to Toledo with a plan of sorts—you had to be inclusive; you had to be communicative; you had to reach out to the entire community . . . to business, to labor, and to the education community. And you had to communicate to General Motors that they were very important to this community."

A number of approaches emerged as plausible for reaching across boundaries in the greater Lansing community. It was clear to Ray Tadgerson, however, that Mayor Hollister's approach was that "we need to take this public. We need to do what Toledo did. We need to make a statement, if to no one else, at least to our constituents, that we are trying to do something." The bottom line here was that Mayor Hollister, as effectively messaged to Ray Tadgerson, intended to show the Lansing community "that we are trying to accomplish something that maybe can't be accomplished, but we're going to give it our best shot."

An influential local "helper" in this endeavor of reaching across boundaries was Michigan State University. Virtually no one in the local community had competing goals with the nonprofit university, with its large presence and regional financial impact. Michigan State University could play a unique and neutral role in boundary-spanning competitiveness that seeped into the fabric of what the community really needed to do. University president Lou Anna K. Simon pointed out as much: "One of the roles that universities play or can play in this is a bit of a neutral broker. Particularly when there are a number of governmental units involved. One of the things that Steve Webster [MSU's vice president for Governmental Affairs] did, and he should get enormous credit for, was helping to gain support from some 40 partners [governmental units] to the Keep GM endeavor that might not have agreed to sign on if they were approached in a different way [see the Appendix]. But by the university getting behind it, and seeing it as a community priority, MSU was able to sort of leverage its assets to get others to join in."

Seek Out Champions, Leaders, and Expertise

Seeking out champions, leaders, and expertise sounds like a straightforward task. Unfortunately, too many chefs making a meal usually results in a lot of ingredients being mixed without much of a taste at the end. And what is worse, the dish is potentially never finished.

So seeking out champions and leaders necessitated finding the right people with the passion to commit and stay involved for the long haul while also representing meaningful partnerships that could work for the region's benefits and not their own individual goals. Given the fractionalization of the community that Jack Davis alluded to earlier in this chapter, finding and involving the appropriate leaders became paramount for the ultimate success of keeping GM in Lansing.

Expertise is related to but in many ways also different from champions and leaders. In the case of keeping GM in Lansing, though, expertise had to be added in. Ray Tadgerson, with a strong engineering background, became the right-hand person for Mayor Hollister. He was not an obvious "expert" to help Hollister bring together the community, but he was the right person to be part of the leadership team.

Ray Tadgerson spelled out nicely what had to be done: "It's one thing to have the challenge, but have it taken on by someone. There has to be a champion, and the champion in this particular case was Mayor David Hollister. He was willing to take on the challenge and willing to try to figure out what we can do differently; what can be done to save GM from leaving Lansing. He had the insight. He had the courage to go forward and to recruit a team of folks who were previously adversarial to him, working with a difficult Lansing City Council and working with Delta and Lansing township leaders who had a different agenda. That was difficult, but it took someone like Dave with his leadership skills, and with the talent, expertise, and experience he brought to the table." Tadgerson summarized it succinctly and perfectly by saying: "That's what it takes. That's the key. That's probably the most important element to anybody trying to undertake a model like this and to make it work."

Tadgerson elaborated on this point by very directly stating that "the first thing is making sure you have a good champion in place— somebody who is influential, somebody who is a recognized leader in the community—put together a really good team, a strong team, a collaborative team. People who have a vision similar to the champion." Now champions are selected or sometimes even select themselves!

Tadgerson explained: "One of the things we identified first was the fact that the Lansing Chamber was about to launch their own program, but they wanted to keep it very quiet and non-public, and to keep politicians out. The Lansing Chamber obviously labeled Dave as a politician; he was after all the sitting Lansing mayor. So, Dave's first request of me was, 'Let's start a conversation with the Lansing Chamber.' So, I spent a lot of time trying to bring the two factions together. We ultimately did, and one of the outcomes of that was to have Jack Davis be a co-chair with Dave Hollister and also Peter McPherson."

At the time, and along each step of the process, it may not have been clear who the true champion was at all times. But history has a remarkable way of rewriting and crystalizing itself and giving credit where credit is due and honorably earned. David Hollister now gets tremendous credit and accolades for his efforts, and his championing of the process, goals, and very meaningful community partnerships can serve as a nice lesson beyond the community of greater Lansing.

For Hollister, "The key was the trip to Toledo and what we learned from them. Now the key message there was hire an engineer.

Don't try to speak to General Motors in political language. They don't understand it, so speak engineering." So, he said, "We engaged Ray Tadgerson to be that lead person. I would look to him for the expertise on that; that was critical to our whole process."

Hollister continued: "You need to have a champion, and the group is the champion for the region, but you need a champion. At that point it was me playing the role as mayor. Jack Davis was our lead public face to the project. Jack and myself together with Peter McPherson from Michigan State University became the original lead team. So you need a champion who brings a clear definition of the goal, what the goal is and why are all in this together." This is where Ray Tadgerson entered the mix.

But even before that, Hollister realized that "critical, critical, critical, Jack Davis was the Chairperson of the Lansing chamber. The strategy was to say to business, which was suspicious of me, we'll make Jack the spokesperson. He was the recognized person as the Chairperson, the spokesperson, our public face with the campaign." Plus, "Our labor leaders, Art Baker, Ralph Shepard, Tiny Sherwood, and others had their finger on the pulse of the UAW. Mark Hogan and Ed Donovan had the pulse on the leadership of General Motors, although publicly they were miles apart." The team had a plethora of champions, leaders, and now also expertise—it was time to practice inclusiveness.

Practice Inclusiveness

Inclusiveness had to be realized, not just perceived, among the community leaders involved in the "Lansing Works! Keep GM!" campaign; otherwise old adversaries and competing goals would very likely come to the forefront and flourish in a negative way. Practicing inclusiveness became the norm for developing meaningful partnerships across boundaries in the community and even with identified champions and leaders. In that sense, the champions and leaders—even Mayor Hollister—became facilitators of a much larger, more grandiose endeavor than any community member could have foreseen at the beginning of the campaign.

Mayor Hollister is the perfect person to comment on practicing inclusiveness. He said: "You need a transparent, collaborative, participatory process that looks at win-win situations. It wants to build on the strengths of the community. In our particular case, it was our history of great labor-management relations and a highly skilled workforce that had a hundred-year history of being problem solvers."

But he also identified a unique and very important component of the "Lansing Works! Keep GM!" campaign: "The team is absolutely essential. It's essential that people feel like they're being heard, that their interests are being listened to and balanced—but there will be winners and losers. As we saw in the outcome, Lansing Township was a major loser. But the political leadership from the township had enough understanding of the impact of General Motors in the entire region and in the community. Even though their plants were closed, many of their people would be employed in the new plants. By keeping General Motors here, they're going to be contributing to Big Brothers, the churches, and the grocery stores. So they felt they had been heard and it was participatory. That enabled John Daher, who was the Lansing Township Supervisor at the time, to actually endorse, embrace, and support the outcome."

Perhaps amazingly to some, but in great harmony, John Daher echoed Hollister's sentiments: "Mayor Hollister and Joe Drolett simultaneously approached me and said 'You're a key player in the community.' You know, I never considered myself to be a key player. I always thought I was a supporting cast. I always felt we had a role, and I wanted to participate in any way I could. Dave and Joe embraced me and said that we need to do whatever we can to keep GM here in this community. So, they took me on. And, in retrospect it was probably one of the better things that ever happened to me."

Joe Drolett, Delta Township supervisor, explained: "We had to do something, and we had to work together. So anything we could do. I know Delta Township was invited in to the campaign right away when Dave Hollister was working with General Motors downtown. David came to me one day and he said 'Joe, give us first shot.' And I said, 'I'll give you more than that.' When General Motors was sitting in the room, I said, 'We want downtown first.' We cannot afford to have a decaying central city. I and my board members understand that a strong central city is good for us."

John Daher, Joe Drolett, and Jack Davis (chair of the Lansing chamber) became some of the key converts early in the process. Jack Davis bought into the arguments and later pointed out that "Dave Hollister decided to get real active on it [the campaign], and he wanted to bring about a community, regional effort. So, he decided he would turn to the Lansing Chamber for business support. He obviously had UAW's support, and he went to Michigan State University and MSU's President at the time, Peter McPherson, and Peter pledged a lot of support and was very active." Today's MSU president, Lou Anna K. Simon, illustrated this effect in her earlier remarks in this chapter: "One of the roles that universities play or can play in this is a bit of a neutral broker. Particularly when there are a number of governmental units involved. One of the things that Steve Webster [MSU's Vice President for Governmental Affairs] did, and he should get enormous credit for, was helping to gain support from some 40 partners [governmental units] to the Keep GM endeavor that might not have agreed to sign on if they were approached in a different way [see the Appendix]. But by the university getting behind it, and seeing it as a community priority, MSU was able to sort of leverage its assets to get others to join in."

In some ways, practicing inclusiveness ultimately became "easy." David Hollister noted: "We decided that we had the resources in this community. We had the brainpower, institutional knowledge, commitment of the university, state government, local governments, regional governments, and most of the community to give it a shot."

Build Trust and Mutual Respect

Now, how could the campaign reach across boundaries, seek out champions and leaders who could facilitate the "Keep GM" effort, and at the same time practice inclusiveness without building trust and mutual respect? It could not! Building trust and mutual respect became essential to developing meaningful partnerships in the community, partnerships that GM took seriously and believed in enough to reverse a decision that was already made. Keep in mind, GM rarely if ever reverses a strategic decision it has already made. Lansing was in unusual territory here, but what the Lansing team did know was that building trust and mutual respect had to be embedded in the fabric of doing business.

Jim Donaldson, Michigan Economic Development Corporation's vice president of Michigan Business Development, captured the sentiment that laid the ground for what had to be a change in the climate: "There was somewhat of distrust from City Hall across from the Romney building of the Governor's Office. Could Michigan's Governor Engler be trusted? The UAW certainly didn't trust him. And, I think the Governor's Office was also thinking, could Dave Hollister be trusted to really deliver and is he really the guy to lead the charge on this? So, there was some feeling out during that timeframe; and the Governor's Office asked Doug Rothwell to sit on the board for the Blue Ribbon Committee for the retention of General Motors. Doug asked me to represent him when he couldn't go, and quite often that meant I was at the meetings. Eventually trust was built between both City Hall and the Governor's Office."

At the time, Jack Davis (prominent Lansing attorney and chair of the Lansing Chamber) said: "We had mayors that would be totally

Lansing's mayor David Hollister and Michigan's governor John Engler shaking hands for a great partnership across the political aisle, with Los Angeles Lakers Hall-of-Fame basketball player Kareem Abdul-Jabbar watching in the background

ineffective at this [running a campaign]. I can't think of a mayor that would be as effective as David that we've had in Lansing. He understood that it was, it had to be, a community effort, regional effort. He understood that he was going to have to go along with certain leadership aspects that may not be exactly what he would have done. But, he became very trusted; he was clearly the leader of the whole thing." Keep in mind that trust also had to be built between Jack Davis and the Lansing Regional Chamber on one hand and the Lansing mayor on the other. The Lansing chamber after all had supported Hollister's opponent in the most recent election.

Not only did the Davis-Hollister partnership work out beautifully; so did the community relationships. As corny as it may sound, in many ways partnering became the de facto solution, even though the goal of keeping GM was the focus at all times. Perhaps this partnering and trust is best captured by Dave Hollister's view that "you need a pretty sophisticated communication strategy. First, you have to have the trust of the community, because if they don't trust you, nothing is going to happen anyway. And, you are continuously communicating something." Ultimately, Hollister said: "There were many groups of people on board, and they were honored to get on board. They were, initially, pretty suspicious. They got on board just to keep track of what I was doing and protect their own turf." Whatever reasoning community leaders had initially for being on board the "Lansing Works! Keep GM!" campaign, they got to a point where trust and mutual respect overrode their initial concerns and perhaps competing goals.

Perhaps the fabric for trust and mutual respect did exist deep down but needed to be brought to the forefront. The "Lansing Works! Keep GM!" campaign did just that. "In the 90s you could really notice a difference in attitude, but Lansing has always been a little bit unique," said Bruce McAttee, Community Action Program coordinator of the local United Auto Workers. He continued: "You have other communities where they were very militant from the beginning. I don't think that Lansing would be categorized as a militant community. There were places within GM, Ford, and Chrysler where you didn't even acknowledge your supervisor if you walked past them. It was almost like us against them. We always had the attitude in Lansing from the time I worked there that we were all in this together."

Randy Thayer, GM's Regional Plant manager, echoed Bruce's understanding: "What's unique about labor-management relations here in Lansing is the shared goals. The union here never had anything in mind except job security. They overlap between, when you get right down to it, the management's worried about job security too, right? So, the overlap was huge. It wasn't 100 percent—don't, can't sugarcoat it. I mean you have differences, but the overlap was much more than in most places. And, the local UAW union knew that it took them being a part of it to make anything successful."

Share Common Goals and Vision

The problem—or opportunity, if you want to be optimistic from the get-go—is that any team effort has to evolve into shared common goals and vision. Reaching out across boundaries is fine, but boundaries are there, or have been there, for a reason. Boundaries by design suggest differing goals, at least in many areas. Likewise, seeking out champions and leaders means that by the basic nature of selecting certain champions and certain leaders, others are excluded from those roles. At the same time, practicing inclusiveness is a key to success, and this success and inclusiveness is very much rooted in the trust and mutual respect that can be created among team members. All this is easy to spell out and identify but obviously not easy to realize and implement. How do we then reach a stage where we have shared common goals and vision?

Sometimes it takes brutal strategies to achieve some semblance of shared goals. Jack Davis laid it out from both a political and a practical perspective: "The other thing besides starting a campaign that happened was the Lansing City Council got word of the possibility of not having GM production, and two or three of the city council members let it be known that if GM was going to require tax incentives or breaks from the city to stay or increase production or retain production here that they were going to vote against it. So, Dave Hollister asked the chamber to get some candidates. They would have to be from the business-oriented community and then we [Lansing Chamber] had to fund a campaign in order to beat the three who were saying that."

Perhaps this is not the normal or even politically correct way of developing shared common goals and vision. But think about it—the greater Lansing community got more than 50 major community leaders and organizations together for a common goal, that of keeping GM in town. Continuing Jack Davis's storyline, David Hollister explained: "Do you think as someone who was in city office, working in state government, it is hard to turn off that part of your brain? Are you always kind of thinking about how things could work out, how the city could be better, the state could be better? You're always considering process and large goals. My goal at that time was a world-class city."

Hollister identified the outlook, and it was not good if three obstacles, or members, of the Lansing City Council remained on the council. Partly due to the Lansing chamber's efforts, and the community's support, of course, Hollister realized his intended remake of the Lansing City Council, a much-needed makeover to develop a shared common goal and vision among the rest of the more than 50 community leaders. In an irritated tone, Hollister pointed out the remarkable statements made by three Lansing council members, as described by Jack Davis: "It became public right away, because of what the three council members said publicly, 'Well, if GM leaves us, leaves with no production, it's not a big deal. We'll become a wine-drinking community like Ann Arbor instead of a beer community like we have always been. That was quoted in the paper [*Lansing State Journal*]."

Larry Meyer, Lansing City Council member and prominent Lansing businessperson, explained: "It was the Mayor who put together the community, put together regional forces, and put together a collaboration of a lot of like-minded people that said, 'Okay, for this particular mission we are all united. It can work.' Key to the council, we went from 5–3 votes to 8–0. That doesn't mean we didn't deliberate. That doesn't mean we didn't collaborate. It doesn't mean there was not a lot of give and take, but we were united and we worked together. We were working toward solutions. It wasn't about just raising a ruckus; it was about working toward solutions."

What people making a statement like "wine-drinking community like Ann Arbor" perhaps did not realize is the tremendous bullwhip effect and its escalation on jobs in the community a move like GM's leaving town would mean: a gigantic number of first-tier suppliers to GM and their partners of second-tier suppliers and third-tier suppliers, and so on, would translate into hundreds if not thousands of small and medium-sized companies and thousands of people employed now being out of a job. This means fewer businesses and services in the community, a weakening tax base, and a huge hole in the financial prospects for the city. It was not just one company (GM) leaving; rather, it would have become an infrastructure crashed and a cultural fabric shattered.

Keep Disputes Private

It should (almost) go without saying that trust and mutual respect cannot materialize, or at least stay, if disputes are not kept private in a major undertaking such as the "Lansing Works! Keep GM!" campaign. But let's say it anyway! Partnering across the community and building meaningful relationships that can make the greater Lansing area thrive now, and especially back in the "Lansing Works! Keep GM!" campaign days, it required that disputes be kept private among the involved team members.

This politically charged topic is illustrated, as before, by Paula Cunningham, executive director of the Michigan AARP: "There were many ups and downs. Just like everything, politics gets in the way—what the unions wanted, what management wanted, what the Delta Township wanted, and what the Lansing Township wanted." Cunningham continued: "And [when] you sit at the table, when you get inside it's like you see the sausage getting made. Oh, this is never going to happen, but there was always that common denominator, that common goal of General Motors will leave if we don't get our act together." This was "the unifying force for us that we had to figure it out, a way to work through whatever the issues were. . . . And that's what I saw happen, week after week after week, that we would leave really angry with one another or something, and then the next week we would come back to the table again, or even the next day."

In regard to not publically airing disputes, Bob Trezise, CEO of the Lansing Economic Area Partnership, has a great point: "I think people should not be tricked into thinking, 'Boy, how do those guys be so in love all the time?' We weren't, we were just normal people, but had a very abnormal process that kept people in check and really worked, internally, kept things internal. To the public, to the outside like GM, it really did look like we were all in love." In many ways, it helped that the Quick Response Team was relatively small (compared with the Blue Ribbon Committee). "The Quick Response Team met every Monday morning in my office," said David Hollister, and it "included a very small group of people, Joe Drolett, John Daher, Jack Davis, Dennis Sykes, Bob Swanson, Mel Kent, Trygve Vigmostad, and Ray Tadgerson." Tadgerson, of course, became the right-hand person for the mayor on this team, on the Blue Ribbon Committee, and in almost any endeavor on the "Lansing Works! Keep GM!" campaign.

Tadgerson's commentary on the topic of keeping disputes private is important as well. He was entrenched in the project, its many storylines, and its many players. "Before we announced the Blue Ribbon Committee, Dave and I and a couple of Dave's key department heads [Bob Swanson and Dennis Sykes] were meeting to strategize how this was going to work and how we could get the community involved," he said. Tadgerson added: "He [Hollister] had a public relations person working with him, Steve Serkaian. Between members of this group, we decided that every week, we would decide how we're going to roll out certain pieces to the Quick Response Team and the Blue Ribbon Committee. But, before that, we had to figure out what was the Blue Ribbon Committee. Who would be involved? How often would they meet? What was their charge? So, Dave asked me to put together a plan. I put together a strategic plan and identified various segments of the community: labor relations, finance, community, neighborhoods—all of the constituencies that would be affected by the campaign."

Obviously this caused stress, and it also entailed keeping disputes private, even in the beginning before any shared common goals and vision could be established. Tadgerson said that "it was a strategy session to figure out what we were facing this week, how we were going to accomplish this, how do we spin it to the public, what do we release to the public. In our conversations with the unions, they would often tell us, 'What we are telling you can't go outside this room.' Some of the things they told us, we really had to keep confidential, and in the Quick Response Team, we would decide what we were going to say to the public, and what we were going to say to the Blue Ribbon Committee. How we say it and how much information we are willing to share, because whatever we said could put the whole campaign at risk."

Provide Hope and Courage

Chapter 6, titled "Celebrating: Mark Successful Milestones," discusses a number of the ultimate outcomes—intermediate and bigger celebration–related—and the hope and courage associated with the campaign. But hope and courage also entered into the equation when developing partnerships in the form of meaningful relationships that could strategically be leveraged, be nurtured, and be good in a timely way for the greater Lansing region in keeping GM. In effect, people on the Quick Response Team and the many individuals on the Blue Ribbon Committee fed off each other and the hope and courage exemplified by everyone involved.

The natural extension is, of course, that the larger community then, in turn, fed off what publicly came out of the Quick Response Team and the Blue Ribbon Committee. Hope and courage are what Hollister exemplified, for example, in deciding to launch a public campaign even in the face of more potential adversity, given that the vice president of GM's Car Group North America, Mark Hogan, had stated he wanted no such public Toledo-like campaign for the Lansing area.

But hope and courage also have to be brought to the forefront and nurtured to flourish. Commentary from Ed Donovan, director of Government Relations for General Motors, illustrates these issues: "I would suggest to anybody in America, here's your answer to finding that magic lock to these problems. Is it easy? No, it's not easy. I think that I met Mayor Hollister, I want to say, around January or February of 1994. At that time, I had little hope for where this was going, and look where we are today." Donovan continued: "We now believe Lansing holds the potential to make significant investments and be the future of General Motors. It really began happening during that time frame [late 1990s and early 2000s]. It wasn't just one day it happened; it took three, four, five years for that to really transition from where it was to where it ended up. Unless there's something we can't predict in the global economy, that time frame opens the door for a vibrant presence of GM in the Lansing region in the auto manufacturing area to 2050."

Ray Tadgerson, from earlier in this chapter, elaborated on the hope and courage: "It's one thing to have the challenge, but have it taken on by someone. There has to be a champion, and the champion in this particular case was Mayor David Hollister. He was willing to take on the challenge and willing to try to figure out what we can do differently, what can be done to save GM from leaving Lansing. He had the insight. He had the courage to go forward and to recruit a team of folks who were previously adversarial to him; working with a difficult Lansing City Council; and working with Delta and Lansing township leaders who had a different agenda. That was difficult, but it took someone like Dave with his leadership skills, and with the talent, expertise, and experience he brought to the table." Tadgerson summarized it succinctly and perfectly by saying: "That's what it takes. That's the key. That's probably the most important element to anybody trying to undertake a model like this and to make it work."

Much of the hope and courage also rests in integrity and a specific goal-driven objective that can be shared among community leaders from all walks of life. Hollister illustrated the importance of integrity: "This is about creating a process and the integrity that you bring to the process, and then a vision and goal and working on it and bringing partners together. You might win some, you might lose some, but the important thing is that you are committed to a participatory process with collaboration and win-win with people coming together. If not solving a problem, addressing the problem, so that I feel that this is a community I want to be proud of, and all my family would be proud of. I want to be proud of it myself and brag about it and live here and enjoy the recreation, the schools, and the businesses and just be a member of a thriving community."

Many communities like Lansing take their infrastructure and existence for granted. Bo Garcia, dean of Community Education and Workforce Development at Lansing Community College, helps us better understand that this should not be the case: "It is imperative that we remain conscious, appreciative, and take inventory of all the assets on a regular basis: small businesses, midsize, large, all the stakeholders of the community, elected officials, educational systems, and the whole nine yards. Just kind of make sure we are covering all the bases as it relates to supporting, growing, enhancing, identifying, and addressing issues that may have an adverse impact, if not today, tomorrow."

Today's leaders in Lansing agree. MSU president Lou Anna K. Simon noted: "You can never take what you have for granted, particularly in this very complex global marketplace where you're not the center of corporate decision making. You have to continue to show value for what you're doing. You can't just wait for something bad to happen, in order for the community to mobilize and continue to both promote what you have and the quality of the workforce that you have, at the same time looking for new opportunities. People thought we won, so we relaxed, and now in this world, you can't do that. You've got to continue that kind of structure and that kind of regional focus on creating new things and keeping what you have."

At the same time, Debbie Stabenow, U.S. senator from Michigan, remains in selling mode to GM and other manufacturers in Lansing and in the rest of Michigan: "I think, first of all, knowing that General Motors understands how critical Lansing is, the teamwork, the workforce, the leadership, the community coming together, is very significant, but these benchmarks, seeing the Camaro come in 2015, the North American Car of the Year, ATS, and seeing Cadillac moving ahead with the CTS and others, means we have a very strong future in Lansing and it is all about General Motors, and that the future of the best cars and trucks in the world is going to start right here."

Today's Lansing mayor, Virg Bernero, agrees: "We're making award-winning cars here; that's part of not just our legacy, but our future. When you're making great cars that are selling, those are leaders of the flagship. We are selling the flagship of the GM fleet here in Lansing. It's produced right here in Lansing. That's job security for hundreds of people. That gives me a very good feeling about Lansing's future. I think GM's future and Lansing's future are intertwined. If I have anything to say about it, they'll be here for years and decades to come."

PARTNERING SUMMARY

Perhaps combining the eloquent and important viewpoints of MSU president Simon that "you can never take what you have for granted, particularly in this very complex global marketplace," with the optimistic and sales-oriented pitch of U.S. senator (and MSU alumnus and Lansing native) Debbie Stabenow and current Lansing mayor Virg Bernero makes for a great outlook for the future. Remember where we have been and nurture where we are going, and do it via meaningful relationships and partnerships that can get the tasks accomplished— no matter how big!

David Hollister, the Lansing mayor at the helm during the "Lansing Works! Keep GM!" campaign, is also optimistic, and his friends in the Lansing community are as well: "The story is just beginning. We've secured the future for the next 50 years, and now it's up to the next generation to build on that and make something better," he said. In fact, he went even further: "There's no limit to what this community can do. You've got state government and all the brainpower. You've got the university [MSU] and all that brainpower. You've got strong neighborhoods with people committed to this community. You've got within the region enough economic and population density to make it pretty much whatever you want it to become."

But Hollister also warned today's community leaders: "The challenge will be to overcome those regional turf issues and continue to build a more strategic economically feasible governmental operation. There are some enormous challenges, but what we've been able to achieve shows that it can be done. Just have a vision, have a process, and go to work."

What we captured in the story of more than 800 pages of interview notes tends to agree with Dave Hollister. His team set the tone for how to partner and how to develop meaningful relationships across boundaries, seeking out champions in the process, practicing inclusiveness as much as possible, building trust and mutual respect, creating shared common goals (even at the cost of some members), keeping disputes private, and always providing hope and courage as a part of the encouragement.

———— ❖ ————

CHAPTER 4

BUILDING

CONSTRUCT YOUR STRATEGY
AS YOU GO

While the community was in agreement with the goal of keeping GM, it had no mechanism to engage in regional problem solving and definitely no mechanism to build a clear strategy for doing so. It became a necessity to construct the strategy along the way as Mayor Hollister and his team went about keeping GM. They wanted GM to keep building cars in Lansing in the same robust way it had been done for more than 100 years. But nothing was robust about the strategic start. The team had no other choice, as time was of the essence and being responsive to GM and the community demanded strategic thinking at the highest level. It was just that this highly complex, involved, and partner-oriented strategy had to be constructed "as we go."

Strategically, the starting point to build some form of coherent strategy was launched with the fact-finding trip to Toledo on January 13, 1998. A delegation of business, labor, and community leaders joined Mayor Hollister on the trip to learn how that community reversed Chrysler's decision to move its Jeep assembly operation out of the city. Hollister summarized the group's findings in a memo to the Lansing City Council: "Mayor Finkbeiner appointed David Wallace, a respected businessperson and engineer, to coordinate all community efforts and to report to him directly. Mr. Wallace organized a proactive technical work group that included all federal, state and local agencies involved in site development and began weekly

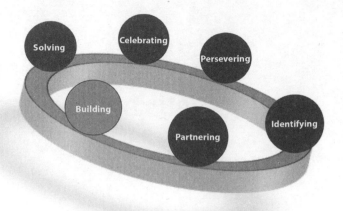

Figure 4.1   The Second Shift Model—building

meetings. Mr. Wallace worked with the mayor to develop a Quick Response Team. This community effort, united by the mayor, was made up of political, educational, business, service, and community leaders to begin a public campaign to retain Jeep." Figure 4.1 illustrates the Second Shift Model, highlighting the "building" component discussed in Chapter 4.

It became almost a literal "construct your strategy as you go" undertaking. Going to Toledo set off the "starting gun" for the race to keep GM in the greater Lansing community. On the return trip to Lansing, Hollister asked Ray Tadgerson if he could put together a similar plan for Lansing. Tadgerson said yes, and within two weeks the Blue Ribbon Committee to Keep GM was announced. Toledo and Chrysler became Lansing and General Motors, but the Lansing story has complexities and nuances that carry deeper and into more fascinating areas than what could be expected from the Toledo learning experience. Nevertheless, Toledo was the starting gun to think strategically and act deliberately for the Lansing community.

The "construct your strategy as you go" approach really worked well for the Lansing community. Building a strategy and sticking with it would not have provided enough flexibility to solve all issues that came up (more on that in Chapter 5), and it would also not have allowed for appropriate identification of problems at all stages of the ordeal (Chapter 2) or created win-win situations for the community's strategic partners in this endeavor (Chapter 3). The latter notion of win-win is important.

Without any doubt, the primary goal of the campaign was to create a win-win scenario whereby all the involved parties felt the region was benefiting from the effort to retain GM. This required unique communication strategies for each specific constituency, e.g., surrounding city and township governmental units, the Lansing City Council, the business community, GM, local and regional UAW units, the media, state government, Michigan State University (as the large Big Ten university in the region), Lansing Community College (as the core workforce development trainer in Lansing), neighborhood associations, the nonprofit community, and the general public. Basically, there were a lot of entities that had to be in on the win-win strategy, and they had to feel and know that win-win was the primary goal of the "Lansing Works! Keep GM!" community engagement campaign.

If anything, the core strategy was to bring the most influential team members on board to help with the campaign. While a difficult process, to say the least, the most influential members had to buy in, had to work hard, and had to be passionately involved. There was no strategy, not yet a shared vision (although that would come soon), and so constructing the strategy on the go depended on the brightest minds in the region and the most diverse set of people being involved to cover all essential and potential topics that could come up. Look no further than to the major challenges and obstacles highlighted in Chapters 2 to 7, and it is easy to realize that a dynamic strategy was essential to survival.

Now some were more than willing to help, while unfortunately others joined just to see what was going on and to potentially protect their turf. Nearly all had their own agenda and constituencies to represent. As expected, it took several different strategies, several different tries to build a strategy, to address these various agendas. Given that it was a one-of-a-kind campaign (with a starting point from the Toledo case), nearly all planning was developed on an "as you go" basis.

BUILDING NARRATIVE

The public announcement of a regional problem-solving committee dedicated to retaining GM was greeted with interest and skepticism.

The tri-county area (Ingham, Eaton, and Clinton Counties) had over 130 taxing units and virtually no history of local units of government collaborating to attract or retain businesses. Turf, animus, and suspicion, not collaboration, were in the region's DNA. One would think that this is not the typical, and certainly not preferred, setup for building the strategy to save GM in the greater Lansing area.

Mayor Hollister's drive to retain GM as a major employer in the region was launched when he announced the formation of the Blue Ribbon Committee to Keep GM in his 1998 State of the City Address. While continued community skepticism was expressed in a *Lansing State Journal* editorial on February 25, 1998, its conclusion reflected the general consensus: "There is little to lose by making a united pitch to General Motors to keep its car making operations here. If it takes a Blue Ribbon Committee to forge this united front, so be it."

The Blue Ribbon Committee that was announced impressed skeptics because of the high-level leaders involved, particularly Jack Davis representing the Lansing Regional Chamber of Commerce and President Peter McPherson of Michigan State University. It is noteworthy that President McPherson was not your typical academic; he and Jack Davis formed a magnificent "brand" for the initial strategic efforts.

The Blue Ribbon Committee roster of more than 50 people (the initial list included 28 community leaders but was later expanded to in excess of 50) represented the "who's who" of regional stakeholders and also a very high collective IQ about the region and its manufacturing. Six subcommittees covered the broad range of issues and challenges facing the community and included diverse and often conflicting points of view.

A unique and very important part of the ongoing efforts to build the appropriate strategy—what we would call a dynamic strategy in academic terms (although not even President Peter McPherson would have used that language)—was the creation of the Quick Response Team. The initial Quick Response Team included Jack Davis, Mayor Hollister, Melvin Kent, Peter McPherson, Ray Tadgerson, and Trygve Vigmostad; later Joe Drolett, Jim Donaldson, and John Daher were added (when Melvin Kent and Trygve Vigmostad were dropped).

The leadership group developed a two-part strategy—first, to create a business case that would convince GM that investing in mid-Michigan made the best business sense and, second, to educate the community about the importance of maintaining auto manufacturing in the region and collaboratively designing and delivering a comprehensive community strategy to show that Lansing could compete with and exceed any other place in the world. This became the starting point for the "Lansing Works! Keep GM!" slogan. Lansing was, after all, to be pitched as the city and region with the best-qualified and most highly competent auto workforce in the world.

Beyond the normal operating procedures of signing confidentiality agreements around the table, the Intergovernmental Subcommittee chaired by President McPherson put together a resolution that was circulated to area governments. The resolution strategically recognized that:

- The Lansing region was the birthplace of the automobile manufacturing industry in part due to RE Olds's accomplishments.
- All Lansing-region communities have benefited economically from the 100-year history of building quality automobile production.
- Excellent labor and management relationships between the United Auto Workers and General Motors have been a hallmark of the Lansing plants.
- The current plants and skilled workforce made the Lansing area the "Car Capital of North America" in terms of both the quality and quantity of cars produced.

Think about this for a minute. By signing the resolution, each local government was making a pledge to set aside narrow provincial issues and make the retention of General Motors a top priority. Most importantly, perhaps, was that these oftentimes competing communities had to agree to a strategic and collaborative effort among units of government in the Lansing region to keep General Motors.

Bob Swanson was the Quick Response Team liaison with the Economic Analysis Team and knew from both local and state experience that incentive packages with corporate tax breaks were very controversial but essential when competing with other states and nations for manufacturing jobs. Swanson knew that local politicians would question the wisdom of forgoing property taxes on one of the nation's largest corporations.

Anticipating the hostility of some Lansing City Council members, Swanson convinced members of the subcommittee to engage distinguished University of Michigan professor George Fulton (director of the Institute of Labor and Industrial Relations) and his colleague Donald Grimes to do a study of what the economic impact of GM closing the plants would be. Fulton and Grimes were well-respected researchers and had developed a model for measuring investments, incentives, and job creation. They were also based in Ann Arbor at the "friendly competitor" to the local Michigan State University. For some, this disconnect of Fulton and Grimes to the local Lansing community actually helped make the case (at least it seemed very objective).

Fulton and Grimes concluded that the outdated existing plant currently producing the Grand Am and Alero employed 7,000 GM workers and was responsible for 20,000 total jobs in the greater Lansing region and nearly 50,000 jobs statewide. This represented 7 percent of the total jobs in the region and 1 percent statewide. Bottom line, the stakes for Lansing and the region in getting a replacement plant for the existing facility were huge. Fulton and Grimes also concluded that GM plant closings would result in a loss of $4.5 million in annual tax revenue and $11.2 million in property taxes and school taxes. "The importance of a replacement facility in the region cannot be overstated. The local tax incentive of $188 million . . . will lead to an increase of $37.3 billion in personal income growth statewide over the next ten years—or $200 for every dollar invested."

This study became a critical tool to build strategic support and overcome opposition to the incentive package being developed. Amazingly, the Lansing City Council had already begun to question the role of General Motors in the community. One council member suggested that GM couldn't afford to leave because of all the investments it had made over the years, and talk of its leaving was just a strategy to scare the community and get enhanced concessions. The current president of Michigan State University captures this council member's ignorance perfectly in her general thought about renewal: "You can never take what you have for granted, particularly in this very complex global marketplace where you're not the center of corporate decision making. You have to continue to show value for what you're doing. You can't just wait for something bad to happen, in order for the community to mobilize and continue to both promote what you have and the quality of the workforce that you have, at the same time looking for new opportunities."

Another council member suggested that Lansing would be better off if General Motors left. Strangely, this sentiment was not unheard of in the community, and it percolated to the top again in the 2008–2009 economic downturn that hit the globe and especially the U.S. automakers. From our vantage point, such sentiment is economically ridiculous and not operationally logical. Thankfully, the Fulton and Grimes report, and lots of data subsequently, made it clear what the stakes were and provided useful data for the Blue Ribbon Committee as it developed and refined its campaign to keep GM. It became known as the "construct your strategy as you go" approach, but in reality, data, passion, drive, stubbornness, and incredible political savviness set the tone for the dynamic building of strategy that ensued.

REFLECTIONS ON BUILDING

David Hollister

As I thought about the stark reality that GM was planning to end its auto manufacturing operation in the region, I was determined to do everything in my power to reverse that decision. GM had concluded that the outdated and inefficient production facilities could no longer be justified; foreign competition was cutting into market share and profits. GM was downsizing everywhere it could; the odds against us were overwhelming, and the task and challenges were daunting, but something about this region was unique. We had a great workforce with a 100-year history of excellent labor-management relations, and that workforce had continued to produce quality, award-winning products in these old, outdated plants. As mayor, I had no power to change GM's mind, but I could use the bully pulpit and my passion for collaboration to unite the region in a focused, problem-solving effort built around our number one asset: our skilled entrepreneurial workforce.

Ray Tadgerson

A well-defined communications strategy and a well-thought-out action plan are the two most important elements of a successful campaign. Having open, transparent (to the highest degree possible) communications with the various stakeholders was critical to create trust. Virtually all of them wanted to know what was going on and felt like they had a right to know.

At times there was so much happening, it necessitated discussion and action between the Monday meetings, and occasionally there was no opportunity to get "clearance" from the QRT members or the Blue Ribbon Committee. Some of those actions or decisions had to be shared after the fact. However, by doing so, the process reinforced the trust element.

The Monday morning team (my designation) was very proactive and worked together successfully to identify challenges early on and formulated strategies to address. My role at the time as project manager and project director was to create agendas for all meetings, draft minutes for those meetings, and monitor the execution of tasks defined by the team. I also had the responsibility to monitor and oversee the various subcommittees of the Blue Ribbon Committee, which included the Labor Advisory Committee, Government Advisory Committee, Regional Focus Team, Technical Team, Economic Analysis Team, and Public Relations Team. I had written the strategic plan for the mayor and had included the roles and responsibilities for each of the subcommittees. Each subcommittee met on an as-needed basis to address specific challenges and develop a plan of action for the mayor and his team to consider.

MAJOR CHALLENGES AND OBSTACLES FOR BUILDING

A summary of the major challenges and obstacles we faced include:

1. The members of the Lansing City Council were somewhat divided on whether to try to keep General Motors in the city, and they were also sharply divided on whether to provide incentives and tax abatements. The differences were encapsulated in the "wine and quiche" versus "beer and bowling" town comments from the council members.

2. Convincing the Lansing City Council and community representatives that keeping GM was worth the effort required an economic impact analysis to demonstrate the impact of losing GM. It also included the potential impact of building one new plant and, later, building a second plant.

3. The Lansing mayor, the Lansing Regional Chamber of Commerce, and the United Auto Workers union backed candidates for the Lansing City Council who were known to be favorable to the mayor's agenda to keep GM to replace those who were not in favor of even trying to keep GM. The result was three new council members.

4. The Lansing mayor felt that changes were also necessary on the Lansing School Board and actively sought new candidates. The result was Jack Davis being elected to the Lansing School Board, which became controversial due to a question about his residency. The school board issue was important because the board was a solution to addressing GM's concern about having an educated labor pool.

5. The launch of the Alero on the second shift was initiated by plant manager Jim Zubkus and UAW leader Art Baker. This approach was very unorthodox (no one launches new car models on the second shift!) and a high-risk effort. GM's corporate leaders were skeptical about a second shift launch (during second shift, essential personnel are working, and a bulk of the engineers and other skilled employees are not). Zubkus prevailed, and the launch was ultimately hailed as the most successful in GM's history.

6. As result of the successful Alero launch, Mark Hogan stated that General Motors would look at Lansing as a potential site for a new plant. The constraint, though, was that General Motors needed 300 acres for the new construction. There was no 300-acre location in Lansing that would meet GM's criteria for build-

ing a new plant (ultimately the plant was built in an incredibly efficient manner on 70 acres).

7. Controlling the media was an issue. The local newspaper, the *Lansing State Journal*, was outright negative about the campaign initially. To a lesser degree, the local TV stations were also skeptical about the "Keep GM" campaign. The *City Pulse* also had a skeptical, negative perspective about the campaign. These are writers, not manufacturers, but they had to be on board to share the vision. All hands had to be on deck in the community, including media, to make this a successful reversal of GM's decision to shut down the Lansing operations.

SEVEN COMPONENTS OF BUILDING

Given the dynamics of the situation, there was no time to pause and develop a strategy. GM needed to move forward with its plans to construct a new plant to build the newest line of Cadillacs. The cities and townships in the region needed to move forward with a response. The result was a dynamic strategy development process. This entailed, unfortunately but appropriately, constructing the strategy as the team went, and this focused on seven building components: (1) start from research and data-driven best practices, (2) plan communications strategies proactively, (3) take inventory of strengths and weaknesses, (4) build on assets, (5) practice delegation with accountability, (6) take prudent risks, and (7) share credit and accept responsibility (Figure 4.2).

Building
(Construct Your Strategy as You Go)

1. Start from Research and Data-Driven Best Practices
2. Plan Communications Strategy Proactively
3. Take Inventory of Strengths and Weaknesses
4. Build on Assets
5. Practice Delegation with Accountability
6. Take Prudent Risks
7. Share Credit and Accept Responsibility

Figure 4.2   The Second Shift Model—components of building

Start from Research and Data-Driven Best Practices

The "building narrative" in this chapter clearly laid out the need for data-driven arguments. Compelling vision, ideas, and even justifiable thoughts were not enough. The starting point had to be research and data-driven best practices. The reason was multifold—ranging from hostility on the original Lansing City Council (or at least on the part of three of its eight members) to the *Lansing State Journal's* skepticism and the varied goals and wishes of community members. The best way to tackle this negative sentiment was with research-based data.

This is where University of Michigan professors George Fulton and Donald Grimes came in, having been commissioned to do a study of the resulting economic impact if GM closed the Lansing plants. As previously mentioned, Fulton and Grimes were well-respected researchers and had developed a model for measuring investments, incentives, and job creation. Their base in Ann Arbor brought in a larger community and some degree of objectivity to the Lansing project.

As noted earlier in the chapter, Fulton and Grimes concluded that having GM in Lansing meant having 7,000 GM workers in town, or a total of 20,000 Lansing workers when suppliers and support services were considered (and nearly 50,000 jobs statewide). They also suggested that the proposed local tax incentive of $188 million would lead to an increase of $37.3 billion in personal income growth statewide over the next 10 years—or $200 for every dollar invested. Perhaps impressed with his own findings, George Fulton pointed out that he was "a big advocate of research-based public policy. And, this was a great of example of research-based public policy in action, to be able to bring numbers to bear that are credible is important. It really expressed the urgency of the issue and also the possibilities."

These numbers are impressive! And Mayor Hollister learned quickly that being prepared with firsthand research and data was a minimum requirement to be able to construct strategy as he went. The depth of research and constant new data being gathered offered a short-term substitute for a clearly outlined and detailed strategic plan for the next few years. Hollister commented on this: "I was on a pretty steep learning curve trying to learn as much as I could about General Motors and its hierarchy and its decision making."

Ray Tadgerson agreed: "It's critical that you get to know not only your adversary in an adversarial situation, but who can be your advocate as well. So, this entailed getting to know the people from General Motors and picking up on those folks who had worked in the Lansing plant and who were now executives in General Motors. They could now become advocates for us because they understood the work force and the ethic here. They did become advocates for us. Within General Motors' executive circles, to have people speaking on our behalf was so important, so very, very important."

"As a community leader, you always want to learn from others," said Hollister. This also worked well in the data and knowledge gathering that needed to be done. Learning from others, perhaps even getting their buy-in, and then ensuring that the community was on top of the latest knowledge, became a staple of the campaign. "If there's something we can do, we'll do it . . . what are the best practices?" Hollister, being the "champion" of the "Lansing Works! Keep GM!" campaign, had to morph himself into the astute politician, community leader, and savvy businessperson in one outfit.

The key, according to Hollister, was that "if you can demonstrate with credible data and expert testimony, you can minimize the political rhetoric." Hollister explained further: "There always will be political rhetoric. I mean, there will always be people posturing, but you use data to build the correlation. Part of what you do in this [Second Shift] model, you educate yourselves, the team. You've got to make sure your team is informed. You've got to inform the community, and we had a PR operation to do that. This is a bottom line economic decision, and we got the data to show it."

Tadgerson agreed: "It's all about identifying the right resources within a community and how to bring those resources together, utilizing the energy that's available to pull together in a way that normally wouldn't happen and allow things to transpire over time so that it comes together in the right way." Hollister concluded: "We decided we had the resources in this community. We had the brainpower; we had the institutional commitment of the university, the state government, the local government, the regional government, labor, and most of the community to give it a shot."

Plan Communications Strategies Proactively

Another important strategy-building task was to develop an appropriate, proactive communications approach. The goals were to develop the trust of the community. As Hollister said: "You need a pretty sophisticated communications strategy. First, you have to have the trust of the community, because if they don't trust you, none of this is going to work anyway." This included being relatively inclusive and transparent so that the stakeholders felt their issues were being heard and addressed. This was sometimes a balancing act because there were certain confidential matters (e.g., national negotiations between GM and the United Auto Workers) that could not be publicly shared.

In the communication mix, Steve Serkaian served as the mayor's public relations advisor and was the liaison to the Public Relations Team. Serkaian's firm had been with Hollister since he first ran for mayor, and he enjoyed the mayor's complete confidence. His firm had led the effort to design a new city seal, creating a new image for the city. Now it was his responsibility to harness the brainpower of the public relations community to create a comprehensive communications strategy both to convince GM to stay and to persuade the local community to support the incentive package and other components necessary to be successful. Serkaian summarized the situation by saying: "Knowing more than you can communicate has been a part of my career. In the conversations with the union, the union leaders would often tell us, 'What we are telling you can't go outside this room.' It had to stay inside the room, because whatever was said could put the whole campaign at risk."

As Blue Ribbon Committee member Chris Holman said: "It's like asking, 'When is D-Day?' You just don't tell people when D-Day is. Otherwise you compromise the success of the operation. I think we shared enough for the media to tell the story, to inform the community, without compromising the outcome of the story."

The campaign needed to apply a number of communication tactics that would capture the spirit and the imagination of the region. As Serkaian explained: "Unlike a retail advertising campaign, there was no product to sell other than the amorphous notion of keeping General Motors. This was accomplished through a variety of media.

Remember, when this communication strategy was conceived, the Internet was in its infancy. E-mail was not as pervasive as it is today. Social media was nonexistent. So it was necessary to use traditional media to communicate the messages and strategy. The campaign symbols, tactics, collateral material were all intended to demonstrate to GM that the region wanted them to stay, and more importantly, to communicate to the Lansing region the value of the corporation and its jobs."

The result was the "Lansing Works! Keep GM!" campaign made up of billboards, bumper stickers, radio and TV public service announcements, a jingle praising the local workforce, and regular press releases updating the media on recent developments. The mayor officially kicked off the campaign in his 1998 State of the City Address. To demonstrate the positive and lasting relationship between the city and GM, the speech took place at GM's Oldsmobile headquarters just blocks from Lansing City Hall.

Each week the Quick Response Team would decide what would be shared with the Blue Ribbon Committee and the public. This strategic discussion was very important because whatever was said could put the whole campaign at risk. Getting support from the media was difficult initially due to their belief that the campaign was a waste of time, money, and energy. The prominent local newspaper, the *Lansing State Journal*, even rejected the mayor's offer to have a reporter sit in on the Quick Response Team's meetings, as the newspaper wanted full and free access to information generated and to retain the right to print any and all stories as it saw fit. Obviously such freedom could not be strategically granted by the mayor.

The *Lansing State Journal*'s negativity was not unusual early in the process. Similarly, in one issue, the weekly *City Pulse* newspaper took a dim view of tax breaks and incentives and posted a caricature of Hollister on its cover. The Fulton and Grimes study was not initially persuasive enough, perhaps! So instead of turning to what they said they covered—tax incentives and what they may mean for the community (that is, the proposed local tax incentive of $188 million likely leading to an increase of $37.3 billion in personal income growth statewide over the next 10 years, or $200 for every dollar invested)—the newspapers focused on the suggestion that the mayor was turning a blind eye to environmental concerns at two of the local plants. Fortunately, the local TV stations were quite neutral in their reporting and later became very supportive of the campaign.

The other significant challenge affecting various strategic decisions was how to deal with GM and its position of not wanting Lansing to mount a public campaign like the one Chrysler faced in Toledo. Mayor Hollister's research of the hierarchy within GM uncovered which leaders were the decision makers and whether they had risen within the GM ranks via a history of assignments in the Lansing plants. It turned out that many of the upper leadership had spent time in Lansing and were employed in various roles throughout the organization. Although GM vice president Mark Hogan had not been a plant manager in Lansing, he was spending a considerable amount of time meeting with Jim Zubkus, the Lansing plant manager, in late 1997 and early 1998, overseeing the planning of the Alero launch scheduled for the spring of 1998. The mayor also worked with the leadership of UAW Locals 652 and 602, the largest unions in the region representing the body shop on Verlinden Avenue and the main assembly plant on Townsend Street. Through discussions with Zubkus and the United Auto Workers leadership, primarily Art Baker, Ralph Shephard, and Tiny Sherwood, the mayor and the Quick Response Team were able to identify leaders within the GM hierarchy who might be sympathetic and helpful with the direction of the campaign.

Beyond the traditional role of promotion and messaging, the communications team became a significant strategic partner, advising Hollister on how to navigate between his pledge of transparency and his need to protect confidentiality, how to celebrate achievements, how to avoid public disputes, how to maximize local assets, how to be optimistic and hopeful in periods of doubt and setback, and how to communicate the uniqueness of the region's workforce and leadership. While developing an appropriate communications strategy is often difficult, this one was particularly so due to the broad number of stakeholders and the history of distrust.

Take Inventory of Strengths and Weaknesses

Another strategy-building task was to take inventory of the regional strengths and weaknesses. The first lesson to take away from the

Lansing experience is that you want to be proactive. It is imperative that regional politicians remain aware, be appreciative, and take inventory of all the assets on a regular basis: small, midsize, and large businesses, all the stakeholders of the community, elected officials, educational systems, and the whole nine yards. It is important that the scope of the assessment cover all the bases as it relates to supporting, growing, enhancing, identifying, and addressing issues that may have an adverse impact for the local industries for today and tomorrow.

It is also important that a region not wait for an emergency or crisis to happen or to hear through the grapevine that a regional employer is expecting to move. Increasingly, it is important for regional politicians to connect with what's going on in the world around them because that's the economy we live in. It doesn't take a lot of insight to know that virtually every manufacturing industry is global and therefore must compete globally.

Plus, in order to remain competitive, capital-intensive industries such as automobile manufacturing must continually assess the global environment to consider the changes in technology, labor, taxes, demand shifts, and regulations. And if the auto manufacturers have to assess such a global environment, the local community in which these companies—GM in our case—operate, then the local community (ideally in tandem with the company) should do so as well. The result is that investments in plant changes and upgrades are going to happen in a very mobile, flexible way. So it is important for regional developers to anticipate what the needs are, get out in front of them, and organize themselves to deal with contingencies. If the region is proactive, then in the long run, it is going to be in pretty good shape. It's the regions that are reactive, that hear about things for the first time in the newspaper, have never talked to the businesses before, or don't have a sense of what the global trends, that have problems—once they get in that situation, it's almost too late to deal with it.

Michigan State University president Lou Ann K. Simon offered a broad perspective regarding the importance of being proactive: "You can never take what you have for granted, particularly in this very complex global marketplace where you're not the center of corporate decision making. You have to continue to show value for what you're doing. You can't just wait for something bad to happen, in order for the community to mobilize and continue to both promote what you have and the quality of the workforce that you have, at the same time looking for new opportunities. People thought we won, so we relaxed, and now in this world, you can't do that. You've got to continue that kind of structure and that kind of regional focus on creating new things and keeping what you have."

This proactiveness, along with stressing innovative and entrepreneurial behaviors, is directly tied to the speed and complexity of today's global business environment. Lansing is not local per se; it is a global hub of auto manufacturing. So don't act local when you are seen as global! This requires continual monitoring of the regional and global changes influencing business decision making. In addition to the traditional factors of demand, location, availability of raw material, labor, and production cost, today's firms need to consider numerous factors regarding sustainability (energy and water), regulations and compliance, and the political and tax environment. While the assessment reviewed a number of the factors, there was one factor that was regularly identified as a potential competitive advantage: the knowledge and skills of the Lansing workforce.

Build on Assets

The Lansing region had to figure out how to build on the strengths that were identified, most notably the very skilled and knowledgeable workforce (and perhaps also the 100-year entrenchment of GM in the community). As one example, Detroit's strength is that 85 percent of all the automotive engineers in the United States are located in southeast Michigan. When GM decided to move the Oldsmobile research and development operation from Lansing to Detroit, it was difficult for the Lansing region to argue against it, given all the expertise in southeast Michigan. Mayor Hollister wondered if the same argument could be used in reverse for the Lansing region by demonstrating that the Lansing assembly operations had the best labor-management relations and the best-quality workforce.

It's all about identifying the right resources within a community and bringing those resources together, utilizing the energy that's available to develop resource synergy that allows the necessary initiatives to transpire in the right way over time. It's critical that you not only get to know your adversary in an adversarial situation, but also identify the members of the adversarial team who might have some knowledge and respect for the region as well. So there was an obvious need for the Lansing team to get to know the people from General Motors and pick up on those GM executives who had worked in the Lansing plants. The Quick Response Team believed that these former Lansing plant executives might now become advocates for the region because they understood the workforce and the ethic there. Ultimately, they did become advocates for the Lansing region. More broadly, it was also critical to determine the people it was necessary to know in General Motors, to pinpoint the people the committee needed to meet and talk to, and to recognize and engage those in the community who could help in this process.

One of the critical local assets was the two union locals in Lansing. Sean McAlinden, vice president for Strategic Studies and chief economist at the Center for Automotive Research, said: "First of all, these two union locals in Lansing, 602 and 652, were considered to be the most cooperative and some of the smartest union locals that GM had in the United States or Canada. And second, Lansing had an excellent reputation on training programs, going their own way to be competitive and ignoring the sort of common, international, approach to your plant situation." This training approach created a labor pool that better understood how labor and management collaboration can enhance industry performance.

Thankfully, an understanding of the strong workforce was echoed by General Motors. Mark Hogan, GM's vice president, summarized the situation by saying that "we were blessed with a great workforce. The Plant Manager, Jim Zubkus, was probably one of the best plant managers General Motors ever had, maybe in their history. And, he had a great management team and a great working relationship with the local unions, and the people of Lansing have always prided themselves about being great car builders."

Hogan also made an interesting observation regarding the Lansing workforce. He said: "Typically you don't have your most talented people on the second shift. It has a lot to do with experience, not just of the team members, but of your management team on the floor. Normally there are two shifts. The day shift has always been looked up to as the smart shift because it had all the engineering and all the support activities. Alternatively, the night shift would come in and have merely car builders without the experience and management support provided on the day shift."

Hogan continued: "While most assembly plants have the most experienced management and labor on the first shift due to seniority rules, Lansing is blessed with a deep bench on both the first shift and second shift, and it would be difficult to tell the difference from either an experience or enthusiasm perspective. It was another example of the Lansing team being just fantastic, and we were very blessed to have such a great workforce. So, the typical approach was to always assign any new product introduction launches to the day shift. To demonstrate the recognition and appreciation of Lansing's second shift, the GM manufacturing team decided to take a chance and have the launch of the new Oldsmobile Alero on the second shift. It was the most successful launch in GM history." As a strategic knowledge and skill asset, the Lansing community could not have been portrayed in a better light.

Once again, President Simon provided the broad perspective when she said: "We touched a number of people in the community who may have taken manufacturing for granted. And so when it's easy to say that people who work in plants should advocate for keeping plants, or a city that could benefit from the taxes of plants should advocate for keeping plants, I think when the university voice was added to that, and whatever resources that we could provide and intellectual capital for the Keep GM effort, it set a different message about why this was important for the success of the region."

Practice Delegation with Accountability

The Blue Ribbon Committee to Retain GM needed to decide how to organize the Lansing regional resources to both influence GM's decision and convince the region to support the committee. The construction of the baseball stadium and the success of the minor league baseball team provided the mayor and his team with some credibility. Before the Blue Ribbon Committee was announced, the mayor and Ray Tadgerson and some of the mayor's key department heads (Bob Swanson and Dennis Sykes) met to strategize how to organize the team and how to get the community involved.

It became a matter of understanding what they wanted each Blue Ribbon subcommittee to do and when they wanted the subcommittee to have it done. Given the scope of the project and the lack of a unified organizational perspective, it was necessary to develop a clear definition of each subcommittee's role and responsibility and assign appropriate accountability. It was critical that each subcommittee be provided feedback on whether it really was accomplishing what it was being asked to do. So it is a matter of managing the process as well as directing it.

There were a number of separate challenges that the Blue Ribbon Committee and Quick Response Team needed to deal with to move the "Keep GM" initiative forward. For example, Bob Swanson, Lansing's finance director, illustrated one of the requirements for responsibility and accountability: "We [GM] are going to build the Oldsmobile Alero here, and we're going to invest a couple hundred thousand dollars in the plant to retool for that. And, of course, we would like a tax abatement for that. So, that was my first experience, after I took the job of Finance Director, dealing with the city council on a General Motors tax abatement. It was a little bit complicated. It's sort of hard to say, on the one hand, we're going to close these facilities, but give us a tax break. So, we had a couple challenges at that point. But, all that aside, the abatement just passed by the minimum number of votes on the council, and it was very iffy right up to the end. They needed five of the eight council members to vote for it, and that's the vote in the end."

Delegation of authority also became a neighborhood thing. The story of how David Wiener, chief of staff to Mayor Hollister, became the "designated neighborhood lead" is a case in point. As a backdrop to the story, General Motors talked about expanding the production at the Verlinden plant and also at the Lansing Craft Center. The company was going to produce the SSR, a specialized Chevy pickup truck. GM had a formal hearing to get a permit from the Michigan Department of Environmental Quality, but the neighborhood people objected because they were concerned about odors and healthcare issues, and they had support from the Michigan Environmental Council and the Michigan Ecological

Center. This pushback was a real concern, as it might suggest to GM that there would be significant challenges for any new construction in Lansing. Mayor Hollister had pulled all these community leaders together (e.g., the Blue Ribbon Committee to Retain GM), and all of sudden here was a wrench thrown into the machinery of that process. Mayor Hollister said, "Well, we need to get the neighborhood people together to try to figure out how we can overcome this problem." Enter David Wiener. Because David lived near the plants and was a friend of many of the citizens concerned about the environment, the mayor asked him to talk to them and develop a process to work through this situation. Wiener ended up with a nine-month process involving a series of excellent discussions with General Motors and environmental engineers along with the local health department, state health department, state department of environmental quality, and the schools. It became a very positive interaction that helped allay the concerns that a number of people had and also made them feel comfortable in allowing General Motors to go forward with its plans.

Take Prudent Risks

The strategic business partnership between Mayor David Hollister and Ray Tadgerson resulted in synergy and appropriate risk taking. Some risks had to be taken to create an environment where GM would reverse course and decide to stay, but it had to be calculated risk taking with a relatively good chance of succeeding while minimizing the risk to the community if GM kept to its decision to leave. Ray Tadgerson commented: "It is one thing to have the challenge, but have it taken on by someone. There has to be a champion, and the champion in this particular case was Mayor David Hollister. He was willing to take on the challenge and willing to try to figure out what we can do differently, what can be done to save GM from leaving Lansing. He had the insight. He had the courage to go forward and to recruit a team of folks who were previously adversarial to him, working with a difficult city council, working with township leaders who had a different agenda. That was difficult, but it took someone like Dave with his leadership skills, and with the talent, expertise, and experience he brought to the table. That's what it takes. That's the key. That is probably the most important element to anybody trying to undertake a model like this and to make it work."

Once again proving their vision and leadership skills, Hollister and his team thought it would be useful to demonstrate the skills of the Lansing workforce. The team suggested that one way to do that might be to take a chance on assembling the new Alero on the second shift. As discussed earlier, new models were almost always assembled on the first shift because the engineers were in the plant and the workers were more experienced. This reduced the risk for the new model introduction. Building the Alero on the first shift would not have made any statement since that is the way it was always done.

Zubkus and his team, with the support of Hollister, took a chance in order to demonstrate their confidence in the Lansing regional workforce. A failure in this introduction would guarantee that GM would close its Lansing plants and look elsewhere. Success in this introduction would make a strong case regarding the skills of the Lansing workforce, but it would not provide a guarantee. While it was a risky proposition, Hollister and his team had the vision and confidence to support taking the chance.

Share Credit and Accept Responsibility

With the vision to demonstrate the capabilities of the Lansing workforce, Mayor Hollister and Jim Zubkus, who had the responsibility for launching the Alero, met to discuss the benefits and risks of such a strategy. Zubkus said: "We need to send a message to General Motors in Detroit that this is the best workforce in America. We've heard it. We've said it, but let's prove it. I'm willing to launch the Alero on the second shift." That decision, that single decision, was fundamental to Lansing's success going forward. Launching on the second shift was an important signal that Lansing wanted to send to General Motors, and it turned out the launch of the Alero was singularly the most successful launch GM had ever had to that point.

Plus, in a symbolic and strategically appropriate move, Mayor Hollister and his wife, Christine, actually drove the first Alero off the assembly line, bought by the City of Lansing. Jim Zubkus closed the plant down, and the second shift team lined up. The Lansing

First Shipment of Oldsmobile Aleros
June 4, 1998
100 Years of Quality from
Lansing, Michigan
Best

Mayor David Hollister and his wife, Christine, driving the Oldsmobile Alero off the assembly line at the Lansing Grand River Assembly plant

Eastern High School marching band played "God Bless America" as the Hollisters went down that final assembly. Tears were streaming down people's faces. Everyone was thrilled with the launch, and that launch positioned Lansing to make a case that the city could turn the decision to close the GM plants around.

At the same time, Tadgerson believed that the GM executives were indifferent about GM continuing in Lansing. The market forces were driving them south. Most of the plants were south of the Mason-Dixon Line because the leadership was increasingly concerned with labor unions, and the South had considerably fewer unions. So the Blue Ribbon Committee had to make labor a major asset instead of a liability. Fortunately, the Blue Ribbon Committee had a relationship with some enlightened leadership including Art Baker from the United Auto Workers union.

Baker, chair of the UAW Local 652 Shop Committee, jointly accepted responsibility for GM's future in Lansing with the mayor's teams, but not everyone was on board yet. As discussed earlier, the Lansing City Council was marginally supportive of the incentives for the Alero. The 5–3 vote from the eight-member council was dangerously close to the cliff of not being supportive of GM.

When the city leaders understood the implications of this situation, they began to actively reach out to the community to attract pro-business advocates to run for the council. Larry Meyer, then CEO of the Michigan Retailers Association and prominent Lansing businessperson, was one of those who was really reluctant to run for city council but realized that it was very important for the future of the community and region. With the election of Meyer and two other pro-business council members, community support for business and job initiatives increased a lot. In the case of the council, the votes went from 5–3 to 8–0.

Michigan's governor John Engler provided a great perspective when he said: "I think to General Motors' credit, they were willing to listen to the arguments [made by the Blue Ribbon Committee]. I think there was no way in the beginning that John Moyer [plant controller for GM] thought they were making an investment in Michigan. But the persistence and the power of what came together as a package, and the enthusiasm to retain that General Motors investment, resulted in a big win for the community and a big win for the State. And in some ways it showed what can be done when people cooperate, share credit, and accept responsibility."

Engler also commented about Hollister's tenacity during the campaign when he mobilized the community. Hollister believed that there were a couple of ways to look at economic development. One was to say that this area in the state really needs help, so we should put the investment there. How do we push it uphill and convince GM and the community to make that investment? The other approach was to look around, identify those who were prepared and were doing the necessary work, and determine what was needed to support them. Engler believed that the best approach was to build from strength. He realized that the region and the state needed jobs.

Another example of the necessary responsibility and accountability came from the state legislature, which had to approach the incentives for job retention differently. The legislature had to listen to an argument that said, as illustrated by John Engler: "The premise of this in the past was, net new jobs. Now the premise is to retain jobs, so it was, 'Net from zero,' because zero is what you're going to have if everything went away. So, if you look at it that way, you're going to have to rethink the premise of bringing jobs to the state and instead focus on retaining jobs in the state. With the understanding of the Lansing situation and the support of the governor, the legislative process worked the way it should have by changing the law to allow incentives for job retention versus only for attracting new jobs."

This collaboration of Hollister and Engler stresses the potentially bleak picture and subsequent importance of the "Lansing Works! Keep GM!" campaign. In many ways, Hollister and Engler were adversaries back in their legislative days. However, when they became executives, their attitudes, style, and outlook changed because now they were responsible for everything, not just for what they said. John Engler as governor and David Hollister as mayor became good friends and worked together; they developed a great relationship not only on the "Keep GM" campaign but in many other areas that led to regional development.

Doug Rothwell, then director of the Michigan Economic Development Corporation (MEDC), reflected that he was not sure that there was one obstacle that really stood out, as much as there were many moving parts. What the Blue Ribbon Committee was really dealing with was, first of all, needing to get legislation through to enable the committee to be able to even offer the deal. Then it was being able to offer the deal to GM and having GM feel it was competitive enough to make the deal work. Then the added complexity was whether the facility could actually accommodate the investment.

Rothwell also gave substantial credit to Jim Donaldson of MEDC. He recognized Donaldson as one of the state's economic development gurus. Donaldson had a way about him that built trust with people. Not only did he know the technical side of what it takes to put a deal together, but he also had the ability to develop relationships with people so that they trusted his judgment and his ability to look out for the best interest of the community and the business. That's a rare skill to have. Without a Jim Donaldson, it would have made it a lot harder to get a deal like this put together. Donaldson put in countless hours behind the scenes to make this work, and to

this day this deal remains revered in the halls of economic development in the state.

---------------◆---------------

BUILDING SUMMARY

This chapter reviews the dynamic strategy development process of
the Second Shift Model that was used for the "Lansing Works! Keep
GM!" campaign. The changing environment from the perspective of
the economy, General Motors, and the region required the strategy
to be based on sound data to build credibility and then be refined as
the dynamics changed.

The first step was to commission Fulton and Grimes at the
University of Michigan Economic Analysis unit at the Institute of Labor
and Industrial Relations to conduct a data-driven benchmark study.
The numbers, by most accounts, were staggering and very supportive. The Lansing community had to buy into the idea of going hard
after GM and advocating strategically to GM to change its decision
to leave the community. At risk were 7,000 jobs at GM locally, affecting 20,000 jobs locally and 50,000 jobs throughout the rest of the
state—these are numbers that most people can understand. Overall,
the Fulton and Grimes study provided unbiased and credible information regarding what the GM assembly operation meant to the Lansing
region and what would be the implications if it left. The study also
provided insight regarding what a new assembly plant would mean
to the region.

The second step was to create a communications strategy that
facilitated collaboration between the Blue Ribbon Committee and
GM while keeping the other stakeholders (regional politicians and citizens) appropriately informed regarding the implications of a potential
plant closure. This resulted in the "Lansing Works! Keep GM!" initiative.

The third step focused on identifying the strengths and weaknesses of the region and demonstrating the benefits of those
strengths to GM.

The fourth step was to build on the regional assets by demonstrating the importance of the Lansing regional workforce to GM.

The goal of the fifth step was to delegate the responsibility for change to key members of the Blue Ribbon Committee and make them accountable for successful completion of that element of the initiative.

The sixth step addressed the need to find leaders who had the judgment to prudently manage the process.

Finally, the leadership team had to share credit regarding the successes and accept responsibility for the situations where the strategy was not optimal.

CHAPTER 5

SOLVING

ENGAGE IN CONSTANT
PROBLEM SOLVING

While it was obvious that the greater Lansing community needed to rally to convince GM to reinvest in mid-Michigan, a big challenge was the lack of a mechanism for regional problem solving. GM and its suppliers needed a single place that they could go to in their efforts to confront and resolve the multiple issues facing their transforming businesses and industry. Mayor Hollister established a "single-entry, single-exit" policy to address all issues needing problem-solving and resolution. The single-entry, single-exit policy also meant that all issues were to be directed to the mayor's office and the only official communication would emanate from the mayor's office. If either GM or the community representatives felt that a topic needed to be secret, the mayor's office worked with the organizations and media to keep it secret. Otherwise the policy was to make the discussions transparent to the media and the community. The policy regarding transparency turned out to be, singularly, the most important thing. It was collaborative. It was designed to be a win-win.

At his 1998 State of the City Address, Mayor Hollister announced that he was creating a Blue Ribbon Committee to Retain GM and a "Lansing Works! Keep GM!" community engagement campaign. At a subsequent press conference, the mayor reiterated his vision of convincing GM to change its mind about leaving Lansing and the region.

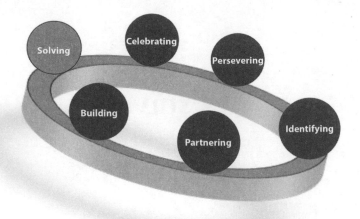

Figure 5.1   The Second Shift Model—solving

The mayor and members of the Blue Ribbon Committee also presented an organizational chart of how the campaign would be organized. The Quick Response Team served as the executive committee for the Blue Ribbon Committee. Subcommittees were also set up to be problem solvers and respond to whatever challenge arose. Figure 5.1 illustrates the Second Shift Model, highlighting the "solving" component discussed in Chapter 5. Ray Tadgerson served as project manager for all aspects of the Blue Ribbon Committee and provided strategic and technical advice and support. Figure 5.2 includes the leadership of the 50-member Blue Ribbon Committee, the committee's six subcommittees, and the Quick Response Team.

Initially, the Blue Ribbon Committee met weekly, then biweekly, then monthly, and eventually on an as-needed basis. With such a large group, 20 to 40 busy, influential people (and more than 50 people involved at one point), it was difficult to get everyone to attend a weekly or biweekly meeting. It was also difficult to reach consensus with so many varied opinions and personal agendas about what needed to be done, and how and when.

Concern existed about confidentiality and leaking of sensitive information to the public and parties who should not have access to such information. To offset the confidentiality risks, the mayor

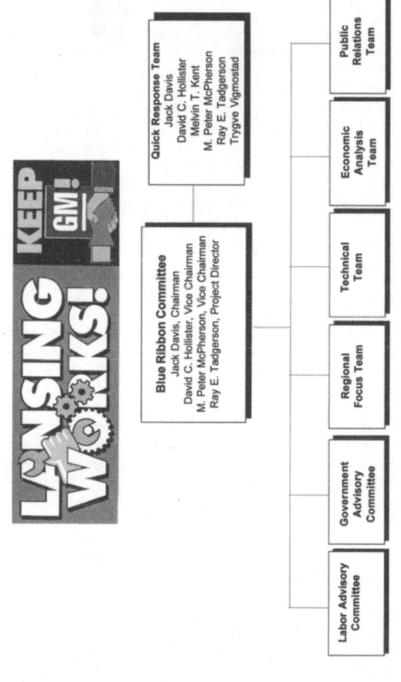

Figure 5.2 Organization Chart—"Lansing Works! Keep GM!" campaign

chose to rely on his closest confidants, dubbed the "Monday morning team," to help identify priorities that would be shared with the Quick Response Team and the Blue Ribbon Committee.

The Monday morning team met early every Monday morning for about 2½ years, and sporadically thereafter, to identify what needed to be done for the coming week, review progress over the past week, and discuss items remaining on the to-do list. The meetings resulted in an ongoing outline of what was "hot" and needed immediate attention as well as a detailed list of all things to be done, big or small. Out of these meetings, an agenda was created for the Quick Response Team. The QRT would then determine who would address the issues and when, and develop the agendas for the larger group of the Blue Ribbon Committee meetings.

SOLVING NARRATIVE

Problem solving was the hallmark of the "Keep GM" campaign, with more than 35 major challenges and a myriad of small ones that the mayor and the Blue Ribbon Committee had to face. Understanding the magnitude of what Lansing as a city and its neighboring region were facing, it was critical to establish a game plan for every challenge. Time was always of the utmost importance. After all, GM had already made the decision to leave.

For each challenge that was identified, an individual or group of team members was charged with addressing it within a defined timeline. To put the challenges and problem-solving solutions in perspective, we highlight the most significant challenges that the Blue Ribbon Committee addressed in this narrative for this chapter. The core list of challenges for the "solving" aspect of the Second Shift Model is outlined later in the chapter as well.

As a start, getting accurate information from a worldwide corporation is always a challenge, and in the case of General Motors, it is particularly difficult, as the company was quietly moving to a Global Platform Consolidation Program modeled after that used by its foreign competitors. The new design would require the support of the United Auto Workers union in upcoming national negotiations and would need to be piloted in a new facility at some undisclosed location.

In early 1996, GM approached the City of Lansing with a plan to invest $600 million at the Verlinden and Townsend plants to launch the Alero. That year the Lansing City Council debated a tax abatement for GM, and some council members made comments critical of GM. After contentious debate, a property tax abatement was approved by a vote of 5 to 3.

In September 1997, the vice president of GM's Car Group North America, Mark Hogan, granted an interview to the *Lansing State Journal* and stated that models in the Lansing Car Assembly small car group were scheduled to phase out between 2002 and 2004 and that GM was considering replacing its outdated 100-year-old Lansing manufacturing facility. There were no guarantees made that it would stay in Lansing or the region. In fact it was unlikely it would stay. The local news headline read: "No production assured in Lansing after 2004." Fourteen thousand jobs were at risk!

Hogan would be a critical partner going forward as he was GM's liaison with Lansing on the Alero launch and the leader of the Global Platform Consolidation Program. Many industry insiders saw Hogan as an "up-and-comer" and potential future GM CEO. And to most, this picture of Hogan as a key decision maker inside GM as he began to oversee the Alero launch was widely supported.

At this stage, it became abundantly clear, after conversations took place between GM management and union leadership, that GM was planning to cease all operations in Lansing and the region after 2004. This began the challenge phase of what was to become known as the "Lansing Works! Keep GM!" campaign. "What can be done, if anything?" wondered the community. It was apparent that the majority of the community felt the game was over, and it would be an exercise in futility to try to change the minds of GM leadership; after all, the "1,000-pound gorilla" had spoken, and it did not change its mind, as the longstanding history could attest.

The next big problem for which an almost immediate solution had to be found was lack of cooperation of influential leaders in the community. A coalition needed to be built; this entailed gathering the "brain trust" of the region and formulating a plan of action. First up were the leaders of the Lansing Regional Chamber of Commerce, who were very much opposed to having the mayor lead any effort because they felt they were primarily responsible for all retention efforts for the region.

There was also a concern about whether the mayor could handle such an effort. Many meetings were held between the chamber leadership and Ray Tadgerson to negotiate a common ground with the chamber and the mayor's office. Subsequently, the mayor, with the creation of the Blue Ribbon Committee, asked Jack Davis, the Lansing chamber's chair of the board, to cochair the committee with Michigan State University president Peter McPherson. Although the group was organized with cochairs Davis and McPherson, the default spokesperson role was largely shared by Davis and the mayor.

Utilizing the influence that the Lansing chamber leadership had on the region, in particular with the business community, the Blue

The "Lansing Works! Keep GM!" campaign leaders: Lansing's mayor David Hollister, served 1994–2003, and Ray Tadgerson, project director

Ribbon Committee began the process of bringing on board others who would become de facto spokespersons within the community. The initial Blue Ribbon Committee was composed of 28 individuals representing nearly every public and private group within the region, including Delta Township and Lansing Township, both of which had GM facilities located within their respective communities.

Another urgent problem facing the team was GM itself, which, through VP Mark Hogan, expressed that GM did not want to have a public campaign put into place and preferred to discuss any of GM's future plans in private. Hogan also said he did not want to work with any politicians. The mayor assured Hogan that he was not the typical politician and would prefer to work with the corporation rather than be adversarial; Hollister wanted an open communication between the two.

The mayor also told Hogan that the Lansing region had to at least make the effort to publicly demonstrate to the region that something was being done to convince GM's leadership to reconsider. The region's acceptance of any final decision was tied to how much energy was put into the retention effort as opposed to "rolling over" and allowing GM's decision to stand. Hogan, although not sanctioning the effort, stated that he understood that the mayor "had to do what he had to do."

"Lansing Works! Keep GM!"

A key to any solution was the formation of a "campaign" that the community could get behind, understand, and see as a positive way to reinforce what was great about Lansing. This became the "Lansing Works! Keep GM!" campaign.

The "Lansing Works! Keep GM!" campaign was officially kicked off by Mayor Hollister in his 1998 State of the City Address. To demonstrate the positive and lasting relationship between the city and GM, the speech took place at GM's Oldsmobile headquarters inside the Plant 1 site near downtown Lansing. The campaign was a major theme of the speech. Mayor Hollister declared that the city's main goal for 1998 was to ensure that the automaker would maintain a strong presence in the Lansing area after 2003. With that declaration, Mayor Hollister established a call to action for the community.

Following the kickoff, an event to formally demonstrate the regional collaboration of the "Lansing Works! Keep GM!" campaign was developed. A resolution was accepted by some 40 governmental units which signified that the retention of GM manufacturing was a top priority and that those governmental units would set aside parochial interests and work collaboratively to keep GM in the Lansing region. Regional partners unanimously pledged their support for the campaign by signing the resolution.

To reinforce the campaign's call to action, every local media outlet was called upon to help explain to citizens the importance of GM to the area and to communicate to GM how much the region valued the company's contributions to the community. Hollister even got the first Lansing-built Alero, purchased by the City of Lansing (and drove it off the assembly line with his wife, Christine), and he recommended that the city purchase more GM vehicles for its fleet as a significant sign of the city's support for the automaker.

To add to the campaign's portfolio, Kolt & Serkaian Communications developed a "Lansing Works! Keep GM!" image video for local TV stations. The TV stations helped out as well and developed service announcements promoting Lansing and GM's presence. A musical jingle was developed for radio stations so they could run promotions for Lansing and highlight GM's local history. The local newspaper, the Lansing State Journal, used the campaign as a backdrop to feature comments submitted by area residents about GM and why the automaker was so important to the area. Ultimately, solving the "Keep GM" problem involved a myriad of community partners, friends, and advocates.

To support this effort and stay on message, press releases were routinely sent to update the media on significant developments in the "Keep GM" effort. Many media outlets developed packaged segments to update their audiences. When negative stories appeared in the media, Kolt & Serkaian Communications reacted quickly by gathering Blue Ribbon Committee members and the media together to provide a focal point for local officials to reassure the community that the retention effort was on track.

Despite the advantages of utilizing the media and their supportive tone, it was still an ongoing problem-solving challenge to work with some of the media, mainly the *Lansing State Journal* and the

City Pulse, both of which had initially chosen a less than neutral or positive position about the campaign. Their initial, early-on position was polar opposite to that of the TV and radio stations, which were promoting either a neutral position or positive message supporting the campaign. This somewhat adversarial position had to be attended to, and broad-based campaign tactics had to be employed.

One such tactic involved the launch of the Alero. In the latter part of 1997, the local Lansing GM plant manager, Jim Zubkus, began planning the launch of the Alero and the Pontiac Grand Am. They were scheduled to go online in the spring of 1998. Zubkus told the mayor he wanted to make a statement about how great the car-building team was in Lansing, and he told GM's leadership he wanted to build the Alero on the second shift, which had never been done before. GM's leadership in Detroit was very skeptical and advised against such a risky move. However, Zubkus and the local UAW leadership convinced the entire workforce that this was their one chance to show the GM leadership in Detroit just how good they were at building cars. No one started a new car line on the second shift. Well, now Lansing did!

This second shift launch also created a unique opportunity for Lansing. Knowing that GM executives and engineers would be traveling back and forth from Detroit to Lansing to monitor and evaluate the launch, the team developed a communications strategy aimed directly at them. The targeted campaign included public service announcements for radio and TV audiences singing the praises of the local Lansing UAW workforce and highlighting the history of great labor-management relations, mass distribution of "Lansing Works! Keep GM!" bumper stickers, and the creation of "Lansing Works! Keep GM!" billboards. The billboards were strategically placed on the most common expressways taken by GM executives in their frequent trips to Lansing.

Some initial positives came out of this campaign idea—maybe the billboards actually projected a reinforcing message! In his first visits to Lansing to supervise the Alero launch, Mark Hogan stated that he was impressed that Zubkus had included Art Baker and his UAW team in their meetings and that the billboards made it clear that the community was serious about a new creative partnership. Thankfully, it wasn't long before Hogan became a true believer in the emerging Lansing solution and a strong advocate internally for reinvesting in the Lansing region.

The success of the launch, considered by GM to be the best launch in GM history at the time, caught the attention of GM's leaders, and Hogan said that they would consider building a new plant in Lansing. The door had been opened to the idea of keeping GM in Lansing, small as the opening may have been at that time.

But now the problem solving had to start. For one, Hogan told the mayor that GM would need 300 acres to build a new facility. The mayor put Ray Tadgerson and his city staff to work on it. The finding was that there was no 300-acre site in the city suitable for a new plant unless the city chose to declare eminent domain and begin the process of relocating homes and businesses. Because this seemed so difficult, it appeared as though GM would have to locate the new plant somewhere in a neighboring township.

However, Zubkus was in possession of a blueprint for a new GM plant that had been built in South America, coincidentally under the supervision of Mark Hogan. Zubkus called Ray Tadgerson and asked to meet with him privately. Zubkus showed Tadgerson an aerial map of the assembly site on Townsend Street known as Plant 1. He pointed out that there were many buildings on the eastern part of the site that were empty and could possibly be torn down to create enough room for a new plant. Zubkus gave Tadgerson some photo-copies of a plant built in Brazil, code named "Blue Macaw." Zubkus said he didn't know if it would fit and asked Tadgerson to check it out. After several days of examining the nearly illegible photocopies and creating a "new" metric scale for the site, Tadgerson determined the site in Brazil was on 70 acres. Via CADD, Tadgerson overlaid the Blue Macaw site on the Plant 1 site, which clearly demonstrated that the new state-of-the-art plant layout would work after tearing down the unused buildings.

This was creative problem solving at its best! Zubkus arranged for Tadgerson, the mayor, and his team to make a presentation to Hogan clearly demonstrating that the old brownfield site of Plant 1 could be transformed to a next-generation common platform facility that Hogan had responsibility for developing and implementing. Hogan was shocked that the mayor and Tadgerson had gotten their hands on the top-secret blueprints of the Blue Macaw in Brazil but also was deeply impressed with the technical findings. It was a turning point. From that day forward Hogan considered the Blue Ribbon Committee a part of his problem-solving team.

We dig into this new plant story further in the chapter on celebration, with parallel and celebratory details. But, in a nutshell, on a handshake the mayor and Hogan agreed to begin the work and agreed that the city would be reimbursed once the new UAW contract was approved. The city invested over $7 million in infrastructure to prepare the Plant 1 site for a new plant, to be called the Grand River Assembly plant, home of a new Cadillac line.

Remarkably, after the construction of the Blue Macaw footprint was under way in Lansing, GM made it known it was considering building a second assembly plant somewhere in the region. Tadgerson worked closely with the GM real estate group to find a suitable site. For this plant, GM wanted 1,200 to 1,300 acres, upping the ante, and also wanted unrestricted access to the interstate highways and access to railroads and the airport. Nearly all "greenfield" sites in the tri-county region were either eliminated due to location or tied up in the government land bank program. Ultimately, the site selected was in Delta Township, and GM secured approximately 1,000 acres on which the new Lansing Delta Assembly plant and a new stamping facility was built.

But back to the original storyline: In order for GM to move forward with the construction of the new Lansing Grand River Assembly plant, it was requesting incentives and tax abatements from the City of Lansing and the State of Michigan. City leaders, after the election of three new city council members, were willing to provide the abatements they could, but the state had no vehicle to do so. Laws needed to be changed to offer abatements and incentives for "retention" efforts as opposed to only new job attraction. Lansing's mayor Hollister and Michigan's governor Engler, longtime adversaries in earlier years in the Michigan legislature, put aside their differences and teamed up to convince the legislature to change the law to allow the state to assist GM.

Among a number of tricky issues and obstacles, environmental concerns over GM plant emissions were among the more controversial problems the region faced. It was a significant concern for the neighbors near the body plant, known as Plant 6, on Verlinden

Avenue, where car bodies were built and painted. Also nearby was Plant 2, where a new GM SSR pickup was to be built. The community and environmental groups wanted the paint odor problem solved prior to the new car launches and the new Lansing Delta plant being constructed. The mayor assigned his chief of staff to work with the neighborhood group, environmental groups, GM, and local school officials. It took several months to reach consensus, but GM eventually changed the paint chemistry, thereby eliminating the offensive odors. Plant problems solved!

REFLECTIONS ON SOLVING

David Hollister

While I had led several collaborative initiatives as a state legislator in the past, prior to taking on the "Lansing Works! Keep GM!" community engagement campaign, the "Keep GM" campaign was the most high risk, complicated, and consequential of any I had undertaken. The entire Lansing region's economic future was at stake.

The Blue Ribbon Committee's collaborative model was tested against one of the largest corporations in the world. It proved to be effective and successful because the Blue Ribbon Committee's participants embraced the following seven problem-solving principles:

- *Shared goal.* All parties stayed focused on the overall goal and understood how they fit into the whole.
- *Collaboration.* All parties agreed to share information and relevant expertise, identify issues, seek common ground, generate ideas, keep an open mind, evaluate options, and strive for win-win solutions.
- *Trust.* Honesty, credibility, and communication were treated as essential to building trusting relationships.
- *Accountability.* A single-entry or one-stop structure was put in place.
- *Inclusiveness.* All stakeholders were invited to be part of the process regardless of their position on issues.
- *Mutual respect.* All parties' viewpoints were encouraged, heard, and respected.

- *Transparency.* All parties had a clear understanding of the goals, objectives, process, and ability of stakeholders to participate at appropriate levels.

Ray Tadgerson

The issues and challenges facing the region were many and necessitated a multifaceted approach to solving each and every one. When the mayor asked if I would play a role similar to the engineer in Toledo, my response was, "Absolutely."

My subsequent reaction was, "Wow, how on earth am I going to do this?" I then reflected back on my similar response and reaction when the mayor asked if I could take on the challenge of locating the baseball stadium downtown. I knew if we had the right people on board, we could do what we had done with the stadium. However, I considered that convincing the "1,000-pound gorilla" to change its mind was a much greater challenge.

When we began the campaign, we really had no idea what we were facing or what we would face as new challenges evolved over the next several years. It truly was a team effort with all the right people in the right seats at the right time. In looking back at that time in history, it is apparent that with each new mountain we climbed, there was another beyond to conquer.

Oftentimes the team was attempting to climb several mountains all at the same time. There were numerous balls in the air at any given time, and it took the collective brainpower to solve the many problems faced. The region was fortunate to have the mayor and the leaders of the Blue Ribbon Committee focused on the big picture of retaining GM. Special recognition should be given also to the Quick Response Team, who mostly behind closed doors zeroed in on solving problems and ensuring that the team got the right things done on time.

The solutions effort started with a strategic plan, which provided the basis for the structure for the Blue Ribbon Committee and the Quick Response Team. We also had a map for what was envisioned to be accomplished by the effort. As the campaign matured and as the team members gained trust in one another, the interaction among the members of the team solidified and gained momentum through the success of the problem-solving process. A Second Shift Model evolved, without it being the goal initially, which demonstrated how a group of like-minded individuals can assess problems at hand and solve them for the greater good of the local community for what may turn out to be the next 50 years.

MAJOR CHALLENGES AND OBSTACLES FOR SOLVING

We identified a dozen major challenges and obstacles:

1. The mayor had an internal advisory group that met nearly every Monday morning for over 2½ years to strategize on how Lansing as a city should handle the various challenges as they popped up. The group included Dennis Sykes, Bob Swanson, and Ray Tadgerson on a regular basis. Others who attended periodically were Patty Cook, Jim Smiertka, and Steve Serkaian.

2. The Blue Ribbon Committee, initially with 28 members, grew to some 50 people and, at that stage, proved to be unwieldy in terms of orchestrating meetings and responses to new challenges. An executive team of six leaders was formed and called the Quick Response Team (QRT), making some Blue Ribbon Committee members feel left out. But to create effective and efficient solutions in a timely manner, the QRT had to be instituted. The broad objective of the QRT was to respond to GM's questions and concerns quickly and thoroughly to ensure that all communications lines were maintained and even nurtured.

3. As result of GM's successful Alero launch in Lansing, Mark Hogan stated GM would look at Lansing as a potential site for a new plant, but it needed 300 acres for the construction of the plant. There was no 300-acre location in the city that would meet GM's criteria for building a new plant. Mayor Hollister assigned to Ray Tadgerson the task of locating a suitable site within the city.

4. Determining whether a new plant could be built on the existing Plant 1 site in Lansing was difficult due to virtually unintelligible photocopies of a smaller facility in Brazil to work from,

along with determining the number of buildings that could be torn down while maintaining the current production levels. Ultimately, the solution was the construction of the Grand River Assembly facility—a state-of-the-art and "nimble" production facility on a much smaller than normal lot but with incredibly sophisticated building structures.

5. GM wanted tax incentives from the state, but the Michigan Economic Development Corporation was handcuffed by state law, which prohibited dollars being spent on retention efforts like keeping the GM operations in the state. At the same time, the number of jobs would still be reduced if a new plant were to be built in Michigan. All in all, the Michigan legislature would need to change the law, which, of course, became a highly debated and political issue.

6. Designing and building the necessary infrastructure without a firm commitment from GM due to the lack of a national contract with the United Auto Workers union was a risky task and required creative and gutsy solutions. Basically it was a handshake between Mayor Hollister and Mark Hogan to proceed. The city spent over $7 million on utilities, roads, and environmental cleanup prior to the GM Board of Directors' approving the construction of the new plant.

7. The environmental groups in Michigan wanted to increase the emissions standards for the paint facilities at the body plant, Plant 6, also known as the Fisher Body plant, and Plant 2, site of the new SSR pickup assembly. The neighbors agreed with the environmental groups and also wanted standards beyond the EPA standards, which the Department of Natural Resources eventually enforced. The process was months long until GM changed its paint system, which enabled an agreement to be made among all parties.

8. With the success of the siting of the Grand River Assembly plant and the approval of a national UAW agreement, GM wanted to locate a second assembly plant and a stamping plant potentially in the Lansing region as well, but it required a greenfield with traffic stipulations, railway access, and access to the airport. Now instead of 300 acres (which became only 70 acres when the

plant was built per the Brazil model), GM wanted at least 1,000 acres, and preferably 1,200 to 1,300 acres, to provide options for future development. Locating a suitable site of this size meant examining every potential site in the tri-county area, which took several weeks.

9. GM was looking for additional incentives from Delta Township, and it appeared to reach a dead-end over a $1 million commitment that was needed. The GM representative walked out of the meeting and left the building. There was no point of return it seemed, but Mayor Hollister chased him down, lightly grabbed him by the arm, and convinced him to return. After that, negotiations went well.

10. The second plant also required Public Act 425 and Public Act 328 agreements between the City of Lansing and Delta Township, resulting in Lansing's extending utilities to the new plant. Both were groundbreaking agreements and took extensive negotiations. Townships often compete; this collaboration and extension of services was unusual and very positive.

11. The township also did not have enough resources to adequately handle the plan review for the new plant in a timely fashion. Ultimately it ended up being a shared responsibility, with the City of Lansing negotiating to have the authority for building plan review.

12. GM was concerned about workforce training and was seeking an expanded training program. It first linked with Lansing Community College. The result was the creation of Lansing Community College West Campus, a development that was widely debated before happening, largely due to cost and perceived benefit. The Ingham County Intermediate School District, United Auto Workers union, and GM created a program called the Lansing Area Manufacturing Program, which was a program for high school students to enter into the manufacturing field. This continued the solutions-oriented approach to ensuring a skilled workforce in the region. Another program that focused on skilled labor was the CLASS program started by Mayor Hollister, an initiative to improve the quality of education through mentoring and assistance in Lansing school classrooms.

SIX COMPONENTS OF SOLVING

Engaging in constant problem solving and involving the region's leaders in business, labor, education, and local and state government, as well as citizens at large, when needed, are objectives that call for having a great infrastructure and go-getter mentality. The Blue Ribbon Committee and the Quick Response Team provided the core infrastructure, but challenges and obstacles came from a variety of places and needed to be tackled accordingly at all times. To engage in constant problem solving required them to (1) anticipate challenges, (2) maintain capacity to respond in a crisis, (3) look for collaborative win-win solutions, (4) manage communication, (5) establish a unified voice with a single point of entry and exit, and (6) build more partnerships (Figure 5.3). In this portion of the "solving" chapter, we take a closer look at the six solving components and build on what community leaders who were involved at the time pointed out in our interviews.

Anticipate Challenges

Perhaps there is nothing as important as anticipating challenges and then being prepared to solve them as they come in your direction. When the challenges hit the larger community, as in Lansing in the case of General Motors' anticipated withdrawal from the community, then the anticipation has to be universally applicable to the community and supported by a broad-based and shared common vision.

Solving
(Engage in Constant Problem-Solving)

1. Anticipate Challenges
2. Maintain Capacity to Respond in a Crisis
3. Look for Collaborative Win-Win Solutions
4. Manage Communication
5. Establish a Unified Voice with a Single Point of Entry and Exit
6. Build More Partnerships

Figure 5.3 The Second Shift Model—components of solving

To set the tone for such anticipation mechanisms, Mayor David Hollister said: "I was on a pretty steep learning curve trying to learn as much as I could about General Motors and its hierarchy and its decision making. As a community leader, you always want to learn from others. If there's something we can do, we'll do it . . . what are the best practices?"

Hollister learned, perhaps even anticipated, that "if you can demonstrate with credible data and expert testimony, you can minimize the political rhetoric. There always will be political rhetoric. I mean, there will always be people posturing, but you use data to build the correlation. Part of what you do in this [Second Shift] model, you educate yourselves, the team. You've got to make sure your team is informed. You've got to inform the community, and we had a PR operation to do that. This is a bottom line economic decision, and we got the data to show it."

Anticipation also involves knowing and understanding the various players that may influence an outcome. Ray Tadgerson said: "It's critical that you get to know not only your adversary in an adversarial situation, but who can be your advocate as well. So, getting to know the people from General Motors and picking up on those folks who had worked in the Lansing plant and who were now executives in General Motors. They could now become advocates for us because they understood the workforce and the ethic here. They did become advocates for us. Within General Motors' executive circles, to have people speaking on our behalf was so important, so very, very important."

Such liaisons also helped in what to anticipate, and perhaps even gave a glimmer of hope or at least advance warning. Tadgerson continued: "If it's General Motors, you better get to know who is in General Motors: who you need to know—who you need to meet, who you need to talk to—and recognize anyone in the community who can help you in this process and get them engaged." A part of the early strategic planning involved a small group. Tadgerson explains, "Before we announced the Blue Ribbon Committee, Dave, myself, and a couple of his key department heads [Bob Swanson and Dennis Sykes] were meeting to strategize how this was going to work and how we get the community involved."

Jim Zubkus, Lansing GM plant manager, explained the value of correctly anticipating or at least having a strategy for anticipating what may happen in the future. He said: "You know no one ever knocked on my door and said, 'Hey, we are going to shut you down.' It doesn't work that way. You get a sense when something is not right. No one has to tell you when something is not right. It is like when your wife is mad at you. She does not have to tell you she is mad at you. You know it without her saying a word. We knew something was wrong because our plants were old. We had a lot of emission problems in the body plant. It was costing us a considerable amount of money to maintain the body shop. We knew GM was going to come up with a new product, and we figured if we could somehow convince them with our efforts and past accomplishments they would recognize us as a viable candidate to bring in their product. And, if they brought their new products in we would need new plants." So in some ways the team anticipated what would happen but also held out hope that it would work out in Lansing's favor.

In some cases, the anticipation had been years in the making. Dave Wiener, chief of staff to Mayor Hollister, said: "General Motors talked about expanding their production at the Verlinden plant and also at the Lansing Craft Center. They were going to produce the SSR, a specialized Chevy. GM had a formal hearing to get a permit from the Department of Environmental Quality under state law. The neighborhood people objected, and they had support from the Michigan Environmental Council and the Michigan Ecological Center. The reason was that they were concerned about odors and health care issues."

Although odor had been an issue, it had not been raised to this extent before, and so the community's anticipatory mechanisms to the issue of environmental quality were on a relatively low sensory level. Wiener explained: "This kind of threw a jolt in all of us. David Hollister had pulled all these community leaders together and all of a sudden here was a wrench thrown into the machinery of that process. He said, 'Well, we need to get the neighborhood people together to try to figure out how we can overcome this problem.' He said to me, 'Okay, Wiener, these are your friends. You live there. You go talk to them and see what you can do to develop a process by which we can work through this situation.'" Ultimately it was solved, but perhaps this issue could have been tackled more easily and more speedily had the community anticipated what had been brewing for years!

At the same time as the greater Lansing community was strategically planning and trying to anticipate what would happen and how it should respond, "the first challenge at hand for GM," according to Mark Hogan, "was to get our ducks in a row internally and inside the company. So, I really wasn't looking for outside help at that time, because I wasn't even sure that we knew what we were going to talk about to Dave Hollister, who was mayor at that time, and his committee, which included Ray Tadgerson, regarding GM in the area."

Hogan continued: "You know, getting our ducks in a row inside the company was really important and not easy because there were critics inside the company that thought we should probably walk away from an old five-story, 100-year-old building, and completely go to another site. In spite of the capability, the workforce, and in spite of the logistics advantages that came with Lansing, we had our own knitting to do."

Hogan also didn't anticipate Lansing's response! But he became a strong convert: "I think it was more the zeal and enthusiasm the team here in Lansing had to retain GM. It was great. It was terrific. I enjoyed it, but again, I didn't want to get the cart before the horse. It was very important to make sure that we had everything lined up internally from a product and plant concept. In those efforts, whether it was from a permit to tax abatement, the support of the Lansing team was incredible, and actually made the job we had at GM a lot easier."

Maintain Capacity to Respond in a Crisis

If everyone is completely occupied at all times, it does not matter how much intelligence, capability, and knowledge exist on the team if a crisis arises. Engaging in constant problem solving is not just about solving the problems at hand, although the word "constant" would imply just that! It also means having the capacity to respond in a crisis, as needed and when needed.

Basically, it is the old, clichéd mentality of categorizing various activities into A, B, and C stacks, where the A stack is given the most importance, followed by the B stack, and then the (unfortunate) C stack. What gets piled on the C stack should automatically be discarded; it's unlikely anyone will care about those items anyway! The B problems should be solved at some point, but the A problems obviously take precedent over any other issues. Now, that is with the exception of the real crisis issues that arise. Maintaining capacity to respond to these crucial A-stack problems is of critical importance, especially in a case such as saving General Motors in Lansing.

Remember, there were a lot of fickle players, decision makers, people initially at odds on how to go about it, and so on. Any misstep at any point in this years-long process could alter the final outcome (or just reinforce GM's decision to shut down in Lansing). David Hollister captures this nicely: "It fell apart several times; you just suck it up, regroup, get your team together, do an analysis of what's going on, and you move forward. If you have a vision, and if you've got a plan, the biggest issue is perseverance, just not getting confused with winning or losing." He continued: "If you've got supportive partners, you can overcome any setback, and you will persevere over time. What you will find is the friendships and partnerships you develop will carry you through the tough times."

Maintaining capacity to respond to a crisis also entails maintaining the relationships with key players, such as GM leadership. Joe Drolett, Delta Township supervisor and Blue Ribbon Committee member, commented: "One of the things when we started this process is we had to let General Motors know that we cared for them. We want them to stay here. We don't take them for granted." And this was not a one-time reaching out to GM. This had to be constantly done, even showcasing that the Lansing mayor, Quick Response Team, and Blue Ribbon Committee had the capacity to respond and solve virtually any issue coming their way. GM had to know this capacity for problem solving, and the message had to be retold, reinforced, and nurtured that the Lansing community meant business!

The core structure for the mayor and the Lansing team to ensure that capacity was maintained to respond to any crises that came up was in the form of the relatively small and nimble Quick Response Team and the larger Blue Ribbon Committee. Tadgerson elaborated:

"Before we announced the Blue Ribbon Committee, Dave, me, and a couple of his key department heads [Bob Swanson and Dennis Sykes] were meeting to strategize how this was going to work and how we get the community involved. He [Hollister] had a public relations person working with him, Steve Serkaian. Between [members of] this group, we decided that every week, we would decide how we're going to roll out certain pieces to the Quick Response Team and the Blue Ribbon Committee."

Tadgerson went on: "But, before that, we had figure out what was the Blue Ribbon Committee. Who would be involved? How often would they meet? What was their charge? So, Dave asked me to put together a plan. I put together a strategic plan and identified various segments of the community—labor relations, finance, community, neighborhoods—all the constituencies that would be affected by the campaign. So, we had to identify all those people and in that [the strategic plan] I had a charge for each area, each subarea. Each subcommittee had a responsibility. A strategic plan for those subgroups and for the larger groups which we called the Blue Ribbon Committee to Retain GM. From that, we figured out that we couldn't have a committee meeting of 50 people and make it effective because there would be just too much discussion; too many people involved in trying to make a decision. Se we created an executive team, which was the Quick Response Team." These two teams created an effective capacity for responding to almost any crisis in short order.

Maintaining capacity also entailed maintaining the relationships with GM, with the community, and among the members involved. Outwardly, in the public eye and in the community, Steve Serkaian's team was critical. Serkaian, Mayor Hollister's communications director, commented on this: "I, in effect, served as Mayor Hollister's press secretary. We, from start to finish, were intimately involved in the effort to keep General Motors. Every step of the way after we kicked off the event at the State of the City, we made sure that if something happened in downtown Detroit with General Motors, we were available at a moment's notice to react to the media in order to keep the community informed that our effort to keep General Motors in Lansing remained on track. And there were some pretty tough things that were going on that we were involved with in this effort, including a strike in Flint, where all things stopped and really put the investment of keeping that plant in Lansing in jeopardy."

A pointed and important example of showcasing to GM that Lansing meant business came in the form of negotiations and discussion regarding the Delta Township plant. Joe Drolett and Ray Tadgerson have unique perspectives on the tenacity that the Lansing mayor showed in this case. As viewed by Joe Drolett, Delta Township supervisor: "We had gone over all those things and I just asked him [Ed Donovan] a question. I said, can we have some discussion on this $2 million water charge? He said, 'Well, we are going to cease negotiations right here. We have to go and think about this,' and he left. Dave turned to me and said, 'We just had the largest corporation in the United States walk out on us.' I said, 'It was just a question, is there anything they can do?' I didn't tell them we were not going to. So, Dave went down and brought him back and I said a couple of words. I said, 'I didn't say no, it was just a question.' He said, 'You mean you'll do the deal?' I said, 'Yeah.' Anyway, everything worked out okay."

Ray's take is a little more colorful: "The mayor went out, chased down the GM guy [Ed Donovan], brought him back to the meeting, and said, 'We're going to do this.' And Joe had to go back to his board and convince them to come up with another million dollars. Fortunately, for the whole region, Joe stuck his neck out, took the risk, and the board backed him, and they came up with the other million dollars. Not that they hadn't already done something, it's just that they had to come up with the other million dollars. And the end result is a billion, two hundred million dollar plant sitting in Delta Township. This is a major, major plant being built there."

Look for Collaborative Win-Win Solutions

If the objective is as grandiose as keeping GM in a town that it had decided to leave, realizing that GM rarely, if ever, changes its mind when a strategic decision such as this has been made, the engagement in constant problem solving also has to include win-win opportunities for most parties involved. This requires collaborative thinking and leaving any "me, me, me" approach at the door. Steve Serkaian captured Mayor Hollister's sentiment on this: "You know, Hollister's favorite phrase from day one was 'creating win-win strategies,' strategies were both sides; all sides can feel good about what's been accomplished. All sides could feel like they're winners." Hollister himself said: "You need a transparent, collaborative, participatory process that looks at win-win situations. It builds on the strength of the community. In our particular case, it was our history of great labor-management relations and a highly skilled workforce with a 100-year history of being problem solvers."

From the GM plant perspective, Randy Thayer elaborated on the win-win approach by pointing out that shared goals drive the win-win mentality: "What's unique about it is the shared goals. I mean the union here never had anything in mind except job security. When you get right down to it, management is worried about job security too, right? So the overlap is huge. It wasn't 100 percent—can't sugarcoat it. I mean you always have differences but the overlap was much more than the differences in most places."

The collaborative aspect of win-win is also important, in addition to the shared goals. If someone wins but was not part of the process, the meaning likely has less importance than if the person was integral in getting to the win-win outcome. This was a point Jim Zubkus stressed: "You have to have collaboration. You've got to remember that people who come through the gate every day to work would rather be somewhere else. You know they are bringing their lunch bucket in and saying, 'I'd rather be fishing,' as everybody would. Well, you got to create an atmosphere where it is not distasteful. You got to create an atmosphere where they feel a sense of contribution."

While we might disagree that we all go to a job wishing we were someplace else, the idea that people come to work with different levels of commitment, passion, and involvement rings true. Joe Drolett echoed Zubkus's sentiments: "We had to do something, and we had to work together. So anything we could do. I know Delta was invited in [to the campaign] right away when Dave Hollister was working with General Motors downtown. David came to me one day and he said 'Joe, give us first shot.' And I said, 'I'll give you more than that.' When General Motors was sitting in the room, I said, 'We want downtown first.' We cannot afford to have a decaying central city. I and my board members understand that a strong central city is good for us." This level of give-and-take, and more give, ultimately reached a super outcome for the greater Lansing region.

Michigan State University's president, Lou Anna K. Simon, illustrated this outcome: "It's hard to argue the campaign's success. Not only did we keep what we had, but we've grown the production capacity. You think we probably couldn't contemplate at that point in time the way technology would affect the number of jobs. So, you have to look at success I think in terms of production capacity and the desire for GM to continue to reinvest in that production capacity in this community, and to value the workers and the quality of work done in Lansing. So, in that sense, it was an enormous success."

In this book, though, we are showcasing the outcome of success while creating the blueprint for Lansing and other communities to stay strong, vital, and important and to have the problem-solving capacity to achieve win-win outcomes. This is what our intention is with the Second Shift Model, and Michigan's senator Debbie Stabenow realized early on the power in such a model: "There is no question this was a model that works . . . it's about people putting aside egos and individual turf and coming together and saying, 'We're going to do whatever it takes, whatever is best for the community, we're going to work together, we're going to respect each other's talents,' bringing them to the place where we can actually get the job done."

Senator Stabenow expanded on the Second Shift Model as an idea for the country: "This is exactly what needs to happen in Washington right now, no question in my mind. We've got to get people out of the corners, blaming each other, and instead saying, 'Let's get together. Let's grow an economy where people can have great jobs so we can make things and grow things and continue to be the world's leaders, because we are benefitting from each other's strengths and not demonizing business or workers or anybody else.' But, saying, 'We have to have everybody. We are all in this together.' What Lansing showed is that when people understand that, great things can happen."

Manage Communications

In the late 1990s and early 2000s, managing communication was both tougher and easier than it is today. In today's social media world, there are no old-fashioned news cycles. News cycles are 24/7, coming in many forms and being consumed in many different vehicles. This makes it easier to get the news out there. But it also makes it tougher to manage communications and stay ahead of the storyline, especially if it is likely to be a bad one.

Regardless, structuring the communication plans, managing when and how news was delivered, still applied just as much in the "Keep GM" campaign. Ray Tadgerson told this story about what eventually was labeled the "Lansing Works! Keep GM!" campaign: "Before we announced the Blue Ribbon Committee, Dave, me, and a couple of his key department heads [Bob Swanson and Dennis Sykes] were meeting to strategize how this was going to work and how we get the community involved. He [Hollister] had a public relations person working with him, Steve Serkaian. Between [members of] this group, we decided that every week, we would decide how we're going to roll out certain pieces to the Quick Response Team and the Blue Ribbon Committee." Ray continued: "It was a strategy session to figure out what we were facing this week, how we were going to accomplish this, how do we spin it to the public, what do we release to the public. In our conversations with the unions, they would often tell us, 'What we are telling you can't go outside this room.' Some of the things they told us, we really had to keep confidential, and in the Quick Response Team, we would decide what we were going to say to the public, and what we were going to say to the Blue Ribbon Committee—how we say it and how much information we are willing to share, because whatever we said could put the whole campaign at risk."

The overarching idea is, of course, that "you need a pretty sophisticated communications strategy," according to Mayor Hollister. But "first, you have to have the trust of the community. Because if they don't trust you, none of this is going to work anyway." Hollister explained that this trust and communication started with having goals and being inclusive. He said: "You really had to identify the goal, and then you had to be inclusive. You had to be transparent so people feel the issue is being addressed and they're being heard. You had to have a communication strategy so you're communicating to the community, to the corporation, and to community interests." Of course, "sometimes the communication's very superficial. We would give an award to one of the GM officials and have them be an honorary Lansing Lugnut. I mean, come on, that's not a news breaker, but we would do it and they would get a lot of coverage. We'd send them a copy so they'd have it in front of their executive bathroom where they would read the papers. We just went out of our way to communicate."

The "Lansing Works! Keep GM!" theme was brilliant. It stressed that the community wanted to "keep GM" while also pointing out that "Lansing works," in the sense of its very skilled labor and powerful, competent knowledge workers. According to Steve Serkaian: "In any campaign, you try to put together a number of communication tactics that will capture the spirit, capture the imagination of this community. Unlike a retail advertising campaign, we had no product to sell other than this amorphous notion of keeping General Motors. We did that through a variety of mediums. I mean remember, back when this happened, the internet was in its infancy. There was no e-mailing as pervasive as it is today. Social media was nonexistent. So, we had to use traditional media, traditional means in order to communicate our messages and our strategy. We did it through public relations and the news media. We did it through bumper stickers. We did through a jingle that Lansing radio stations could play."

Serkaian continued: "The campaign symbols, the campaign tactics, the campaign products, if you will, all those were intended to show General Motors we want them to stay but more importantly, they had to communicate to the Lansing region what the value of this corporation, what the value of the jobs meant to the area." He also said that "knowing more than you can communicate has been a part of my career" but that "no one communication tactic ruled the day. It was a cumulative effect that showed the community that this effort was very important; a little bit for everyone." Mayor Hollister also saw the communications from a big-picture perspective: "The key was not blowing the cover of the UAW and General Motors and their national negotiations."

And as always, information had different meanings, and different players had it! Chris Holman, CEO of the Michigan Business Network, elaborated: "There was a lot of embargoed information at the time. There was a lot of secret information, but you know it's like saying to Eisenhower, 'When is D-Day? I mean, the people want to know.' You just don't tell people when D-Day is. Otherwise you compromise the success of the operation. I think they gave enough for the media to have the story they wanted, to tell the story, to inform the community without compromising the outcome of the story." What Holman said is important, as echoed by Ray Tadgerson: "In our conversations with the union, they would often tell us, 'What we are telling you can't go outside this room.' It had to stay inside this room, because whatever we said could put this whole campaign at risk."

Of course, the media knew that they often did not get the full picture of what was happening or about to happen. Holman pointed out as much: "Let me tell you, by the nature of media they were trying to reach for more and they absolutely didn't feel they were getting the full story, but that's okay, quite frankly. That's the world all of us in media live in. I did straddle the fence because I was a business guy and I was involved in this in some peripheral factions. There were some little things I was able to do kind of outside the realm of media. And so, I think, it was quite honestly, in retrospect, handled very well."

Establish a Unified Voice with a Single Point of Entry and Exit

Engaging in constant problem solving, along with striving for win-win outcomes and collaboration across all possible fences, requires a lot of unity. That unity has to center on a unified voice with a single point of entry and exit to be practical, and that's when the community often loses it. Many individuals would automatically call out a leader for taking charge where charge was not given, questioning why a certain person should be in charge, and so on. Champions of a cause exist everywhere; sometimes they are champions because they are knowledgeable, because they have previous experience, or because they are viewed as being relatively neutral. Very few people were neutral in this story!

Ray Tadgerson captured what needed to be done: "The first thing is making sure you have a good champion in place, somebody who is influential and somebody who's a recognized leader in the community. This person has to put together a really good team, a strong team, a collaborative team—people who have a vision similar to the champion." The obvious champion was Lansing mayor David Hollister, but Jack Davis (chair of the Lansing chamber board) and Peter McPherson (president of Michigan State University) were, in essence, also appointed the champion role by Mayor Hollister. Over time this champion role shifted more and more to just the mayor and Jack Davis as well as deepened behind-the-scenes championing by Ray Tadgerson.

Championing also means tactfully adhering to some of the wishes of the parties involved, although not always! Hollister explained: "We had the signal that our plants were closing at some point in the future and that there was a new plant to be built somewhere. But, Lansing was not on the drawing board. So, then, we began a very comprehensive, community strategy. When I talked with Mark [Hogan], he didn't want us to do anything publicly. He didn't want us to do the Toledo model, which was very public and high profile. I told Mark that we really have to convince this community of the value [of GM]. So, we really had to educate two constituencies, one being the automotive leadership in Detroit and the other was our community."

While a unified voice was important, Hollister also said that sending strong signals to GM was important in many respects. Mayor Hollister told Mark Hogan at GM that "this would be a single entry, single exit, regional comprehensive problem-solving group. There wasn't a single problem that he could bring to us that we wouldn't solve in about a 30-day period of time." Mayor Hollister also took this idea to the local 6 p.m. news: "Topping the 6:00 tonight, Mayor David Hollister feels chances of keeping General Motors here in Lansing may be better if all efforts stem from one common ground." This one-voice idea resonated when Hollister said that it was also supported by constant problem-solving initiatives: "We said, for example [to Mark Hogan], 'Give us a problem and we will solve it. We will try to turn it around within 30 days. Give us a chance.' And, that's all we were asking."

Build More Partnerships

In some ways, the more than 50 people on the Blue Ribbon Committee at its peak point, and the many community leaders that were involved, demonstrated a nice team of collaborative relationships that delivered constant problem-solving solutions. But given the lengthy process, partnerships that initiated the process, solved intermediate issues, and represented the finalizing of GM staying in the community were not going to be exactly the same across the timeline. The constant problem-solving mentality also had to be part of an approach to deciding which partnerships should be nurtured. That way, all the right hands were always on deck!

Ray Tadgerson: "It's all about identifying the right resources within a community and how to bring those resources together, utilizing the energy that's available to pull together in a way that normally wouldn't happen and allow things to transpire over time so that it comes together in the right way." Facilitation is extremely important in bringing community resources together, as pointed to by Bob Swanson in his views of the mayor: "I think Mayor Hollister's ability to work together with people, even people of opposing political philosophies, made it easier for him to deal with John Engler as Governor of Michigan. The two of them had served together in the House. They had a history and relationship, but they were sort of miles apart ideologically. But, in terms of doing what needed to be done that best served Michigan and Lansing, they were together."

The cultural fabric was important. "I think you can see this as a model of regional collaboration where instead of having compromise being a bad word and beating your opponent over the head, you look for win-win situations," said Mayor Hollister. "You look for strategic partnerships. You try to come at the problem holistically."

Some of the top political leadership in Michigan today remarked on this as well, as best illustrated by Michigan's U.S. senator Debbie Stabenow: "I think Mayor Hollister at the time did exactly the right thing. It's in our DNA to fight for what we believe in. And, we know the people of Lansing, the business, labor, work, everybody working together works best. We wanted General Motors here. We knew we had high quality. We were producing some of the best in the country and the world. So, I said, 'Sign me up.'"

She continued: "I remember, the most important thing is the fact that first of all everybody decided to do it [join together to save GM] rather than just saying, 'Gee, they're going to close. Isn't this awful?' Everybody said, 'We're going to change their mind,' and it's not about beating up on GM. It's really about telling the Lansing story, telling the GM story, telling the story of the UAW, of the workers who are, in my judgment, the best workers in the world; bringing everybody together, seeing everybody up on a stage, not just those of us who are elected officials representing the area and living in the community, but to see the business leaders, and the university and the community college. Everybody came together and said, 'We're going to work together and we're going to do whatever it takes to make sure GM stays in Lansing,' and I thought that was pretty cool."

SOLVING SUMMARY

Engaging in constant problem solving became the mantra for the Blue Ribbon Committee, but especially for the Quick Response Team. The process was years in the making, and often without a clear end or outcome in sight, or even, at times, an idea of what the outcome really could or should be. Even with the great unknowns, the region's leaders in business, labor, education, and local and state government, as well as citizens at large, when needed, saw it as their call of duty to engage.

Within the framework of the Second Shift Model, this constant problem solving—regardless of the players involved, and there were many—built on six core areas. These included (1) anticipate challenges, (2) maintain capacity to respond in a crisis, (3) look for collaborative win-win solutions, (4) manage communication, (5) establish a unified voice with a single point of entry and exit, and (6) build more partnerships.

CHAPTER 6

---◆---

CELEBRATING

MARK SUCCESSFUL MILESTONES

To "celebrate" traditionally means doing something special or enjoyable for an important event, occasion, or holiday. It acknowledges and praises individual and group achievements and goal attainment, and it is generally reserved for the end of a process. This is especially true in the individualistic U.S. society, where goal attainment is the ultimate objective and where the process of getting to the goal perhaps takes a secondary focus. But celebration really has a much deeper meaning and potential for uplifting spirits, especially in a community-based project such as the Second Shift story we capture in this book.

Celebration is important because it lifts morale and helps sustain individuals and groups by reaffirming the goal, strategy, plan, and community's resources and assets. Knowing that changing a decision by the GM Board of Directors would be long and complicated, it was important to build celebration into the overall community strategy. Instead of focusing on the end goal that was likely three to five years away, it was decided that the Lansing team would acknowledge and celebrate the region's strengths, resources, assets, and heritage, as well as the progress of the Quick Response Team and the Blue Ribbon Committee.

As time moved on, there were many milestones that gave the Quick Response Team a sense that progress was being made. These needed to be celebrated somehow. However, unfortunately, it was also true that many of the successes achieved could not be shared

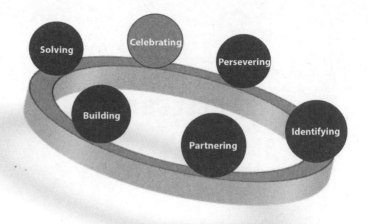

Figure 6.1   The Second Shift Model—celebrating

with the public in the greater Lansing community or even with the Blue Ribbon Committee, for fear of compromising the campaign with General Motors or the United Auto Workers. Also, limits on what could be shared had to be well thought out so as not to create false hopes. Nevertheless, celebrating by marking successful milestones was an important part of what ultimately turned out to be the Second Shift success story. Figure 6.1 illustrates the Second Shift Model, highlighting the "celebrating" component discussed in Chapter 6.

CELEBRATING NARRATIVE

The greater Lansing region had come to take GM's presence in the community for granted. Numerous scenarios and comments by community leaders highlight this unsettling fact. But some cautioned the community not to assume that GM would always be in Lansing or that the economic vitality of Lansing would be sustainable without lots of hard work. For example, Lou Anna K. Simon, president of Michigan State University, says: "You can never take what you have for granted, particularly in this very complex global marketplace where you're not the center of corporate decision making. You have to continue to show value for what you're doing."

She continued: "You can't just wait for something bad to happen, in order for the community to mobilize and continue to both promote what you have and the quality of the workforce that you have, at the same time looking for new opportunities. People thought we won, so we relaxed, and now in this world, you can't do that. You've got to continue that kind of structure and that kind of regional focus on creating new things and keeping what you have."

Perhaps more importantly, and even more unsettling, GM had come to believe that Lansing was just another manufacturing community with outdated facilities that could no longer justify the investment needed to make them profitable and competitive. Unfortunately, there was no mechanism for the Lansing area leadership to realize and plan for GM's strategic decision to leave the community it had been in for some 100 years.

When the realization hit home, the mayor directed the public relations firm of Kolt & Serkaian to develop a two-part communication plan that would (1) continually educate the Lansing region about the importance of keeping advanced manufacturing operations in mid-Michigan and (2) persuade GM officials that the region's unique assets, particularly its quality workforce, merited their continuing investment. Kolt & Serkaian recommended that the Blue Ribbon Committee create a "Lansing Works! Keep GM!" campaign designed to acknowledge and celebrate every asset, every event, and every achievement that distinguished the greater Lansing region.

This was a way to place a positive sentiment, build a positive community fabric, and send a message to GM and other manufacturing organizations that "Lansing Works" and works well. The community strategically plans to be a manufacturing leader for years to come, and now we are showing it off by celebrating and marking successful milestones in the community's efforts to keep General Motors.

The first milestone achieved was the mayor's launch of the Blue Ribbon Committee to Keep GM and the "Lansing Works! Keep GM!" campaign in his 1998 State of the City Address. The address—of utmost importance to the region as a message maker and unique opportunity for a positive signal—was carried live by a local television station and also highly publicized in the Michigan media.

Billboards, bumper stickers, and a "Lansing Works!" jingle highlighted the Lansing workforce, its tradition of great labor-management relations, and its quality products. This public showcase of celebration, combined with the fact that the community, including the Lansing mayor, believed Lansing had reasons to celebrate its efforts to keep GM, was against the wishes of the vice president of GM's Car Group North America, Mark Hogan, who had clearly stated that he wanted no such public Toledo-like campaign. But in small ways, it worked early on.

Let's step back a bit and look at some celebratory milestones with respect to Lansing and General Motors in this late 1990s and early 2000s time period. As a starting point for the celebratory story, in the fall of 1997, Jim Zubkus (plant manager for GM's main assembly plant and the Fisher Body plant in Lansing) recommended, and Art Baker (shop chair of the United Auto Workers) and Mark Hogan agreed, to make a statement to GM's leaders about the high quality of the Lansing workforce by launching the new Alero on the second shift, something that had never been done in GM history.

While the August 1997 centennial anniversary celebration for Oldsmobile attracted thousands of car enthusiasts to Lansing to celebrate its past, the decision to build the Alero and also the Grand Am on the second shift was a celebration of the region's skilled workforce. The focus was on the future. Then, in February 1998, Zubkus and other UAW leaders organized an "All Employee Enthusiasm Meeting" to rally workers around the goal of making the launch the "best ever," thereby improving the Lansing area's chances to build cars in the future.

At the ceremonial launch in June 1998, Zubkus closed down production so that all the second shift employees could participate and see the Eastern High School band lead the mayor and his wife as they drove the first Alero down the assembly line. The event was also widely covered by local media. The City of Lansing purchased the first Alero and bought several more for the city's vehicle fleet. David and Christine Hollister drove it off the assembly line on June 4, 1998.

General Motors recognized the Lansing autoworkers with the "Best Launch Ever" award. Along with that came a $25,000 prize, which Zubkus and UAW leaders decided should go into a plant-wide drawing for an education scholarship, thereby supporting the mayor's school improvement efforts.

Given the great success of the launch, Hogan told the mayor and Zubkus that GM would consider Lansing as a possible site for a new plant as long as the city could make available 300 acres. This was good news, but no celebration could take place until 300 acres was found. Unfortunately, Ray Tadgerson and his staff concluded that no sites were available in the city without using the politically challenging process of eminent domain. It began to look like GM would have to seek a site outside the city.

Not long after the pronouncement by Hogan, Zubkus called Tadgerson and said he wanted to talk with him privately. Zubkus pointed out that the main assembly plant, Plant 1, had many empty and underutilized buildings. He also showed Tadgerson a set of photocopied drawings that were footprints for two state-of-the-art GM plants recently built in South America. Zubkus said he knew the plants, code named "Blue Macaw," were built on smaller sites, but he was uncertain whether such a plant could be built on the Plant 1 site when and if the existing buildings were torn down. He also shared that Hogan was directly involved with the construction of the South American plants. Zubkus then asked Tadgerson to explore whether the new-style plant could fit on the Plant 1 site.

Tadgerson took several days to complete the analysis. First, the drawings were not to scale and were virtually unreadable. There were a few dimensions on the copies, which served as a starting point. A new "metric scale" had to be created, and the size of the site had to be verified in several ways to ensure the new drawing file was indeed correct. Tadgerson asked one of his firm's draftsmen to create a drawing without a scale on the firm's CADD system. He then asked to have the Plant 1 site drawing put on CADD, captured from files provided by Zubkus. Once a scale was created, it was validated by scaling the trucks and other features on the photocopies. Then the new CADD drawing of the Blue Macaw could be overlaid on the new Plant 1 CADD drawing. The end result was discovering that the site in Brazil was a 70-acre site, far smaller than the 300 acres requested by GM. Tadgerson called Zubkus to tell him that Blue Macaw would fit on the Plant 1 site and immediately went to meet with Mayor Hollister. After seeing the drawing, the mayor exclaimed, "We have to show this to Hogan!"

Zubkus then called Hogan and asked him to come to Lansing, as the mayor's team had information the team wanted him to see. The meeting took place in Zubkus's office on May 8, 1998. The Quick Response Team met with Zubkus and Hogan and presented the business case, outlined in a three-ring binder, for GM to construct its next state-of-the-art plant in the Lansing area. Seven different possible sites with the Blue Macaw superimposed on them, including the Plant 1 site, were presented. Hogan immediately asked, "Where did you get that [the Blue Macaw footprint]?" Tadgerson responded, "Research." Hogan was clearly impressed but noncommittal.

Several months later Hogan called Zubkus and the mayor to say that GM would be building the new plant on the existing Plant 1 site. Time for celebration? No, because the national contract with the UAW was not finalized, and the official announcement would have to wait until the contract was approved, signed, and ratified. In the meantime, GM began the process of tearing down buildings and asked the city to begin infrastructure improvements. The city then bid a multimillion dollar infrastructure project to prepare the site for the eventual construction of the new plant, which began in 1999 and produced the first Cadillac in 2001. The unique aspect of the infrastructure project was that it was undertaken on a handshake agreement between Mayor Hollister and Mark Hogan. This too had to be kept under wraps until the UAW contract was completed.

Finally, in January 2000, then GM CEO Rick Wagoner unveiled a model of the new "Blue Macaw" plant, announcing it would be built right on the Plant 1 site. Now this was a reason to celebrate! There was a big press conference where all in attendance witnessed a major milestone for Lansing and the region. As a way of continuing the celebration of this milestone, GM agreed to the Blue Ribbon Committee's request that cameras be installed at the site so that the public would have online access to progress that was made.

It seemed as though it was happily "game over"—Lansing and the region had won. However, Hogan had made it known that GM was interested in building a second assembly plant somewhere in the region. Tadgerson worked closely with GM real estate officials to identify 1,200–1,300 acres in the tri-county area, preferably in a greenfield and with unimpeded access to highways, railroads, and the airport. They found one site in Delta Township known as the Creyts Farm that met GM's criteria. An agreement was reached with the Creyts family to purchase the land but allowing the family to retain a small parcel.

After a major groundbreaking ceremony was held at the Delta Township land, GM began the construction of a metal stamping plant that would supply the Grand River Assembly in downtown Lansing and other GM facilities. The construction of the Lansing Delta Assembly plant began much later, after the conclusion of lengthy contract negotiations. In 2006 the assembly plant launched its first vehicles—all crossover SUVs.

A few years following the seminal "knock on the door," the Lansing region had the unique and well-earned distinction of being the only community in the world where an auto company had committed to building three new state-of-the-art manufacturing facilities, thereby ensuring Lansing's prominent role in auto manu-facturing for decades to come. Public grand opening ceremonies were held to celebrate the completion of these facilities.

Below is a list of the most notable celebrations, large and small, public and private, that occurred over the duration of the "Lansing Works! Keep GM!" campaign:

- Fact-finding trip to Toledo.
- Lansing mayor's unveiling of the "Lansing Works! Keep GM!" campaign at the January 1998 State of the City Address at the Oldsmobile headquarters.
- Successful "Best Launch Ever" of General Motors' Alero car in April 1998.
- Announcement by vice president of GM's Car Group North America Mark Hogan that there would be an assembly plant built somewhere in the world.
- Determination that a South American plant model, code-named "Blue Macaw," would fit on the Lansing Plant 1 site.
- Presentation to GM's Mark Hogan on May 8, 1998, at the Verlinden plant (Plant 6) providing him with information about Lansing and the region with seven potential sites, including Plant 1, with the Blue Macaw footprint superimposed upon each.

- Mayor Hollister's meeting in the summer of 1998 with GM officials at GM's Tech Center. This was the first time GM had ever invited a government official into the top-secret planning center.
- Private announcement by GM's Mark Hogan to the Lansing mayor and Zubkus that the new plant would be built on the Plant 1 site, but the city would have to make infrastructure improvements on only a handshake commitment and without public announcements.
- Signed and ratified national UAW contract.
- Public announcement by Rick Wagoner, CEO of General Motors, that a new plant would be built on the Plant 1 site.
- Construction of the Grand River Assembly plant beginning in 1999.
- Public grand opening for the Grand River Assembly plant in 2001.
- Mayor David Hollister and his wife, Christine, driving the Oldsmobile Alero off the assembly line at the Lansing Grand River Assembly plant. Announcement by GM's Mark Hogan that a second assembly would be built, possibly in the Lansing region, which would require 1,200–1,300 acres on a greenfield.
- Laws changed by the legislature to allow abatements and incentives for job *retention* not just job *attraction*.
- GM changing its paint chemistry in response to a neighborhood concern about plant emission odors that held up the production of the SSR pickup at Plant 2 and would potentially stop the Delta facility; the result was that neighborhood and environmental groups signed off on the permitting process, thereby allowing the projects to go forward.
- GM's purchase of approximately 1,000 acres in Delta Township for the construction of a second assembly plant and a metal stamping facility.
- A new GM-UAW labor agreement that was delayed several times but finally ratified and signed, allowing the Lansing Delta facility to proceed with construction.
- The Delta Assembly construction completed in 2006, and the first of the Saturn Outlook, Buick Enclave, and GMC Acadia vehicles rolling out of the 2.4 million square foot LEED gold–

certified facility. This was the first such manufacturing facility to be LEED designated.
- A 425 agreement for tax sharing that was worked out between Lansing and Delta Township.
- The Delta Assembly plant being built after construction was started and stopped several times while waiting for ratification of a new UAW agreement.

REFLECTIONS ON CELEBRATING

David Hollister

As I approached the significant challenge of reversing the decision by the GM board to close our outdated assembly plants, I knew it would be a multiyear process with setbacks and challenges. While the "Keep GM" goal was clear and unifying, the larger task was to create a new mechanism for regional problem solving.

The Blue Ribbon Committee became the vehicle to achieve our goal. It worked because we were able to establish trust by making it inclusive, comprehensive, diverse, and transparent. People bought in because we were committed to win-win outcomes, data-driven analysis, shared credit, and continual communication. We empowered and respected all participants and celebrated behind the scenes and publicly at every opportunity. We proved that our collaborative model works!

Ray Tadgerson

I have been told that thousands of GM workers, supplier employees, and business owners across the state were praying GM officials would change their minds, and obviously, those prayers were answered with the building of the three state-of-the-art facilities. Lansing was and remains the only community in the world to successfully change the minds of, at that time, the largest corporation in the world.

Was it the campaign that did it? Not totally. The local UAW units, namely 652 and 602, understood what was at stake and worked tirelessly with General Motors to get the new plants, even when it meant fewer jobs. The collaboration model created by the

Lansing mayor and his team did capture the attention of GM's leadership and demonstrated that the local community, the UAW, and the corporation could work together to do something that had never been done before or since.

When the mayor asked if I could run a campaign like this, I said, "Absolutely!" but I had no idea about whether I could succeed. Relying on the experience of putting a team together to help the city build a baseball stadium downtown, I believed that with the tremendous amount of brainpower in Lansing, we could at least give it our best shot. Fortunately for Lansing and the region, it came together as close to perfection as it could. It became apparent later that throughout the campaign the right people had to be in the right place at the right time with the right attitude for any kind of success to occur; they were, and they did!

As for my role in this monumental task, I feel humbled and blessed to have been a part of something so meaningful and beneficial for many generations to come. I had what I refer to as back-to-back lifetime experiences, and I have Dave Hollister, the city, and the region to thank for providing me the opportunity. It is not often one gets to participate in something so large that it is hard to describe or wrap your arms around, and it was so gratifying!

MAJOR CHALLENGES AND OBSTACLES IN CELEBRATING

Throughout this book, we have discussed major challenges and obstacles, all elements requiring solutions and what we have come to call the Second Shift Model. Effectively, the challenges encountered along the way were reiterated in the first five chapters of the book. And there were lots of them!

For celebrations to occur, in many cases even small ones, each challenge had to be overcome. So with more than 35 major challenges and a myriad of smaller ones over the course of the "Lansing Works! Keep GM!" campaign, there were times when the team wondered if it would ever have a celebration.

Ultimately, the greater Lansing region won a major battle in spite of the considerable challenges and obstacles. The model that was developed brought the community together and exhibited the heart and DNA of the region in a "never give up" and "win-win" way through collaborations, cooperation, and support via a transparent and inclusive plan.

The true celebration came with the realization that the vast number of challenges were met, and the first vehicles rolling off the lines in both state-of-the-art assembly plants were more than symbolic of the successful effort. This also signaled a very bright future for thousands of employees who nearly lost their jobs and, for future generations, a secure future for decades to come.

THREE COMPONENTS OF CELEBRATING

It may seem odd to include "celebrating" as a dimension in the six-dimensional Second Shift Model. After all, celebrations happen at the end of a project. Mayor Hollister and Ray Tadgerson, and their team, thought otherwise. For a variety of reasons we have discussed, don't wait for the end to celebrate, instead recognize meaningful progress at the time, and then have a bigger celebration at the end. Such a progression of celebrating is always a morale booster and recognizes the dynamic nature of the Second Shift Model (Figure 6.2).

Don't Wait for the End

It seems so logical and even compelling: don't wait until the end of a project to celebrate. But how many people really get in the habit of celebrating small milestones? Perhaps we celebrate big milestones of a larger project, but small ones, usually not. The Second Shift Model calls for celebration of both small and big milestones—some publicly and others perhaps only within the Quick Response Team.

Celebrating
(Mark Successful Milestones)

1. Don't Wait for the End
2. Recognize Meaningful Progress
3. Then Have a Bigger Celebration

Figure 6.2   The Second Shift Model—components of celebrating

Sometimes milestones and opportunities to celebrate present themselves. For example, David Hollister pointed out: "General Motors assigned Mark Hogan to oversee the project [the launch of the Alero], and he was coming to Lansing on a regular basis. With Jim [Zubkus] doing the work behind the scenes and with the good labor-management relations that we had, it turned out the launch of the Alero was singularly the most successful launch they'd [GM] ever had. The plant won a $25,000 award for the successful launch." Mark Hogan's regular visits to check up on progress also, de facto, created an opportunity for celebration of the progress he was in Lansing to check up on!

Maybe some successes or milestones are relatively small in some people's eyes, but they can also be symbolic of the environment and willingness of people involved to "drive" the extra mile to make things happen and to celebrate. "As a part of that strategy [to convince GM to change its decision] the City of Lansing bought the first Alero for me as Mayor," said David Hollister. He continued: "And then we bought one for our cabinet. We not only like this automobile; we're going to purchase it, and I'm going to drive it."

"My wife, Christine, and I actually drove the first Alero off the assembly line," said Hollister. He elatedly explained that "Jim closed the plant down, and that second shift team lined up. We had the Eastern High School marching band playing 'God Bless America' as we went down that final assembly, and tears were just coming down people's faces. They were so thrilled with the launch, and that kind of positioned us to make a case that we could turn that decision around."

Another seemingly small issue for the larger community (but very important for at least a portion of the community in the plant's geographic proximity) was the paint odor environmental issue that came up in the planning for a new plant. David Wiener, Lansing's deputy mayor, explained: "We started off with a commitment to the neighborhood. As the Lansing Mayor's Office, we said that we're going to use our role and our position, our relationship with General Motors, to make sure that we're all talking together. We decided we really needed to look at some of the health care issues. We really needed to dig in and see, are there really health care problems that result from those emissions?"

Wiener continued: "Long story short, we ended up, through a nine-month process, going through a series of very excellent discussions with General Motors, their environmental engineers, the local health department, the state health department, the state department of environmental quality, and the schools. There were a lot of offshoots that came out of these efforts just because we were working together, and we were getting to know each other. And, we were getting to be sensitive to each other's needs; we were learning what each other's assets were. I think that people felt good about being a part of the process. It was really a way of reaffirming our relationships and that we are a part of one community worth living and being in." Who knew that the resolution of a paint odor environmental issue could be cause for celebration—small for many in the community and large for those closely affected.

So whether it be small wins, small successes, or some in the large variety, the idea was don't wait for the end to celebrate, and showcase the celebration when appropriate and when it could be done for public consumption. Steve Serkaian said: "My role was to publicize Hollister's and the Keep General Motors efforts on a day-to-day basis. And, really for 18 months, besides helping communicate the day-to-day activities and accomplishments of the city administration, that's what I did along with other projects. It was intense. It was different than working on a political campaign that had an end. Once we kept GM in effect, and won the official announcement of

Model of the Lansing Grand River Assembly

Grand opening of the Lansing Grand River Assembly

the Lansing Grand River Assembly plant, we moved on to more. That's when we changed the logo from 'Lansing Works! Keep GM!' to 'Lansing Works, Keeping GM.'"

Serkaian further explained: "'Keeping' connoted progress, at the same time that there was still work to be done. There was work still to be done because once the Lansing Grand River plant was announced and the girders were going up, you could officially talk about now being the new plant. Now the effort was to secure a second plant, a larger plant, a bigger operation. Now that Lansing has its investment, let's get an investment for suburban Lansing, for the region."

Recognize Meaningful Progress

Now, there can always be a debate about what is really meaningful progress and whether it should be recognized in a milestone fashion with some celebratory event or accolades. There has to be sincerity here as well. If select individuals are celebrated for their accomplishments, but not others achieving similar feats, then sincerity is lost in the process. Spread the wealth of recognition of meaningful progress, but make sure that it is meaningful progress toward the ultimate goal that is being celebrated.

Jack Davis (chair of the board of the Lansing Regional Chamber of Commerce) noted: "We, the City of Lansing, were happy [with the decision by GM] to build there; it was a major triumph. I was very happy with it and probably would have been satisfied with it. But, on the other hand, the other leadership we had on the Quick Response Team saw this as just the first step. So we didn't celebrate the major triumph when the first plant was built. We felt we had to get a second plant."

Some would, of course, say that getting that first plant built was a remarkable, significant achievement—and it was. But the years of making progress on one plant had been celebrated in step-by-step occasions. Now, having the first plant success allowed for greater strategic thinking and a focus on a second plant.

"That's where David [Hollister] collaborated to the full extent possible with Joe Drolett and the labor movement in getting production out in Delta Township," said Davis. "So, it wasn't like we celebrated the first plant as much as you would think, because we still had to get the second plant. And that was going to be difficult."

Then Have a Bigger Celebration

The recommendations of "don't wait for the end" and "recognize meaningful progress" work to the satisfaction of the community only if the end result is a "bigger celebration" of mission accomplished. This sounds like it brings us full circle to focus squarely on the ultimate objective or goal of a project, in this case "Lansing Works! Keep GM!"

But this is not the case; we do believe "don't wait for the end" and "recognize meaningful progress" are important milestones as well. Oftentimes, such milestone celebrations recognize individuals and accomplished intermediate goals and even identify new target goals. They are also motivating and may lead to greater accomplishments, which eventually lead to reaching the end goal. That said, a bigger celebration is ultimately the goal, but interim goals should also be celebrated.

Such an interim goal can be illustrated by Dave Hollister: "We met with Jim Zubkus, the plant manager for the small car group, who had the responsibility for launching the Alero. Jim said to me,

'We need to send a message to General Motors in Detroit that this is the best workforce in America. We've heard it. We've said it, but let's prove it. I'm willing to launch the Alero on the second shift.' And, that decision, that single decision, was fundamental to our success going forward, because when Jim said that, he said it to the employees. 'We're going to do this on the second shift' meant that launching on the second shift was an important signal that we wanted to send to General Motors. It turns out the launch of the Alero was singularly the most successful launch they'd ever had."

Hollister is also very proud of the fact that he and his wife drove the first Alero off the assembly line. Perhaps this is not considered a big celebration by some, but for the Hollister family it was, and that family includes almost everyone in the greater Lansing region today!

The Alero launch was so effective, it led to more strategic thinking. "Mark [Hogan] came to us and said, 'You know the launch of the Alero was so successful, we will take a look at Lansing. I need 300 acres.'" Hollister recounted how he shouted back, "'Mark, where the hell am I going to find 300 acres in Lansing? You have to close more than one golf course, which I didn't want to do for minor league baseball,' and he laughed and said, 'That's right. It's 300 acres.'"

This is where Ray Tadgerson came in again: "They wanted 300 acres. There was no 300-acre site in the City of Lansing anywhere. I looked everywhere. The mayor and his staff looked everywhere. We couldn't find a 300-acre site."

Jim Zubkus agreed: "I knew the location where a new plant would be built was really tight, really tight, would be really tight. It would take an engineering genius to fit it in, but if you have the guy to fit it in, who Tadgerson was, he would find a way to do that. So, I got these plans, these prints from another plant and reviewed them as best I could, because I am not an engineer, to try to figure out would this operation be able to fit the amount of acreage I had over around the south side of town. Tadgerson was the guy. So, I asked him to come to my plant. I gave them to him. I said there are only two people who know about this, you and me and then, 'I don't want anybody else to know about it.' Tadgerson said, 'Can I talk to the mayor about this?' I said, 'Absolutely, so now there are three of us.' I said, 'But, this is us, this is it for right now,' and that's where it started."

"Well, Tadgerson took those plans, and I would assume he was able to convert a lot of what he had on those plans into what he was going to actually do with the amount of acreage he had available. It was a footprint for him. It was a base from which he could start, and he is a genius at this kind of stuff. So he took it from there," said Zubkus.

Tadgerson explained: "The Brazil site was on 70 acres. Seventy acres I could make. We planted a model from Brazil right on that [Plant 1] site."

"The beauty of what Ray did is to come in and say, 'Okay, this can fit here and it doesn't interfere with the ongoing production that is going to be happening for the next five years if you are still building cars around this,'" said Bob Swanson. "Then we had to figure out how to stage the demos and the infrastructure work so as to not interfere with the existing production, on a pretty tight plant site, but it was doable obviously."

Whether it was figuring out how to build a 300-acre plant on 70 acres or a myriad of other unique accomplishments, "Lansing has always been a little unique," said Bruce McAttee, Community Action Program coordinator of the local United Auto Workers. McAttee also said: "In the 90s you could really notice a difference in attitude. I mean you have some other communities where they were very militant from the beginning. I don't think that Lansing, at the time I worked there, would be categorized as a militant community. I never had a problem coming in and saying, 'Good morning' to my supervisor. There were places within GM, Ford and Chrysler where they didn't even acknowledge you if you wanted. You know, it was like an us against them."

Sean McAlinden, vice president for Strategic Studies and chief economist for the Center for Automotive Research, also suggested that Lansing was unique, but in a different way as it related to GM: "These two union Locals in Lansing, 602 and 652, were considered to be the most cooperative and some of the smartest union locals that GM had in the United States and Canada. Lansing had an excellent reputation on training programs and going out of their way to be competitive." The can-do attitude is illustrated by Tim

Podat (WLNS reporter) on air: "Art Baker has been on the UAW Bargaining Committee for 27 years. He's spent his whole life writing local union agreements. None of them have involved modular assembly, but he's already preparing for what he feels is inevitable."

The bottom line and cause for ongoing big celebration is that "General Motors doesn't have another place in the country that puts out the quality and/or productivity that an employee here in Lansing does," said Art Baker. "This has to be the number one spot that General Motors would look at to put a modular plant." Rick Wagoner reinforced that sentiment as the then CEO of GM: "It's going to be built right here [Plant 1 site], right where we are today, in Lansing, Michigan." David Andrews (WLNS anchor) reported that "the $560 million plant will employ around 1,500 workers when it opens late next year. A streamlined assembly line with increased efficiency, all without alienating the United Auto Workers whose goal is job security." This changed the focus, as Art Baker pointed out: "When a plant is efficient, it stays in business. Staying in business keeps us in jobs."

A reporter from WILX described the event: "So as GM executives mingle with regional leaders in front of the new factory, they credit the workers back in the old ones for securing Lansing's future as the car production capital of the state, the country, and perhaps soon, the world." "It was a completely fresh start for Cadillac and therefore, the future of the entire brand name depended on the success of this Lansing plant," said Sean McAlinden.

The last "big celebration" story carries lots of dollar signs. Dave Hollister tells the story: "We [Ed Donovan and I] had a personal relationship. He didn't enjoy that kind of relationship with [Joe] Drolett. It was more of a professional one. So when Joe pushed back and started renegotiating [the local costs for the Delta plant location], which we thought was going to be the final meeting, and, we were going to wrap this thing up and take it to the various groups for ratification, at least the broad outline, he [Donovan] lost his patience and said, 'Okay, we are done.'

"Joe was stunned. I was stunned. He [Donovan] picked up his stuff, and he goes out the door. And I turned to Joe and I said, 'Joe, do you realize what just happened? That's the number one corporation in America, and they just walked out the door. What the hell are you doing? This is not worth $2 million. We have got to get him back. I'm willing to go get him. I'll try to get him back, but are you willing to back off?' Then I assured him we would have a done deal.

"Joe had to balance that because he was getting pressure from his own board, and they were not in the negotiations. So Joe kept them informed as best he could, but they were pretty much in the dark. They just wanted the best deal they were elected to do for their community, and Joe's trying to balance his obligation to his board with the larger region. So he was kind of pushing the local issue when the larger region was in play.

"I looked at him and said, 'Joe, what are you going to do?' And he said, 'I just asked a question. I wasn't renegotiating; can we put this back on the table?' I said, 'Joe, yes or no?' He said, 'Well, go get him.' So, I chased him, Ed, down the damned street and I said, 'Ed, you've got to come back to the meeting.' He said, 'Nah, I've had it. I've got to take this back. I told my people, we'll wrap this up today.' I said, 'Ed, this is too important. You've got to come back.' I put my arm around him and said, 'Come on, give it another try.' And he came back, and Joe apologized and said, 'I didn't say, why don't we open the negotiations? I just wanted to represent my board who had some concerns.' Ed said, 'Well, I know you got pressure, I got pressure. Let's get this behind us.' And that's how it kind of played out." A long time in coming, but time for a bigger celebration again.

From the vantage point of Ray Tadgerson, "The Mayor went out, chased the guy [Donovan] down, brought him back to the meeting and said, 'We are going to do this.' Joe had to go back to his board and convince them to come up with another million dollars. Not that they hadn't already done something. It's just they had to come up with another million. Fortunately for the whole region, Joe stuck his neck out, took the risk, and the board backed him. They came up with another million dollars. And the end result is a billion and two hundred million sitting in Delta Township; a major, major, major plant being built there." And again, big celebration!

❖

CELEBRATING SUMMARY

Celebrating by marking successful milestones is critically important for building and maintaining morale and motivation and recognizing individuals at the time of certain important achievements. This stresses the importance of not waiting until the end to celebrate, when warranted; recognizing meaningful progress; and then capitalizing, of course, on bigger celebratory events at the conclusion of large-scale projects. The focus is community celebration—in a true Second Shift Model spirit—where everyone can celebrate and be involved.

The celebratory story of the Lansing Delta Assembly plant can serve as an appropriate "celebration conclusion" for this chapter. As narrated in the *Second Shift* film: "Finally, in March of 2003, the Regional Stamping Facility was complete and ready to begin operations." More pointedly, Art Baker said: "The metal is here and ready to punch. We're ready to put up the second assembly plant now and build cars."

Randy Thayer also commented on this metal issue: "Two brand-new plants, full-sized 16 hour type assembly plants. And of course, the stamping plant, there's four press lines in there. Usually when you build a stamping plant for an assembly plant, you have two. The whole idea was to make the metal for Grand River. It actually makes metal for both and ships some metal out to other assembly plants because it's more productive than they ever thought it was going to be."

Randy continued: "The new plant, we put in all the latest modern robots for welding and the body shop; same thing in the paint shop and the conveyors and general assembly with all the latest technology. The latest technology for the paint shop went in. The general assembly we put in what we called skillets in which we had the best ergonomically designed conveyor devices you can do, adjustable height between every station, lots and lots of ergo devices on the physical side. Those kinds of improvements were made, but probably the biggest thing was getting it all under one roof."

And people also noticed that they were needed, said Thayer: "A lot of people think they're going to walk into the general assembly and see a lot of robots putting cars together. I think there were a total of three. So there are very few robot cells in general assembly, what there are is a lot operator assistants, a lot of hoists, a lot of ergonomic devices. Just lots of things that help the employees do the work in a quality way and also be very productive."

Perhaps then governor Engler said it best from a big celebratory standpoint: "It couldn't be more important to have the Car of the Year being produced here in Lansing, and it really reinforces what I think General Motors has always known. And what I did always appreciate actually. They had a superior workforce or high-quality workforce. It's a hardworking group of workers here in the Lansing area. But, the structure had to change and the way they did their work had to change."

Engler went on: "So it's a big deal for the state; it's a big deal for Lansing. It's a big deal for the company. I think for a lot of people who didn't have a familiarity of twenty-first century manufacturing in America, you walk into this incredible, bright, clean, well-organized, quiet, and highly functioning facility and you are just blown away by how transformed it is. And I think, like it or not, want to admit it or not, when you see that, you kind of understand what the company was facing, the challenge they had, and what it takes to compete in a global industry that's as competitive as the auto industry is." Lansing now celebrates being at the very cutting edge of auto manufacturing plants as well as having among the most skilled auto workers in the world—not bad, not bad at all!

CHAPTER 7

—◆—

PERSEVERING

ADAPT AND ENDURE

Failures, setbacks, delays, and missed opportunities are part of any major initiative and should be expected and planned for. This is where perseverance comes in, with a focus on almost constant adapting to and enduring what is likely to come our way. Some may even call it stubbornness! For the Quick Response Team, in particular, but also the Blue Ribbon Committee, perseverance had to be a core trait. Too many people, too many issues, and too many major challenges and obstacles stood in the way of a successful outcome of having GM reverse course and stay, and the "Keep GM" campaign would not have worked without this tenacity, willingness to adapt, and commitment to endure.

Perseverance is not just an individual phenomenon and should not be monitored simply as such. Constant monitoring of group behavior is also required to detect strains in stakeholder relationships or breaks in the collaborative process. If any of the classic defense mechanisms are detected (scapegoating, rationalizing, backstabbing, projecting, or displacing), it should be assumed that participants have lost sight of the goal, don't understand the strategy or plan, or lack the courage to act or have lost hope.

The role of a leader or champion is to quickly detect the dysfunction and to continually articulate the goal, explain the strategy, demonstrate courage, and offer hope while addressing the particular issue causing concern. It is imperative that the integrity of the collaborative process be preserved and that the stakeholders feel engaged, empowered, and relevant. Preserving the collaborative problem-

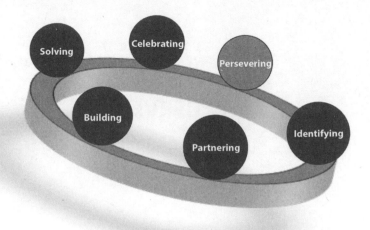

Figure 7.1　The Second Shift Model—persevering

solving process is essential to overcoming any setbacks or defeats. Figure 7.1 illustrates the Second Shift Model, highlighting the "persevering" component discussed in Chapter 7.

PERSEVERING NARRATIVE

One of the best examples of how to persevere, adapt, and endure was the leadership shown by Lansing Township supervisor John Daher. Daher faced a difficult political decision. His township included two of the aging GM plants (Plants 2 and 3) that were scheduled to be closed, and there was little likelihood that GM would rebuild in the township.

Daher's township was deeply suspicious of Lansing and had actually recalled and removed from office one of his predecessors for having a single meeting with Lansing officials to discuss possible consolidation of their separate fire departments. Regardless of these political barriers, Daher accepted the invitation to participate in both the Blue Ribbon Committee and the Quick Response Team and played a key role in the evolution of the regional collaboration.

Importantly, Daher steadfastly defended the goal of keeping GM and signed the pledge to work collaboratively for the region's best interests. Instead of criticizing and complaining about his closed plants, he continually pointed to the study by George Fulton and Donald Grimes that documented the benefits that would accrue to his township and the region with GM's continued presence. Daher became an unsung hero of the entire "Keep GM" collaborative.

Daher's collaborative spirit and confidence found a match at GM as well. As GM's Mark Hogan (vice president of GM's Car Group North America, point person on the Alero launch, and corporate leader for GM's next-generation platform and facility) immersed himself deeper and deeper in the launch of the Alero, he grew increasingly confident in the effectiveness of the Blue Ribbon Committee's "one-stop problem-solving ability." Hogan began to advocate internally for other divisions of GM to take a look at partnering with the new regional collaboration.

In the fall of 1999, Hogan had been given the additional assignment of leading GM's fast-growing e-commerce division, which had the responsibility of integrating information technology into the global platform assembly-line process, increasing productivity, cutting costs, facilitating customer online shopping and financing, developing smart car technologies, and streamlining product development processes. Within months Hogan had authorized members of the Quick Response Team to meet with and explore the potential of moving and consolidating its new e-GM operation to the Lansing region.

This was a positive turn of events and perhaps also the game changer needed. Mayor Hollister's staff began the process of laying out a rationale and business case that could be presented to Hogan and his e-GM team in early 2000. In April, Hogan was taken on a tour of five sites that met his specifications and received presentations from the Lansing Regional Chamber of Commerce, the Capital Area Michigan Works IT Council, Michigan State University, and Lansing's Planning and Development Department.

It was obvious by every measure that talent and a skilled workforce were the region's "competitive advantage." From the first "knock on the door" by Ed Donovan, virtually every conversation covered some aspect of worker training, workforce development, technology skills, and the aging workforce. Hogan was aware that Mayor Hollister had made school reform a major emphasis of his administration and had dedicated his 1998 State of the City Address to school improvement and the creation of the Commission on Lansing School Success (CLASS).

General Motors had partnered with the mayor and the Lansing School District to implement several science, technology, engineering, and math programs and had received three prestigious President's Awards for CLASS, Galaxy, and the Lansing Area Manufacturing Program. Partly due to this strong focus on talent and a skilled workforce, Hogan suggested that GM should consider locating a new North American Training Center in Lansing to leverage the significant reinvestment GM was considering in mid-Michigan.

Discussions were well under way with both the e-GM and North American Training Center when market conditions changed. On December 20, 2000, Ray Tadgerson received an e-mail from Hogan's office stating that "we must discontinue any talks regarding the possibility of relocating portions of our e-GM operations to Lansing. We would however like to reserve the right to contact you in 2001 if the situation changes." Shortly thereafter, all discussions on the North American Training Center also ended, neither project to be resumed. While disappointed, the Blue Ribbon Committee continued to innovate and problem-solve to mitigate its losses and nurture the collaborative relationship, which further gained Hogan's confidence.

Hogan was under pressure to complete the Alero launch and construct a new plant with the global platform. Tadgerson's transposition of the Blue Macaw blueprint on the old Plant 1 Townsend Street site had persuaded Hogan that Lansing was best suited for this critical corporate initiative. But while Hogan had presented his recommendation to the GM board, nothing could be finalized until the national labor agreement was adopted.

Anticipating the delays, Hogan undertook two additional initiatives designed to speed up the construction process. On a handshake with the mayor, Hogan agreed to reimburse the city for costs associated with upgrading the infrastructure at the future Lansing Grand River Assembly site if the project failed to get final board approval, and he persuaded Marilyn Nix of GM's World Wide Real Estate department to contact and encourage GM's suppliers to use the Blue Ribbon Committee's Capital Area Response (CAR) Team.

In December 2000, Marilyn Nix (then GM's director of Acquisitions & Portfolio Strategies) wrote to all suppliers: "We have been given your name by Worldwide Purchasing since you will be a supplier to our new plant in Lansing. As you make your siting decision to serve the new GM manufacturing facilities near and around the Greater Lansing Community, based on our experience, we encourage you to utilize the CAR Team to assist you during your site selection process. This group is dedicated to supporting GM's entire enterprise in the Lansing region and can bring bottom line value to your project."

Nix continued: "The CAR Team is a joint organization made up of the Michigan Economic Development Corporation (MEDC) and the Lansing Regional Chamber of Commerce (Capital Choice), and regional governmental leaders. The CAR Team will work with you in complete confidentiality. The CAR Team is set up to provide you with the following: one-stop-shopping, objective information on sites, economic incentives, labor availability, government support, housing, etc. Several suppliers who have already utilized the CAR Team have raved about the support and the relationship they have developed with local leaders, in particular Lansing Mayor Hollister. Through the CAR Team you will meet the right people, the right leaders—at the right time—who will guarantee you total customer service satisfaction."

In January 2001, Nix received a letter from Steve McNeal (CTI Logistics), which read: "Dave Kulik has forwarded to me your letter of December 18, 2000, introducing the CAR Team and suggesting the group as a resource for site selection in the Lansing area. Actually, we completed the construction of a 140,000 square foot warehouse facility in Lansing this past summer. We utilized the CAR Team for site selection and feel the success of our project and being able to meet GM's operational time-line was a direct result of the support received from Mayor Hollister and Bob Trezise. It was a pleasant surprise to find this support group in place. From my personal experience, the CAR Team is a great idea that is working."

Based on the Hogan-Hollister handshake, GM began demolishing buildings and clearing the unused portions of the Plant 1 site. Lansing officials undertook a $10 million infrastructure improvement project that would service the new "Blue Macaw" plant even though no public announcement had been made. So some positive movement was being made, and the Quick Response Team and the Blue Ribbon Committee started feeling more optimistic.

At the same time, from the outside it was a period of confusion and anxiety. The region mourned the loss of the Oldsmobile management and engineers, and later the nameplate. The region welcomed and embraced the Alero–Grand Am production but worried about what the silence from GM, the UAW, and the Blue Ribbon Committee meant. Even Blue Ribbon Committee members were shaken by the termination of the e-GM and North American Training Center initiatives and were fearful that market forces were putting the entire "Keep GM" initiative at risk.

Few community members fully understood the power of the collaboration and the trust and professionalism that each of the stakeholders brought to the endeavor. GM's invitation in July 2001 to Mayor Hollister to visit the top-secret "war room" at the GM Tech Center clearly symbolized the acceptance of him and the Blue Ribbon Committee as full problem-solving partners worthy of trust and investment. Perseverance had paid off.

REFLECTIONS ON PERSEVERING

David Hollister

Little did I realize how the "knock on the door" conversation with Ed Donovan in 1996 would challenge me and my regional partners to create a new culture of collaboration and regional problem solving to preserve our auto heritage and our way of life. For the next five years, the task of guiding the fragile regional effort never left my mind. However, what was later to become known as the Second Shift Model was time tested and proven, and my role was to nurture it, trust and empower the various stakeholders, insist on win-win solutions, remain optimistic, and provide hope!

Ray Tadgerson

At times, the campaign process was slow and methodical, and at times it seemed to be going at breakneck speed. It was therefore critically important to keep an eye on virtually every aspect of the campaign to be assured people remained on board and didn't try to do an end run to position themselves for their personal aspirations or for their respective constituents. The mayor did a great job of "herding the cats," keeping them "on the ranch," and making sure there was no "jumping off the ship."

One of the ways of ensuring loyalty to the campaign was through frequent meetings to keep everyone informed and engaged. With many moving parts, the Blue Ribbon Committee, or BRC as I liked to call it, remained intact and grew from the initial 28 members to about 50 at the peak. They all wanted to know what was happening and wanted to be a part of something so meaningful, and especially as time went on when successes were identified.

It seemed as though I was constantly assessing what was working and what was not. The mayor, the Blue Ribbon Committee, and I were vigilant about trying to understand and react to an ever-changing landscape. A classic case was when we learned that GM was going to go forward with the Grand River Assembly plant on the existing Plant 1 site. But we could not tell anyone because GM was still in negotiations with the national and local United Auto Workers union.

Since GM wanted to move quickly, Mark Hogan asked the mayor to proceed with the necessary infrastructure improvements

The Lansing Grand River Assembly complex began
construction in 1999 and began production in 2001

on a handshake agreement to reimburse the city if the plant did not get approved by the GM Board of Directors. At the time, this was viewed as a significant challenge and potentially a major risk for the city. The City Economic Development Corporation retained Capital Consultants (now C2AE) to design the multimillion dollar improvements and to oversee the construction of the projects (which ultimately were finished on time and on budget).

Perseverance was essential due to the need to have patience when the process was developing slowly and it seemed like nothing was happening. The community always wanted to know what was happening and if the campaign was successful. Tweaking the community strategy to share what could be shared was almost a daily occurrence at various times accomplished by multiple phone calls during a given day and through the weekly team meetings. Adapting to changes was an ongoing process that required careful thought and dialogue among the Monday morning team and the Quick Response Team.

It was a major sense of relief for the Blue Ribbon Committee when announcements could be made and the community could be made to feel good about the success of the campaign. Although never spoken, there was also a privately held feeling of pride and a "thank goodness we did it" feeling, especially when remembering those who openly discounted the effort as a waste of time, energy, and money. But it was more than that; it was knowing what the team felt all along—that we could do it, that we could accomplish this and make a difference for decades to come!

MAJOR CHALLENGES AND OBSTACLES FOR PERSEVERING

In the last five chapters, we have covered the major challenges and obstacles in the development and implementation of five of the dimensions of the Second Shift Model: identifying, partnering, building, solving, and celebrating. While these dimensions are discussed in detail in Chapters 2 through 6, we give a brief overview here:

Identifying in Chapter 2 addresses the notion of naming the challenge and its impact. Chapter 3 with its focus on partnering stresses the fact that meaningful relationships in the community need to be developed. Building in Chapter 4 is the strategic orientation that has to be adopted, with a "construct your strategy as you go" mantra (since time and resources demand quick action). Chapter 5 focuses on solving problems and issues that demanded that the Lansing team engage in constant problem solving. Celebrating in Chapter 6 is rather self-explanatory; the key is to mark and celebrate successful milestones in addition to what is hoped to be a successful final outcome.

That brings us to the final dimension. Perseverance is the topic of our current chapter, with a specific emphasis on adapting and enduring (which fits with the dynamic strategy focus tackled in Chapter 4).

Before we move on to the five components of persevering, we discuss the collection of major challenges and obstacles encountered in Chapters 2 through 5. After all, persevering applies to all obstacles and challenges associated with identifying, partnering, building, and solving. Plus, the components of persevering are really important drivers of the successful implementation of the Second Shift Model.

To set the stage for why the major obstacles and challenges in Chapters 2 through 5 became connected to identifying, partnering, building, and solving, we need to take a deeper, definitional look at the "-ing" portion of each of those key words. The basic form of a verb is called the infinitive. Such a verb form occurs when the word "to" is put in front of the verb, e.g., as in "I want *to identify* the challenge and its impact" (to play off the Chapter 2 title focused on "identifying"). Continuing this logic, we learned in school that verbs change according to which tense is being used. The past tense refers to things that happened in the past, and this verb form occurs (typically) when we add "-ed" to the end of the word (e.g., "identified").

Now, importantly, in the case of our framework for the Second Shift Model, the present participle refers to things that are still happening. To make the present participle, the ending "-ing" is added to the infinitive ("I am *identifying* the challenge and its impact"). The emphasis on "-ing" words in the Second Shift Model clearly stresses the ongoing ("happening") nature of the model, with the implication that resting on laurels, thinking you are done, not planning ahead, and so on, are often fatal flaws to a successful outcome. "To identify," "to partner," "to build," "to solve," and "to celebrate" imply that these activities could be done once, and then they would be accomplished. Obviously the "Lansing Works! Keep GM!" campaign called for much more "happening" than that, and thus the Second Shift Model and its ongoing focus on "-ing" became the preferred and most viable community-engaging business model. In fact, this logic also fits with the later slogan change from "Lansing Works! Keep GM!" to "Lansing Works! Keeping GM!" which was made after Lansing "won" the first plant and while trying to secure the second GM plant.

The major challenges and obstacles that were actively in focus throughout the development and implementation of the Second Shift Model came from the groupings offered in Chapters 2, 3, 4, and 5: identifying, partnering, building, and solving. The list that follows captures these major challenges and obstacles in one place in this persevering chapter; after all, persevering was something that had to be done through all these 34 challenges and obstacles.

Identifying

1. GM was ceasing operations in Lansing by 2005 due to facility age and cost of operations. The greater Lansing community and the region had never faced a major problem like this. General Motors had been a presence in town for more than 100 years.

2. Mayor David Hollister and the Lansing Regional Chamber of Commerce disagreed on how to approach GM and address the problem. It was a lengthy process to get the chamber on board to pursue the plan of "Lansing Works! Keep GM!"

3. The surrounding townships were historically at odds with the capital city of Lansing, and if GM decided to build locally, the townships would likely want a new plant to be built in their community. A shared vision for the region across neighboring communities did not exist.

4. The "Toledo Loves Jeep" campaign worked for Toledo, Ohio, but Lansing faced a totally different set of challenges. Lansing would need to create a new strategic plan that not only specifically addressed the city's issues but also involved its neighboring townships, and thus it would need to build a strategic, common-vision partnership where minimal collaboration had been present previously.

5. Mark Hogan, vice president of GM's Car Group North America, stated that he and General Motors did not want a public campaign like "Toledo Loves Jeep" and wanted no politicians involved. Both issues were a challenge to overcome—Lansing would involve politicians (with Mayor David Hollister as the champion) and would mount a full-court press in a "Lansing Works! Keep GM!" campaign. Hogan ultimately came around and became a strong supporter of the "Keep GM in Lansing" movement.

6. The Lansing mayor had an internal advisory group that met nearly every Monday morning for over 2½ years to strategize how the city should handle the various challenges as they emerged. The group included Dennis Sykes, Bob Swanson, and Ray Tadgerson on a regular basis. Others who attended periodically were Patty Cook, Jim Smierka, and Steve Serkaian. This Monday morning team spun into two critically important groups: the Blue Ribbon Committee and the Quick Response Team. The former had more than 50 community leaders at its peak, and the latter served as the "executive team" for the movement.

7. The members of the Lansing City Council were divided on whether to try to keep GM in the city. They were also sharply divided on whether to provide incentives and tax abatements. The differences were summed up with the "wine and quiche" versus "beer and bowling" comments from the council members.

Partnering

1. Moving into uncharted territory, Mayor David Hollister formed the "Blue Ribbon Committee to Retain GM," made up of notable leaders from the greater Lansing region. Many of these influential individuals had longstanding conflicting ideas and thoughts about how to address a number of issues in the community, including the looming future of GM leaving Lansing. The mayor also retained an engineer, Ray Tadgerson, to manage and direct the effort of getting everyone in agreement regarding GM's existence in the community. Hollister and Tadgerson had previously worked together on what was then called Oldsmobile Park (and now is called the Cooley Law School Stadium).

2. The Blue Ribbon Committee, initially with 28 members, grew to more than 50 people and ultimately proved to be largely unwieldy in terms of orchestrating meetings and responses to new challenges as they arose almost on a daily basis. As such, an executive team of six leaders was formed, called the Quick Response Team (QRT), but with the consequence that some Blue Ribbon Committee members felt left out. This did not help the idea of developing meaningful relationships, but it was a necessity to adopt a quick response mentality when tactically needed. Strategically, the Blue Ribbon Committee was still at the core, but the feeling of being left out created a major challenge and obstacle. Overall, though, the QRT was to respond to GM's questions and concerns quickly and thoroughly to ensure the communications lines were maintained.

3. A campaign slogan—"Lansing Works! Keep GM!"—was created and designed to have a twofold purpose: to communicate with the community and to send a message to GM. The effort included billboards, bumper stickers, a jingle, a video ad, and even license plates. Many in the community thought it was over the top and too expensive. Plus, of course, Mark Hogan had already sent a clear message that he wanted no public campaign similar to the "Toledo Loves Jeep" campaign. Lansing's challenge was to make the issue public and get community involvement while not alienating GM even more.

4. Raising money for the all-out effort to retain GM was a monumental challenge. It was estimated that Lansing needed "hundreds of thousands of dollars" for the total campaign effort, with obviously no certainty in the outcome to be achieved. At the conclusion, the fund-raising campaign brought in more than $250,000 from local organizations and the private sector along with some contributions from the local government.

5. Having a dialogue with General Motors and the United Auto Workers was a challenge in that both were concerned that the conversations among the parties would be leaked to the public or played out in public forums. What large companies say publicly becomes the rule, or the truth, and what large and influential unions such as the UAW say becomes the talking points and

strategy for members. This could have been a public relations nightmare in the making!

6. The relations between the local Lansing-based UAW and GM were known to be among the best in the country (to this day GM stands by its saying that the Lansing GM plants have among the best and most qualified workers in the company and also in the auto industry). However, the beginning of the "Keep GM" campaign also aligned with employee contract time, and GM was looking for some concessions in the new contract to become more competitive with Asian- and European-manufactured vehicles, namely fewer jobs by virtue of robotics and highly efficient plant operations. GM also wanted a two-tier wage structure and, importantly, a certain set of work rules. Without going into the technical details of these issues, these were highly contentious concessions, as viewed by the UAW, and remained in the background of the "Keep GM" campaign efforts.

7. Meetings with local UAW union leaders at the time—Art Baker, Tiny Sherwood, and Ralph Shepard—were often held behind closed doors with the understanding that whatever was said could not be shared outside that room. This level of trust was remarkable and much appreciated by everyone involved. Keep in mind that there were diverse and often conflicting interests at play. So the deal was that if anything was to be shared, it would require a conversation with the involved leaders first.

8. Michigan State University, through the efforts of President M. Peter McPherson and Vice President (for Governmental Affairs) Steve Webster, convinced 40 governmental units to sign a resolution pledging support to the "Lansing Works! Keep GM!" campaign and effort (see the Appendix). As the large, established higher education leader in the community and one of the top universities in the world, Michigan State University could adopt a broker role in getting governmental characters on all sides of an issue and both sides of the aisle to the table and to a resolution agreement. This was vital at the governmental level for the campaign.

Building

1. The members of the Lansing City Council were somewhat divided on whether to try to keep General Motors in the city, and they were also sharply divided on whether to provide incentives and tax abatements. The differences were encapsulated in the "wine and quiche" versus "beer and bowling" town comments from the council members.

2. Convincing the Lansing City Council and community representatives that keeping GM was worth the effort required an economic impact analysis to demonstrate the impact of losing GM. It also included the potential impact of building one new plant and, later, building a second plant.

3. The Lansing mayor, the Lansing Regional Chamber of Commerce, and the United Auto Workers union backed candidates for the Lansing City Council who were known to be favorable to the mayor's agenda to keep GM to replace those who were not in favor of even trying to keep GM. The result was three new council members.

4. The Lansing mayor felt that changes were also necessary on the Lansing School Board and actively sought new candidates. The result was Jack Davis being elected to the Lansing School Board, which became controversial due to a question about his residency. The school board issue was important because the board was a solution to addressing GM's concern about having an educated labor pool.

5. The launch of the Alero on the second shift was initiated by plant manager Jim Zubkus and UAW leader Art Baker. This approach was very unorthodox (no one launches new car models on the second shift!) and a high-risk effort. GM's corporate leaders were skeptical about a second shift launch (during second shift, essential personnel are working, and a bulk of the engineers and other skilled employees are not). Zubkus prevailed, and the launch was ultimately hailed as the most successful in GM's history.

6. As result of the successful Alero launch, Mark Hogan stated that General Motors would look at Lansing as a potential site for a new plant. The constraint, though, was that General Motors needed 300 acres for the new construction. There was no 300-

acre location in Lansing that would meet GM's criteria for building a new plant (ultimately the plant was built in an incredibly
efficient manner on 70 acres).

7. Controlling the media was an issue. The local newspaper, the
Lansing State Journal, was outright negative about the campaign
initially. To a lesser degree, the local TV stations were also skeptical about the "Keep GM" campaign. The *City Pulse* also had
a skeptical, negative perspective about the campaign. These
are writers, not manufacturers, but they had to be on board to
share the vision. All hands had to be on deck in the community,
including media, to make this a successful reversal of GM's decision to shut down the Lansing operations.

Solving

1. The mayor had an internal advisory group that met nearly every
Monday morning for over 2½ years to strategize on how Lansing
as a city should handle the various challenges as they popped
up. The group included Dennis Sykes, Bob Swanson, and Ray
Tadgerson on a regular basis. Others who attended periodically
were Patty Cook, Jim Smiertka, and Steve Serkaian.

2. The Blue Ribbon Committee, initially with 28 members, grew
to some 50 people and, at that stage, proved to be unwieldy
in terms of orchestrating meetings and responses to new challenges. An executive team of six leaders was formed and called
the Quick Response Team (QRT), making some Blue Ribbon
Committee members feel left out. But to create effective and
efficient solutions in a timely manner, the QRT had to be
instituted. The broad objective of the QRT was to respond
to GM's questions and concerns quickly and thoroughly to
ensure that all communications lines were maintained and
even nurtured.

3. As result of GM's successful Alero launch in Lansing, Mark
Hogan stated GM would look at Lansing as a potential site for
a new plant, but it needed 300 acres for the construction of the
plant. There was no 300-acre location in the city that would
meet GM's criteria for building a new plant. Mayor Hollister
assigned to Ray Tadgerson the task of locating a suitable site
within the city.

4. Determining whether a new plant could be built on the existing Plant 1 site in Lansing was difficult due to virtually unintelligible photocopies of a smaller facility in Brazil to work from, along with determining the number of buildings that could be torn down while maintaining the current production levels. Ultimately, the solution was the construction of the Grand River Assembly facility—a state-of-the-art and "nimble" production facility on a much smaller than normal lot but with incredibly sophisticated building structures.

5. GM wanted tax incentives from the state, but the Michigan Economic Development Corporation was handcuffed by state law, which prohibited dollars being spent on retention efforts like keeping the GM operations in the state. At the same time, the number of jobs would still be reduced if a new plant were to be built in Michigan. All in all, the Michigan legislature would need to change the law, which, of course, became a highly debated and political issue.

6. Designing and building the necessary infrastructure without a firm commitment from GM due to the lack of a national contract with the United Auto Workers union was a risky task and required creative and gutsy solutions. Basically it was a handshake between Mayor Hollister and Mark Hogan to proceed. The city spent over $7 million on utilities, roads, and environmental cleanup prior to the GM Board of Directors' approving the construction of the new plant.

7. The environmental groups in Michigan wanted to increase the emissions standards for the paint facilities at the body plant, Plant 6, also known as the Fisher Body plant, and Plant 2, site of the new SSR pickup assembly. The neighbors agreed with the environmental groups and also wanted standards beyond the EPA standards, which the Department of Natural Resources eventually enforced. The process was months long until GM changed its paint system, which enabled an agreement to be made among all parties.

8. With the success of the siting of the Grand River Assembly plant and the approval of a national UAW agreement, GM wanted to locate a second assembly plant and a stamping plant poten-

tially in the Lansing region as well, but it required a greenfield with traffic stipulations, railway access, and access to the airport. Now instead of 300 acres (which became only 70 acres when the plant was built per the Brazil model), GM wanted at least 1,000 acres, and preferably 1,200 to 1,300 acres, to provide options for future development. Locating a suitable site of this size meant examining every potential site in the tri-county area, which took several weeks.

9. GM was looking for additional incentives from Delta Township, and it appeared to reach a dead-end over a $1 million commitment that was needed. The GM representative walked out of the meeting and left the building. There was no point of return it seemed, but Mayor Hollister chased him down, lightly grabbed him by the arm, and convinced him to return. After that, negotiations went well.

10. The second plant also required Public Act 425 and Public Act 328 agreements between the City of Lansing and Delta Township, resulting in Lansing's extending utilities to the new plant. Both were groundbreaking agreements and took extensive negotiations. Townships often compete; this collaboration and extension of services was unusual and very positive.

11. The township also did not have enough resources to adequately handle the plan review for the new plant in a timely fashion. Ultimately it ended up being a shared responsibility, with the City of Lansing negotiating to have the authority for building plan review.

12. GM was concerned about workforce training and was seeking an expanded training program. It first linked with Lansing Community College. The result was the creation of Lansing Community College West Campus, a development that was widely debated before happening, largely due to cost and perceived benefit. The Ingham County Intermediate School District, United Auto Workers union, and GM created a program called the Lansing Area Manufacturing Program, which was a program for high school students to enter into the manufacturing field. This continued the solutions-oriented approach to ensuring a skilled workforce in the region. Another program

that focused on skilled labor was the CLASS program started by Mayor Hollister, an initiative to improve the quality of education through mentoring and assistance in Lansing school classrooms.

FIVE COMPONENTS OF PERSEVERING

Adapting and enduring, and always persevering, in the face of numerous major challenges and obstacles are personality traits that some have and perhaps others do not. Regardless, the Lansing mayor, the Quick Response Team, and the Blue Ribbon Committee had to adopt a collective "character" of persevering at almost any cost. The cost of not persevering was too great, and the long-term prosperity of the community was at stake. The region's leadership (in business, labor, education, local and state government, and citizens at large) knew all too well what could happen (e.g., Flint, Michigan).

Somewhat strange to the Lansing mayor and members of the Quick Response Team and the Blue Ribbon Committee, there was a contingent of people in the community—many quite vocal— that thought General Motors' announcement of shutting down in Lansing was either a negotiation ploy to get better tax deals or perhaps even a good development for the community and its efforts to focus on nonauto activities.

What some of these skeptics did not understand is that GM and its presence in the community created a tremendous multiplier effect. Much has been written about such multiplier effects in the popular press, in business outlets, and in scholarly journals, but a brief explanation here in our perseverance chapter is appropriate. Specifically, there would be the direct effect on employees at GM in the greater Lansing community of not having a job if GM were to close its doors. But there would also be the consequent effect on the contingent of employees at so-called first-tier suppliers, second-tier suppliers, and third-tier suppliers numbered in the thousands. Not only did these multilayer supplier organizations reside in Lansing and mid-Michigan in the thousands, but they also carried presence in much of the rest of the state, in the Midwest, and far beyond.

Persevering took on a superbly important meaning in the face of the adversities that GM's leaving would entail. The customer base in the region would weaken, fewer people would need products,

Persevering
(Adapt and Endure)

1. Honor Sacrifice
2. Mitigate Loss
3. Recognize Trade-Offs
4. Acknowledge Failure
5. Keep Swimming

Figure 7.2   The Second Shift Model—components of persevering

companies supplying products would not send the normal deep assortment of choices to the region's stores, and so on. To alleviate such an outcome and weakening quality of life and customer choices, persevering by adapting to and enduring any and all major challenges and obstacles was captured in five persevering components: (1) honor sacrifice, (2) mitigate loss, (3) recognize trade-offs, (4) acknowledge failure, and (5) keep swimming (Figure 7.2).

In many cases, these five persevering components are simple—at least to understand—but transparency by the Lansing mayor, the Quick Response Team, and the Blue Ribbon Committee in adopting a core focus on persevering by stressing these five components set the tone for what the community had to do to successfully change GM's decision.

Honor Sacrifice

The concept of persevering by adapting and enduring largely implies that some form of sacrifice is needed. With more than 30 community organizations, numerous influential regional leaders, and an infrastructure of the office of the Lansing mayor plus the Quick Response Team and the Blue Ribbon Committee, there was a wealth of history and knowledge among the involved parties. Each had ideas on what to do and not to do! But people have to give up their ideas and be open to other ideas at times.

For Mayor David Hollister, "trust" became the focal point in the sacrifice that was needed among the parties involved. Hollister mentioned this when honoring sacrifice came up: "Relationships are critical. I don't think people realize how important relationships are. Developing trust—trust with your team, trust with the group that's bringing the opportunity or the challenge." The bottom line was that trust had to be virtually at an all-time high to be able to end up where the give-and-take had meaning for GM to lead to a reversal of its decision to leave the community.

Honoring the sacrifice of team members, clearing the air of why and when a sacrifice was needed in each instance, and ensuring that such sacrifice would lead to a win-win for GM and the region were paramount to keeping GM in town. Also, taking someone's sacrifice lightly, and dwelling on one's own sacrifice, was not a choice. Everyone's sacrifice needed to be honored, understood, and appreciated.

Mitigate Loss

Losing is never easy, is usually not planned, and can be demoralizing, especially in efforts with such gigantic ramifications as potentially losing one of the largest companies as an employer in a region. Mitigating loss is both a way to cope with setbacks and a form of perseverance that signals to the community that we take wins and losses in stride and move forward.

This perseverance was embodied by Mayor David Hollister, his Quick Response Team members, and the Blue Ribbon Committee members. In some ways the larger community of the region's concerned citizens and leaders in business, labor, education, and local and state government—in their own mindsets—had to mitigate the losses, small and large, that were simply part of the process. While the community needed to be kept in the loop, at most stages, the community members also had to feel that they were on the team.

Captured nicely by Mayor Hollister: "It fell apart several times. You just suck it up, regroup, and get your team together to do an analysis of what's going on and you move forward. If you have a vision, and if you have got a plan, the biggest issue is perseverance. The issue is just not getting confused with winning or losing."

Winning and losing in an endeavor as important, large-scale, and public as saving GM in the region will happen. Achieving all wins (or all losses) simply is not realistic. If the expectation is to win all parts of the process, then it was not a compelling one anyway (i.e., GM would have stayed no matter what, and that was never the case). If the expectation is to lose every time, then most people would not take on such a negatively skewed activity.

James Butler, an executive with the Michigan State Housing Development Authority and member of Blue Ribbon Committee, remarked on the wins and losses in parallel to this reality: "First of all, you can realize that there's always hope, and the other thing is never give up. You know once you hear, whatever it is, devastating news or whatever, sit down and try to put a plan together. Try to figure out how many other collaborators you can work along with, and hopefully you can pull them together, sit down, and make things happen."

This notion of a strong, supportive, trusting, and perhaps even compassionate team is highlighted by David Hollister: "If you've got supportive partners, you can overcome any setback, and you will persevere over time. What you will find is the friendships and partnerships you develop will carry you through the tough times."

Also, do not undersell the community approach to solving these problems and persevering. Flint, Michigan, was hard-hit by General Motors, which drastically reduced production after a long history there. GM traces its roots to the Durant-Dort Carriage Company of Flint. At one point, Flint had the largest GM complex in the world. Over the past decades, GM plants in Genesee County (of which Flint is the county seat) have experienced renamings, management changes, openings, closures, reopenings, and spin-offs. At the peak, almost 30,000 employees of GM worked in Flint. Now the number is less than 3,000 if hourly employees are counted and just a tad more than 200 if only full-time, salaried employees are counted.

But even with Flint's devolving from an automobile-building headquarters to an almost nonexistent auto entity, Genesee County supported the Lansing efforts to keep GM. Janice Karcher, who represents the Flint and Genesee Chamber of Commerce, said: "We found Lansing to be inspiring and the basis of regional collaboration for our community, and frankly, the whole I-69 National Trade Corridor. To see that communities can succeed by coming together as a region and by focusing on the success, not only the local economies but of specific companies within their economies is very important. And, certainly, a model for how other communities can react and work together."

Karcher continued: "Mayor Hollister has been instrumental in supporting our regional efforts as we've originally needed to have support in convening the parties, and really thinking about the challenge of working together in new ways, and knowing that it's been done successfully in other areas of the state. He and other members of the Prima Civitas team, including Jim Smiertka, have helped to provide technical guidance, have helped convene and facilitate conversations about how we work together in new ways. And have also started to help us tell the story, about the successes that have been achieved so far, and the progress that's being made."

Recognize Trade-Offs

Persevering by adapting and enduring when such a large group of community leaders is involved requires recognizing that trade-offs have to be made from time to time. Perhaps not everything can be performed perfectly every time if finite resources are available. Perhaps not all people can get everything they want in a deal if finite resources are available.

Michigan's U.S. senator Debbie Stabenow hit on these issues in her commentary on the Second Shift Model and the case story of General Motors and Lansing: "We've got to get people out of their corners who are drawing bright lines in the sand, pointing at each other, blaming each other, instead of saying, 'Let's get together. Let's grow an economy where people can have great jobs, where we can make things and grow things and continue to be the world's leaders because we are benefiting from each other's strengths.' What Lansing showed is that when people understand that, great things can happen."

Persevering implies that things do not go your way at all times, and we have discussed and shown trade-offs being made throughout the first six chapters of this book. Adapting to everyone's wish lists and perceptions, enduring the good with the bad, and coming out ahead as a team and as a community were the important aspects of the "Lansing Works! Keep GM!" community engagement campaign. There were bound to be trade-offs, assuming the people involved recognized them, and those trade-offs had to be managed well enough that the target goal of keeping GM in Lansing had the greatest possible chance of succeeding.

Mayor Hollister recognized some of these trade-offs that had to be made. Specifically, as also discussed in Chapter 3 on partnering, David Hollister identified a political trade-off that had to be made, or at least a situation that had to be nurtured for the chance of keeping GM in town. There were three members of the Lansing City Council who simply did not believe that there was a chance to keep GM and that the cost of trying or even succeeding would be too high. This had the potential to become a political nightmare, and Hollister realized that he had to take on the challenge of remaking the Lansing City Council.

With the assistance of the business community, and not necessarily of the political community, Hollister created a trade-off scenario where three members of the Lansing City Council were voted off the council. In an irritated tone, Hollister pointed out the remarkable statements made by the three council members: "It became public right away, because of what the three council members said publicly, 'Well, if GM leaves us, leaves with no production, it's not a big deal." "We'll become a wine-drinking community like Ann Arbor instead of a beer community like we have always been. That was quoted in the paper [*Lansing State Journal*]," Jack Davis said.

So while the trade-off of wine and beer did not sit well with Mayor Hollister, nor frankly with most of the greater Lansing community, the strategic and political trade-off in political clout and perhaps even the political career of Mayor Hollister (and others) had to be taken on to help the cause of saving GM in the community. Larry Meyer, one of the three new council members, greatly helped the business focus of the Lansing City Council. He said: "It was the mayor who put together the community, put together regional forces, and put together a collaboration of a lot of like-minded people that said, 'Okay, for this particular mission we are all united. It can work.' Key to the Council, we went from 5–3 votes to 8–0. That doesn't mean we didn't deliberate. That doesn't mean we didn't collaborate. It doesn't mean there was not a lot of give and take, but we were united and we worked together. We were working toward solutions. It wasn't about just raising a ruckus; it was about working toward solutions." These solutions included trade-offs, but realistic and logical ones, not wine and beer issues!

Acknowledge Failure

For the avid and dedicated reader of this book, you may have noticed that how we have structured and communicated the components of the Second Shift Model has included extensive quotations from critical people in the Lansing community during the time of the "Lansing Works! Keep GM!" campaign and up to today. Interestingly, and perhaps obviously, we do not have any great quotes for this section on "acknowledging failure." Some authors would take that as a sign that we do not need the section, if no content (in our case, quotations) can be satisfactorily integrated into the storyline.

But that would not tell the full story of the Second Shift Model, and certainly not of the notion of persevering by adapting to and enduring anything and everything that might come the way of the Quick Response Team, the Blue Ribbon Committee, the mayor's office, and so on. Acknowledging failure is pretty much a requirement for future success. Strategies are developed based on a logical, compelling, and shared vision among community members, and these strategies are then implemented via concrete and tactically appropriate action at certain risk levels. Basically, if all implemented strategies have succeeded, then you likely did not take enough risks. And this is risky business! It was very clear that the "Lansing Works! Keep GM!" campaign would be complex, strategic, and high risk and would involve failures along the way. Ignoring these failures would send a strong message that perhaps the Quick Response Team and the Blue Ribbon Committee, and everyone else involved, did not operate in the now, or at least not in reality.

So acknowledging failure, elaborating on what went wrong if needed, and then moving on to the next step had to be the operating model. Such an attitude created reality and pragmatism and got the community involved in the right way. Acknowledging failure also sent a strong message that the champion and leaders recognized that a certain activity or negotiation did not go as planned but that they would try even harder and be even more committed next time. Such a "can-do" attitude also resonated with General Motors.

Keep Swimming

Keep swimming is our final component of persevering. Perhaps we should have cutely suggested "keep driving," but that would not really tell the complete story. Driving usually happens above ground on some road, street, or at least reasonable compact dirt or gravel. Swimming suggests that you can actually go under water and even drown if you stay there too long. And drowning was a distinct possibility—after all, GM had already made the decision to leave Lansing. The community was de facto drowning but just didn't realize it yet; the sentiment was more that the community was out for a dive into the abyss or uncharted territory.

The Lansing mayor and his Quick Response Team and the Blue Ribbon Committee knew better. This was about to be a drowning that would have ripple effects for decades to come. The opposite was also true: the ripple effect of GM staying would likewise be felt for decades to come. David Hollister and Ray Tadgerson—the key architects of the save GM team—believe this turned out to be a half a century of stable prosperity for the greater Lansing (and maybe even Michigan) region.

Virg Bernero, the current Lansing mayor, commented on this: "Dave Hollister made us believe that we could impact the decision [by GM to leave the Lansing region], that we could make a difference. And, belief is so important. It motivates everything we do. You know, if you don't believe, why are you going to get up and try something? If you don't believe you are going to make a difference. If you don't believe, you're not going to be able to impact it. So, it started there. And, he changes minds; and he got people to put their shoulder to the wheel and get involved."

Bernero continued: "I think that's a big part of how it rang true, the fact that we make things that make America great. The fact that we have manufacturing coursing in our blood; you've got to build on your strengths. Don't try to do something you're not. Certainly diversify, certainly stay current with it, but build on your strengths and don't be ashamed. You know, blow your own horn!"

So there was a reason to keep swimming, because Mayor Hollister and the community believed Lansing had the solution—it was the best manufacturing community in America, and it was going to let everyone, including of course GM, know about it.

At the same time, Virg Bernero said: "You've got to stay on the cutting edge too. You can't strictly stay with what worked last year. Build on your strengths and take pride. We are excited about autos. We're excited about cars. We love our cars. We love our General Motors. We love our plants. It's not made up. It's not fabricated. This is the real deal. This is the real McCoy. There is an authenticity here and I think General Motors knows it." Who wouldn't keep swimming with that sales pitch?

The bottom line is that, in the words of Virg Bernero: "GM's future and Lansing's future of course are intertwined. And, if I have anything to say about it, they'll be here for years and decades to come."

David Hollister, Ray Tadgerson, and the 50-some members across the Quick Response Team and the Blue Ribbon Committee certainly hope and expect so. As Hollister said: "The story is just beginning. We secured the future for the next 50 years and now it's up to the next generation to build on that and make it something even better." The greater Lansing community keeps swimming, and not upstream; it's downstream at a nice, innovative, and entrepreneurial pace that benefits General Motors and the many manufacturing organizations in the community.

---❖---

PERSEVERING SUMMARY

The core ideas for this chapter centered on the key words of "adapting" and "enduring" and the understanding that they had to be the focal components of the "persevering." Some may take issue with this logic. That is, some may argue that persevering takes tenacity, aggressive pursuit of goals, and stubbornness to achieve aspirations. This almost sounds like a sporting event. But the "Lansing Works! Keep GM!" campaign was not a sporting event; winners and losers could not be the outcome here. It had to be win-win to make it a success. So while tenacity, aggressive pursuit of goals, and stubbornness to achieve aspirations may be positive athletic components, they simply could not drive the perseverance in this case.

Adapting and enduring had to take the front seat in this car! Adapting to shared goals, not individual wishes; enduring patches of unknowns instead of easy scores; and striving for win-win situations and even to make others look good (perhaps even at the cost of yourself not looking so good) were more in line with the perseverance that had to be part of the fabric of the "Lansing Works! Keep GM!" campaign.

Such perseverance is not easy, may require unlearning or at least relearning certain personality traits that have been with community leaders for their whole careers, and by design brings in uncertainty, uneasiness, and oftentimes incompatibility with common logic. "Lansing Works! Keep GM!" was not an easy and normal campaign. After all, Lansing had been married to General Motors for more than 100 years. "Taken for granted" may not be totally accurate, but GM had been embedded in the culture and way of life of Lansing for so long that adapting and enduring were not commonplace when thinking about GM.

CHAPTER 8

THE SECOND SHIFT MODEL

GUIDELINES AND IMPLEMENTATION

The previous seven chapters have reviewed the dynamic process to move the Lansing, Michigan, region from a doomsday scenario, where the major manufacturer in the region (General Motors) would be closing its plants and leaving town, to a storyline characterized by hope and prosperity, where the major manufacturer, GM, would make a major investment in multiple new state-of-the-art manufacturing plants in the region. The potential outcomes were drastically different—no cars being produced in Lansing and thousands of people losing their jobs, or producing the largest number of automobiles in the world with a best-in-class workforce.

This story is set in Lansing—the capital of the State of Michigan with a population of 10 million people. So the context of this story is the capital city of a midwestern state bordering four of the Great Lakes. The landmass of the state contains more than 11,000 inland lakes. The area is spread across the Lower Peninsula, also warmly referred to as the "Mitten" because of its shape (with the mideastern region of the state identified as the "Thumb"), and the Upper Peninsula, affectionately referred to as the "UP." The Mackinac Bridge, a suspension bridge, connects the Mitten and the UP. The symbolism in this description of Michigan has strong and resonating meaning in how Lansing was able to move from a doomsday scenario to an outlook of prosperity. Mayor David Hollister and his right-hand person, Ray Tadgerson, created a dynamic, fluid infrastructure that developed bridges to all corners of the community.

But the story was not simply one of an economic development challenge; it was about getting a fractionalized, internally competitive region to work together and about reshaping the community's understanding of GM and its importance to the community. The blueprint for the civic collaboration that ensued became known as the "Second Shift Model," and the strategically focused campaign theme was communally referred to as "Lansing Works! Keep GM!"

The Second Shift Model provided both the infrastructure and road map for the greater Lansing community to stay unified and focused on the mission of "Lansing Works! Keep GM!" Out of necessity, the six-dimensional framework was constructed to solve complex community problems involving multiple stakeholders with oftentimes multiple goals. Some would see the outcome of such an approach as "being on the same page," "having the same vision," or "driving toward the same goal."

Practically, though, the Lansing community needed a solution to the looming doomsday scenario. The Second Shift Model became it, a model that is theoretically robust, practically relevant, and dynamically flexible enough to be an applicable solution to complex community obstacles and challenges involving multiple stakeholders with multiple competing goals in communities across the country and the world.

While the core dimensions of the Second Shift Model are not necessarily unique per se, they do provide an integrated and elaborate direction and structure for organizing a project with complex political and economic considerations. The six-dimensional framework that makes up the Second Shift Model is captured in Figure 8.1 and includes identifying, partnering, building, solving, celebrating, and persevering.

To recap what has been said throughout the book, *identifying* captures the idea of naming the challenge and its potential impact. *Partnering* refers to developing meaningful relationships. *Building* denotes constructing the strategy as you go. *Solving* captures the engaging in constant problem solving. *Celebrating* is the marking of successful milestones. And *persevering* denotes adapting and enduring to get the tasks done.

Not only is the Second Shift Model (Figure 8.1) appealing in its inclusiveness, but also the name itself has definitional properties

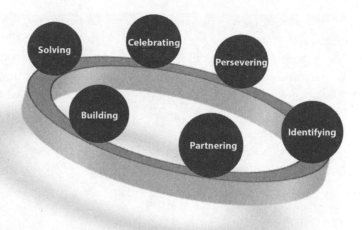

Figure 8.1   The Second Shift Model

that crystalize the sentiment, passion, and commitment of those hundreds of people involved in the "Lansing Works! Keep GM!" campaign. At the core, the Second Shift Model plays off the decision made by Jim Zubkus to launch the Oldsmobile Alero on the second shift, sending a message to GM's corporate headquarters in Detroit that Lansing had the best workforce in the GM arsenal. This captured the initial portion of the campaign theme exceptionally well—"Lansing Works!" Additionally, the Second Shift Model plays off the sociology-based notion of Lansing as a "home" community, with everyone pitching in at "home" to retain GM in the community. This exemplifies the "Keep GM!" motif of the campaign.

Now, of course, these definitional properties and this way of thinking about the "Lansing Works! Keep GM!" campaign have a degree of revisionist history to them, as we frame the storyline in the book. More practically, at the time, the campaign theme was a way to think about the collective efforts needed by the region's leaders in business, labor, education, and local and state government, as well as the emotional involvement that it would take of almost every greater Lansing (and Michigan) citizen, to keep GM in Lansing.

This collective community effort was put to the test in a city that had housed auto manufacturing for more than 100 years. It had become a way of life and was perhaps taken for granted that auto

Mayor David Hollister and Jim Zubkus, plant manager for GM's
main assembly plant and the Fisher Body plant in Lansing, at the
naming of Zubkus Way, a main access road to the GM plant

manufacturing and Lansing would stay married forever. Beyond
the deep passion for the auto sector, the jobs of most of the community depended on GM. There was a 10-to-1 multiplier effect
embedded in the Lansing auto network, meaning that for every 1
auto worker employed on a GM plant site, 10 other jobs in the supplier, transportation, and service sectors were needed to complete
the manufacturing process. Had GM left, this would have been a
massive, costly, and deeply personal divorce. Championed by Mayor
David Hollister and his go-to engineering advisor, Ray Tadgerson,
the blueprint for the solution was created. The Second Shift Model
was born.

BLUEPRINT FOR COMMUNITIES

When Mayor Hollister received the message that GM was going
to shut down its Lansing assembly operations, he could have taken
the position that once a decision is made, the automaker does not

change its mind. After all, that was the GM history, and that was the story told to Mayor Hollister in a direct and nonnegotiable way. While accepting fate would have been the easy road to take, giving up certainly did not fit Mayor Hollister's vision of making Lansing a world-class city.

The Second Shift Model is by design dynamic in nature, with feedback loops, cross-connections between the dimensions, and a reinforcing infrastructure connecting all six dimensions. Each dimension was important as a piece of the "Lansing Works! Keep GM!" campaign, but at the same time, each dimension is individually insufficient for creating the holistic solution needed in these cases. It takes the dynamic interaction and reinforcement of the collective set of six dimensions to successfully develop and implement the Second Shift Model: (1) identifying the problem, (2) partnering with the community stakeholders, (3) building the coalition, (4) solving the problems, (5) celebrating the successes, and (6) persevering through the challenges. We discuss guidelines and implementation issues related to these dimensions next, including key questions that must be addressed for each.

Identifying

The first step in addressing a challenge is to identify its scope. The broad picture of the challenge facing the Lansing mayor and Lansing's community leaders was how to convince GM to remain in the Lansing region after 2005 in light of the GM Board of Directors' decision to close aging, inefficient manufacturing plants around the country. Lansing had the oldest plant in GM's manufacturing portfolio, and the combination of a century-old plant and Michigan's union environment was a ripe situation for GM to shut down its car production as it had done in many other cities.

Carefully framing Lansing's challenge was not just Mayor Hollister's receiving what came to be called the "knock on the door" visit from Donovan in 1996, where the mayor learned about the upcoming GM exit. Identifying and communicating the magnitude of the challenge to the region was much more involved than this. Remember, at the same time, Donovan also gave the mayor the good news that the Oldsmobile Centennial would include a weeklong celebration bringing thousands of car enthusiasts to the region and that the new Alero would be built in the Lansing plant. Within this context, Donovan shared the bad news that, after the Alero had run its course in 2004–2005, there were no products for the Lansing plants, and it was GM's intent to close its Lansing operations. Basically, the Lansing community would receive a lot of mixed messages from General Motors.

The fact that the Oldsmobile Alero was about to run its course in the city and production of GM products would stop after the 2004–2005 period, not until several years after the 1996 meeting, likely would not generate urgency or a do-it-now attitude from the Lansing City Council, nor would it create any form of resolve for action among the myriad regional business, labor, education, and local and state government leaders or the community's citizens. While it was not easy to assemble a team with positive attitudes to become involved, Mayor Hollister ultimately gathered individuals from these groups to join the Blue Ribbon Committee.

For the mayor's leadership team and the Blue Ribbon Committee to move the region forward, it was critical to identify the key constituents and characterize their perspectives. This allowed the team to develop a synergistic approach to meet the various challenges.

Despite the State of Michigan having a history of being collaborative with automakers, the concept of using state funding to retain jobs resulted in many implications that Governor Engler was not initially excited about. An investment to retain a reduced number of jobs in Lansing would open the state up for expectations of similar investments in many more communities around the state. In addition, while the Lansing Car Assembly plant was located in the City of Lansing, there were many other cities and townships, specifically Delta Township and Lansing Township, in the region that benefited significantly from GM operations. The regions' political entities appeared to collaborate, but in reality there was substantial suspicion and distrust. Basically, the City of Lansing, it was perceived, was out to develop a solution that would optimize its financial base while taking resources from the other communities.

In the case of the local populace, there was a wide range of perspectives. There were some who recognized the regional impact of the loss of the plant, while there were others who didn't take the possibility seriously, and yet others who thought GM's departure would be better for the community. It was clear that there was no consensus in the community, and this presented an initial challenge for Mayor Hollister's team. The community really needed to be in agreement and have most of its citizens buy into a shared vision for the "Lansing Works!" Keep GM!" campaign. Thankfully, for Lansing citizens, an eye-opener was the Fulton-Grimes study that illustrated clearly that Lansing faced a dire outlook in infrastructure, finances, and quality of life if GM shut down the plants. This report provided the data needed to develop the required consensus.

The five identifying principles that characterized the constituency group's challenges included the need to (1) understand the corporation (GM), (2) know state policy (tax relief and support), (3) pinpoint regional conflict (among the many townships and neighboring communities), (4) recognize public sentiment (was Hollister believable in his reporting, and even so, did the public think it would matter if GM left?), and (5) quantify the impact of a potential GM shutdown. The mix of constituency groups, regional context, and metrics made the naming of the challenge and its impact unusually difficult given the multiple layers of complexity, stakeholders, and even timing (e.g., elected officials seldom consider the impact of their decisions more than a decade out).

The specific questions requiring answers to identifying the challenges were:

- What is the challenge? GM indicated that it was leaving Lansing—was it really?
- Can the challenge be met and solved, or do we not take on the fight and just let GM go?
- Who are our adversaries among GM, the chamber, the city council, other neighboring townships, labor unions, business, and citizens?
- Who are our strategic advocates?
- Who will lead the charge—the mayor, the local chamber, the state, private enterprise?
- Whom can we learn from? Who else has been through this?
- How can we organize? What is the structure, and who needs to be involved?

- What is our strategic plan and plan of action for team members?
- What is our communications strategy and plan? How do we address the positive and negative issues appropriately?

Partnering

Historically, once the executives at GM decided to close a plant, they did not change their minds, and there was little anyone in the affected communities could do. GM generally deliberated, carefully evaluated, and nurtured any strategic idea internally and under nondisclosure agreement confidentiality until the firm was ready to publicly unveil its decision. In many respects, this is still the operating model for impactful strategic decisions at GM today.

Reversing a strategic decision of the world's largest corporation at the time was a monumental challenge, particularly since the greater Lansing region had no history of or mechanism for regional problem solving. Instead, what the region had—as many regions around the country can relate to—was a relatively large number of community organizations, multiple leaders tackling various community sectors, and a number of business leaders with differing perspectives regarding how to move the community forward.

But the greater Lansing region (and really mid-Michigan) was at risk of losing one of its major employers unless it could set aside old grudges and turf issues and embrace collaborative initiatives. The region's leaders in business, labor, education, and local and state government, as well as citizens at large, needed to come together and let GM know how vitally important it was to the region and why continuing to do business in Lansing was in GM's best interest. This was more than reaching out to GM in a coherent way; this required strategically "selling" GM on the notion that the decision was wrong for logical and compelling business reasons. No one wants to lose a large employer like GM, but the region had to demonstrate why the decision was strategically wrong for the firm; that had to be the position, and very compelling justification had to follow.

With a starting point of a disconnected collection of concerned citizens and regional leaders in business, labor, education, and local and state government, developing meaningful relationships and strategically partnering across "party lines" was a must. Without such unity, why would GM believe it should, or even care to, engage in a dialogue with the greater Lansing community about potentially reversing a strategic decision that had been carefully evaluated? As such, to engage GM in a meaningful partnership would require extraordinary leadership, commitment to the goal of keeping GM, a detailed plan of action, and strong cooperation and collaboration.

Combining the eloquent and important perspective offered by MSU president Lou Anna K. Simon that "you can never take what you have for granted, particularly in this very complex global marketplace," with the optimistic and sales-oriented pitches of U.S. senator (and MSU alumnus and Lansing native) Debbie Stabenow and current Lansing mayor Virg Bernero makes for a great outlook for the future. Simon, Stabenow, and Bernero collectively send a strong message to remember where we have been and to nurture where we are going. Mayor Hollister's win-win mantra and approach to achieving that mantra via meaningful relationships and strategic partnerships that can get the tasks accomplished—no matter how big—follow in the path of this optimism.

Partnering involves (1) reaching across boundaries, (2) seeking out champions, leaders, and expertise, (3) practicing inclusiveness, (4) building trust and mutual respect, (5) sharing common goals and vision, (6) keeping disputes private, and (7) providing hope and courage.

The specific steps for partnering were:

- Begin with a team of confidants to formulate the immediate strategies and communication plans.
- Recruit the most influential team members to help recruit others and deliver the message.
- Utilize the influencers to recruit others and help counteract negativity.
- Identify the team of influencers as a blue ribbon committee (the Blue Ribbon Committee to Retain GM) to emphasize the team's importance and structure.
- Identify the executive team (the Quick Response Team) to be the decision-making body to represent the larger Blue Ribbon Committee.

- Partner with other cities and communities to learn what can be replicated.
- Partner with the local GM leadership.
- Partner with the leadership of the United Auto Workers union to learn about GM's structure and decision making.
- Partner with GM's executive leaders in Detroit to gain their confidence.

Building

While the community generally agreed with the goal of the "Keep GM" effort, it had no mechanism to engage in regional problem solving and definitely no mechanism to build a clear strategy for doing so. It was necessary to develop the strategy at the same time as the team went about keeping GM.

Hollister and his team wanted GM to keep building cars in Lansing in the same robust way it had been done for more than 100 years. However, nothing was robust about the strategic start— "construct the strategy as you go" had to be the way this project was tackled. There was no other choice, as time was of the essence, and being responsive to GM and the community demanded strategic thinking at the highest level.

The starting point to build some form of coherent strategy was launched with the fact-finding trip to Toledo, Ohio, on January 13, 1998. A delegation of 14 business, labor, and community leaders joined Mayor Hollister to learn how Toledo had reversed Chrysler's decision to move its Jeep assembly operation out of the city. The *Lansing State Journal* and all four local Lansing TV stations had staff go along to cover the trip.

Hollister summarized the group's findings in a January 20, 1998, memorandum to the Lansing City Council: "Mayor Finkbeiner appointed David Wallace, a respected businessperson and engineer, to coordinate all community efforts and to report to him directly. Mr. Wallace organized a proactive technical work group that included all federal, state and local agencies involved in site development and began weekly meetings. Mr. Wallace worked with the Mayor to develop a Quick Response Team. This community effort, united by the Mayor, was made up of political, educational, business, service and community leaders to begin a public campaign to retain Jeep."

Mayor Hollister reinforced his sentiments forcefully in his State of the City Address the very next week, on January 26, 1998, when he stated: "My goal is for General Motors to build its new plant right here in the City of Lansing, and I commit to doing everything in my power to make it happen!" The focus was not only on retaining but also on building and reinforcing the relationship between GM and Lansing.

Going to Toledo fired the "starting gun" for the race to keep GM in the greater Lansing community. On the return trip to Lansing, Hollister asked Ray Tadgerson if he could put together a plan for Lansing that was similar to Toledo's. Tadgerson said yes, and within two weeks the Blue Ribbon Committee to Keep GM was announced. Toledo and Chrysler served as a skeleton starting model for Lansing and General Motors, but the Lansing story has complexities and nuances that carry deeper and into more fascinating areas than what could be expected from the Toledo learning experience. Nevertheless, Toledo was the starting point to think strategically and act deliberately for the Lansing community.

From there, the "construct your strategy as you go" really worked well for the Lansing community. Building a strategy and sticking with it would not have been flexible enough to solve all issues that came up, and it would also not have allowed for appropriate identification of problems at all stages of the ordeal, or have created win-win situations for the community's strategic partners in this endeavor. The latter notion of win-win was important.

Without any doubt, the primary goal of the campaign was to create a win-win scenario whereby all the involved parties felt the region was benefiting from the effort to retain GM. This required unique communication strategies for each specific constituency, e.g., surrounding city and township governmental units, the Lansing City Council, the business community, GM, local and regional UAW units, the media, state government, Michigan State University (as the large Big Ten university in the region), Lansing Community College (as the core workforce development trainer in Lansing), neighborhood associations, the nonprofit community, and the general public. Basically, there were a lot of entities that had to be in on the win-win strategy, and they had to feel and know that win-win was the primary goal of the "Lansing Works! Keep GM!" community engagement campaign.

The core strategy was to bring the most influential team members on board to help with the campaign. While difficult, to say the least, the most influential members had to be convinced to buy in, to work hard, and to be passionately involved. There was no strategy, not yet a shared vision, and so constructing the strategy on the go depended on the brightest minds in the region and the most diverse set of people being involved to cover all essential and potential topics that could come up. Look at the major challenges and obstacles described here, and it is easy to realize that a dynamic strategy was essential to survival.

Now, some were more than willing to help, while others, unfortunately, joined just to see what was going on and to potentially protect their turf. Nearly all had their own agenda and constituencies to represent. As expected, it took several different strategies, several different tries to build a strategy, to address these various agendas. Given that the campaign was a one-of-a-kind (with a starting point from the Toledo case), nearly all planning was developed on an "as-you-go basis," and so a key to the "Lansing Works! Keep GM!" campaign's success was the dynamic strategy development process of the Second Shift Model.

The changing environments of the economy, GM, and the region also required the strategy to be based on sound data to build credibility and then be refined as the dynamics changed. The Lansing community had to buy into the idea of going hard after GM and advocating strategically to GM to change its decision to leave the community. First, the Fulton-Grimes Michigan economic analysis study was used to provide credible benchmark data. The numbers, by most accounts, were staggering and very supportive. There were 7,000 direct jobs at GM locally, affecting 20,000 indirect jobs locally and 50,000 jobs in the rest of the state—these are numbers that most people can understand. The bottom line was that for every GM job in Lansing, 10 more people had jobs in related, supporting roles to the GM operation.

Overall, the Fulton-Grimes study provided unbiased and credible information regarding what the GM assembly operation meant to the Lansing region and what would be the implications if it left. After all, Fulton and Grimes were University of Michigan professors, located in Ann Arbor. The impartial and objective study also provided insights regarding the billions of dollars a new assembly plant would mean to the region.

Second, a communications strategy that facilitated collaboration between the Blue Ribbon Committee and GM, while keeping the other stakeholders (regional politicians and citizens) appropriately informed regarding the implications of a potential plant closure, was created. This resulted in the "Lansing Works! Keep GM!" campaign.

Third, the strengths and weaknesses of the region were determined, and the benefits of those strengths to GM were demonstrated. Fourth, the substantial importance of the Lansing workforce assets were demonstrated to GM. Fifth, the responsibility for change was delegated to key members of the Blue Ribbon Committee, making them accountable for successful completion of that component of the initiative. Sixth, leaders were identified who had the judgment to prudently manage the process. Finally, the leadership team had to share credit regarding the successes and accept responsibility for the situations where the strategy was not optimal.

The specific steps for building were:

- Bring the Blue Ribbon Committee together and build momentum by making the campaign very public; communicate to GM and the public that the region was going to do whatever it took to get GM officials to change their minds.
- Emulate Toledo by bringing on an engineer to provide the operational coordination.
- Launch the campaign.
- Maintain the momentum with ongoing and appropriate information sharing.
- Continue to build the team by bringing in additional influences.
- Extend and strengthen relationships across the Blue Ribbon Committee to help carry the win-win message and build support for the campaign.

Solving

While it was obvious that the greater Lansing community needed to rally to convince GM to reinvest in mid-Michigan, the bigger challenge was the lack of a mechanism for regional problem solving. GM and its suppliers needed a single place that they could go to in their effort to confront and resolve the multiple issues facing their business and industry transformation. What emerged was a a single-entry, single-exit, inclusive, comprehensive, regional, collaborative, one-stop problem-solving group committed to win-win solutions.

At his January 26, 1998, State of the City Address, the mayor announced that he was creating a Blue Ribbon Committee to Retain GM and a "Lansing Works! Keep GM!" community engagement campaign. At a subsequent press conference, Mayor Hollister reiterated his vision of convincing GM to change its mind about leaving Lansing and the region. The mayor and members of the Blue Ribbon Committee also presented an organizational chart regarding how the campaign would be organized. The chart included six subcommittees and the Quick Response Team. The Quick Response Team served as the executive committee for the Blue Ribbon Committee. Subcommittees were also set up to be problem solvers and respond to whatever challenges arose. These included the Labor Advisory Committee, Government Advisory Committee, Regional Focus Team, Technical Team, Economic Analysis Team, and Public Relations Team. Ray Tadgerson served as project manager for all aspects of the Blue Ribbon Committee, served on the Quick Response Team, and provided strategic and technical advice and support.

Initially, the Blue Ribbon Committee met weekly, then biweekly, then monthly, and eventually on an as-needed basis. With such a large group, 20 to 40 busy influential people (and more than 50 people involved at one point), it was difficult to get everyone to attend a weekly or biweekly meeting. It was also difficult to reach consensus with so many varied opinions and personal agendas about what needed to be done, and how and when. Concerns also existed about confidentiality and leaking of sensitive information to the public and parties who should not have access to such information. To offset the confidentiality risks, the mayor chose to rely on his closest confidants, dubbed the "Monday morning team," to help identify priorities that would be shared with the Quick Response Team and the Blue Ribbon Committee.

The Monday morning team met early every Monday morning for about 2½ years, and sporadically thereafter, to identify what needed to be done during the coming week, review progress over the past week, and discuss items remaining on the to-do list. The meetings resulted in an ongoing outline of what was "hot" and needed immediate attention as well as a detailed list of all things to be done, big or small. Out of these meetings, an agenda was created for the Quick Response Team. The Quick Response Team would then determine who would address the issues and when, and develop the agendas for the larger Blue Ribbon Committee meetings.

Engaging in constant problem solving became the mantra for the Blue Ribbon Committee, but especially for the Quick Response Team. The process was years in the making, and often without a clear end or outcome in sight, or even, at times, an idea of what the outcome really could or should be, which meant that a constant core focus had to be on problem solving. Even with the great unknowns, the region's leaders in business, labor, education, and local and state government, as well as citizens at large, when needed, saw it as their call of duty to engage.

Within the Second Shift Model, the constant problem solving—regardless of the players involved, and there were many—built on six core areas. These included (1) anticipating challenges, (2) maintaining capacity to respond in a crisis, (3) looking for collaborative win-win solutions, (4) managing communication, (5) establishing a unified voice with a single point of entry and exit, and (6) building more partnerships.

The specific steps for solving were:

- Let GM, the UAW, the Lansing Regional Chamber of Commerce, the Lansing City Council, the townships, and the citizens know there is a plan to partner in a win-win way.
- Solve the resource challenge by raising private funds to support the campaign.
- Gain confidence in the region by developing figures regarding the economic implications of plant closures or openings.
- Develop a communications strategy using billboards, video, radio jingles, press releases, and print media with a message that we are all in this together—everyone can win. (Internet and e-mailing were in their infancy, and social media did not exist.)

- Solve the footprint and site issue by investigating the strategies used in other regions where newer technology has been used.
- Use informal agreements to facilitate site restoration prior to formal agreements.
- Solve the legislative issue by working with the legislature to allow tax abatements and incentives for job retention as well as for new jobs.
- Solve environmental issues by working with all parties including the Environmental Protection Agency, state and local agencies, GM, neighbors, schools, and the public to reach a satisfactory solution.
- Solve the issues of infrastructure and tax sharing using land-sharing agreements between the city and surrounding townships.

Celebrating

To "celebrate" traditionally means to do something special or enjoyable for an important event, occasion, or holiday. A celebration acknowledges and praises individual and group achievements and goal attainment and is generally reserved for the end of a process. This is especially true in the individualistic U.S. society, where goal attainment is the ultimate objective, and perhaps the process of getting to the goal takes a secondary focus. However, celebration really has a much deeper meaning and potential for uplifting spirits, especially in a community-based project such as the Second Shift story captured in this book.

Celebration is important because it lifts morale and helps sustain individuals and groups by reaffirming the goal, strategy, plan, and community's resources and assets. Knowing that changing a GM board decision would be difficult and complicated, it was important to build celebration into the overall community strategy. Instead of focusing on the end goal that was likely three to five years away, it was decided that the community would acknowledge and celebrate the region's strengths, resources, assets, and heritage as well as the progress of the mayor, the Quick Response Team, and the Blue Ribbon Committee.

There were many milestones in the process that gave the team a sense that progress was being made. These needed to be celebrated somehow. Unfortunately, it was also true that many of the successes achieved could not be shared with the public in the greater Lansing community or even with the Blue Ribbon Committee for fear of compromising the campaign, either with GM or with the UAW. Limits on what could be shared had to be well thought out so as not to create false hopes. Nevertheless, celebrating by marking successful milestones was an important part of what ultimately turned out to be the Second Shift success story.

Celebrating by marking successful milestones is critically important for building and maintaining morale and motivation and recognizing individuals at the time of certain important achievements. This stresses the importance of not waiting until the end to celebrate. When warranted, recognize meaningful progress and then capitalize, of course, on bigger celebratory events at the conclusion of large-scale projects. The focus is community celebration—in a true Second Shift spirit—where everyone can celebrate and be involved.

The new General Motors plants included modern robotics for welding and the body shop. Similarly for the paint shop, the conveyors and general assembly had all the latest technology. The general assembly used skillets that had the best ergonomically designed conveyor devices to adjust height between every station. While there were substantial technological improvements, the most significant change was getting it all under one roof.

People also noticed that they were needed. Many thought that they would walk into the general assembly and see a lot of robots assembling cars. However, there appeared to be a total of three. There were very few robot cells in general assembly, but there were many devices to assist operators such as hoists and ergonomic devices— lots of things that help the employees do the work in a quality way and also be very productive. "Lansing Works!" was a direct effort to stress the world-class quality of the Lansing workforce, and these new plants did just that.

The specific steps for celebrating were:

- Celebrate both the small and major victories and both intermediate and final outcome achievements.
- Celebrate overcoming environmental concerns.

- Celebrate the election of political representatives who can represent neutral policy positions.
- Recognize the continued investments by GM in the community (which included an additional $1 billion put into the Lansing Grand River and Lansing Delta Township plants and the relocation of Camaro production to Lansing. The original three plants totaled over $2 billion, and an additional $1 billion has been invested since then).

Persevering

Failures, setbacks, delays, and missed opportunities are part of any major initiative and should be expected and planned for at all times. This is where perseverance comes in, with a focus on almost constantly adapting to and enduring what is likely to come. Some may even call it stubbornness! For the Quick Response Team, in particular, but also among the members of the Blue Ribbon Committee, perseverance had to be a core trait. Too many people, too many issues, and too many major challenges and obstacles stood in the way of a successful outcome of having GM reverse course and stay; and the "Keep GM" campaign would not have worked without this tenacity, willingness to adapt, and commitment to endure. There were many times where some members of the Blue Ribbon Committee felt that they would not be able to overcome the conflicts, but they persevered. The result was a successful ending that allowed everyone to celebrate.

Perseverance is not just an individual phenomenon and should not be monitored simply as such. Constant monitoring of group behavior is also required to detect strains in stakeholder relationships or breaks in the collaborative process. If any of the classic defense mechanisms are detected (scapegoating, rationalizing, backstabbing, projecting, or displacing), it should be assumed that participants have lost sight of the goal, do not understand the strategy or plan, or lack the courage to act or have lost hope.

A leader's or champion's role is to quickly detect the dysfunction and to continually articulate the goal, explain the strategy, demonstrate courage, and offer hope while addressing the particular issue causing concern. It is imperative that the integrity of the collaborative process be preserved and that the stakeholders feel engaged, empowered, and relevant. Preserving the collaborative problem-solving process is essential to overcoming any setbacks or defeats.

Few community members fully understood the power of the collaboration and the trust and professionalism that each of the stakeholders brought to the endeavor. GM's invitation in July 2001 to Mayor Hollister to visit the top-secret war room at the GM Tech Center clearly symbolized the acceptance of him and the Blue Ribbon Committee as full problem-solving partners worthy of trust and investment. Perseverance had paid off.

In the context of the Second Shift Model, persevering entailed (1) honoring sacrifice, (2) mitigating loss, (3) recognizing trade-offs, (4) acknowledging failure, and (5) keeping momentum ("swimming").

The specific steps for persevering were:

- Remember that the campaign is always about creating win-win scenarios for all strategic parties and working through the many challenges that arise.
- Remember that the campaign could have failed many times due to various adversaries feeling that the campaign was a waste of time, money, and energy.
- Build on hope, courage, specific goals, and a dynamic strategy. Doing so, the mayor, the Quick Response Team, and the Blue Ribbon Committee maintained a "never say never" attitude. This meant that even if the GM officials did not change their minds, the effort was built on positives in bringing the region together, which would likely provide future benefits.

CONCLUSIONS

At the time of the GM announcement, there was an initial shock in the greater Lansing community to learn that General Motors really was leaving. The announcement took on added weight when the community started to learn about the 10-to-1 multiplier effect that GM had in the community (for every 1 GM job, 10 more jobs are created) and when it was told that when GM made a strategic decision like this, it never changed its mind.

This was gut-check time. Did Lansing and the region have what it takes to take on one of the largest corporations in the world? In this period, GM was Fortune's number one ranked company at some $168 billion in annual sales. There were times when the challenges and obstacles seemed insurmountable. The "Lansing Works! Keep GM!" team would deliberate every challenge and define a strategy attacking the problem; seek out those who could add expertise, knowledge, or other resources; and then pursue the win-win solution.

In the beginning, there was no strategy, no model, and no infrastructure for a solution. The Jeep scenario in Toledo was a blueprint, given its successful outcome, and there were certainly some takeaways from Toledo; but the "Lansing Works! Keep GM!" effort required a new strategy and new thinking. As a result, a new model was born, the Second Shift Model.

This model was built on team building with an adaptive "think on your feet" strategy to be flexible and reactive to whatever happened. As the campaign evolved, so did the model. As the model was refined through the campaign, the critical components became apparent. The key differentiators are rooted in being regional, being transparent, having a single-entry, single-exit voice, being communicative, and advocating comprehensive one-stop problem solving to design and implement a win-win solution. It has been identified as a model that can be used by communities in the United States and the world to help solve complex challenges with political and economic implications.

David Hollister, the mayor at the helm during the "Lansing Works! Keep GM!" campaign, is optimistic for the future, and his friends in the Lansing community are as well. Hollister said: "The story is just beginning. We've secured the region's future for the next 50 years, and now it's up to the next generation to build on that and make something better."

In fact, he went even further: "There's no limit to what this community can do. With the combination of expertise of representatives from business, state government, academia, and strong neighborhoods with citizens committed to this community, you have within the region enough economic and population density to make it pretty much whatever you want it to become."

Hollister's highlighting of academia is appropriately reflected by then Michigan State University president Peter McPherson. He said, on October 8, 1998, "Michigan State University's GM connection started in the early part of this century [early 1900s], and it continues today— through research partnerships, through our graduates who work for the company, and in many other ways."

Sanjay Gupta, now dean of MSU's Eli Broad College of Business, points out the current significance in the GM-MSU business relationship: "Continuous collaboration between MSU's Eli Broad College of Business, General Motors, and the greater Lansing community has become a way of life and part of the community's fabric."

At the same time, Mayor Hollister also warned today's community leaders: "The challenge will be to overcome those regional turf issues and continue to build a more strategic economically feasible governmental operation. There's some enormous challenges, but what we've been able to achieve shows that it can be done. Just have a vision, have a process, and go to work," he said.

What we have captured in this story of 807 pages, or some 330,500 words, of interview notes involving the best and the brightest minds in the greater Lansing (and Michigan) community, and the countless

Groundbreaking at the Lansing Delta Township
Assembly complex that opened in 2006

hours of capturing and codifying the Second Shift Model, definitely reflects this. Hollister, his right-hand advisor, Ray Tadgerson, and their team set the tone for how to partner and how to develop meaningful relationships across boundaries, seeking out champions in the process, practicing inclusiveness as much as possible, building trust and mutual respect, creating shared common goals, keeping disputes private, and always providing hope and courage.

When they started the process, the members of the Blue Ribbon Committee stated that "Lansing is a great place to invest, live, work, recreate and raise a family." This rings true more than ever! A 35-year, second-generation veteran of GM, born in Lansing, who has been at the Lansing Delta Township Assembly during the 10 years it has been open and, prior to that, at the Lansing Car Assembly for 25 years, summarized it succinctly and appropriately: "Lansing needs GM and GM needs Lansing."

FORTY REGIONAL PARTNERS ENDORSE THE RESOLUTION TO SUPPORT THE LANSING WORKS! KEEP GM! MOVEMENT

NEWS ADVISORY FROM

LANSING WORKS!   KEEP <u>GM</u>!

For Immediate Release
October 8, 1998

Contact: Mayor's Office   483-4141
           MSU Govt. Affairs   355-5060

UNPRECEDENTED REGIONAL AGREEMENT FOCUSES
ON RETAINING GENERAL MOTORS IN LANSING AREA
Forty Regional Partners Endorse Resolution

Michigan State University President M. Peter McPherson and Lansing Mayor David C. Hollister today joined with government officials and organizations from across the Lansing area and announced the approval of a region-wide resolution on intergovernmental collaborative efforts to keep General Motors in the area.

President McPherson, Chairman of the Intergovernmental Subcommittee of the Lansing Works! Keep <u>GM</u>! Campaign, said, "Michigan State University's 'GM connection' started in the early part of this century, and it continues today - through research partnerships, through our graduates who work for the company, and in many other ways. We greatly appreciated the chance to team up now with our local communities, all of whom also have positive and mutually beneficial relationships with General Motors, in this important effort."

Mayor Hollister said, "Never before has the Lansing region united to support such a vital initiative. Every person living in this area will be impacted by GM's decision and I am very proud of the collaborative spirit in this resolution."

Governor John Engler said, "I am in regular contact with GM in an effort to convince them that locating this plant in the Lansing area makes sense for their future and I will be in contact with them again at the appropriate time. What's more, my administration is working closely with Mayor Hollister and other community leaders on the Blue Ribbon Committee to craft a proposal that will convince General Motors that a new plant belongs here."

The resolution recognizes that:
* the Lansing region was the birthplace of the automobile manufacturing industry in part due to R.E. Olds' accomplishments; and
* all Lansing-region communities have benefited economically from the 100-year history of quality automobile production; and
* excellent labor/management relationships between the U.A.W. and General Motors have been a hallmark of the Lansing plants; and
* the current plants and skilled workforce made the Lansing area the "Car Capital of North America" in terms of both the quality and quantity of cars produced.

-MORE-

The resolution commits to making the retention of General Motors manufacturing facilities a top priority and agrees to a collaborative effort among units of government in the Lansing region to keep General Motors.

QUOTES FROM REGIONAL LEADERS ON THE LANSING WORKS! KEEP GM! RESOLUTION:

Joe Drolett, Supervisor, Delta Charter Township
It is imperative that all municipalities in the Lansing region work together to keep GM in the area. We have been working on this important goal for over a year and I trust we are making good progress.

Brett Bernard, Mayor, City of Grand Ledge
GM is an economic cornerstone of Grand Ledge and the entire Lansing region. As one of the area's largest employers, the job loss would be devastating. Many companies provide supplies and services to GM; a move would cause ripple effects throughout the community.

Richard Starck, Mayor, City of St. Johns
Many of our residents work for GM or are associated with companies that do business with GM. Consequently it is vital for us to keep these jobs in the tri-county region.

John Berchtold, City Manager, Charlotte
What happens to GM affects Charlotte because we are part of the regional economy. Our mayor and council strongly support any effort to keep GM in the Lansing region.

Russell W. Whipple, Mayor, City of Mason
General Motor is the hub in the wheel of economic activity from Mason to St. Johns to Ionia to Howell and beyond. As public leaders we must make the effort to understand the needs of GM and to meet those needs to the best of our ability. I do not know what it would take to recover from the devastation to the economy of the region that might result from the loss of GM and we should all shudder at the thought of facing such a challenge. Let's continue to work together to keep GM!

Bruce Little, Supervisor, Meridian Charter Township
We don't have any GM facilities, but we do have a lot of GM employees residing in Meridian Township. We will do whatever it takes to keep GM in the region.

Mary Stid, Chairperson, Tri-County Regional Planning Commission
GM and its employees in the Lansing/Tri-County region assure that we remain economically competitive in a global market.

-MORE-

LANSING WORKS! KEEP <u>GM</u>!

Regional Resolution

To Support Efforts to Retain General Motors

WHEREAS, the Lansing region was the birthplace of the automobile manufacturing industry because of the ingenuity and entrepreneurial genius of R.E. Olds; and

WHEREAS, all of the communities in the Lansing region have enjoyed the economic benefits of a 100-year history of quality automobile production; and

WHEREAS, excellent labor/management relationships between the UAW and General Motors have long been a hallmark of the Lansing plants; and

WHEREAS, our current plants and our skilled workforce have made the Lansing area the Car Capital of North America in terms of both the quantity and quality of cars produced; so now

THEREFORE BE IT RESOLVED, that we commit to making the retention of General Motors manufacturing facilities a top priority and agree to work collaboratively with other units of government to keep General Motors in the Lansing region.

Carl Levin, United States Senator
State of Michigan

Spencer Abraham, United States Senator
State of Michigan

Debbie Stabenow, Congresswoman
State of Michigan

Nick Smith, Congressman
State of Michigan

David C. Hollister, Mayor
City of Lansing

John M. Engler, Governor
State of Michigan

Lansing Regional Chamber of Commerce
300 E. Michigan Avenue, Suite 300
Lansing, Michigan 48933

tel: 517.487.6340
fax: 517.484.6910

Dianne Byrum, Senator
Michigan Senate

Mike Rogers, Senator
Michigan Senate

John J.H. Schwarz, M.D., Senator
Michigan Senate

Laura Baird, Representative
Michigan House of Representatives

Lingg Brewer, Representative
Michigan House of Representatives

Alan L. Cropsey, Representative
Michigan House of Representatives

Frank M. Fitzgerald, Representative
Michigan House of Representatives

Terry Geiger, Representative
Michigan House of Representatives

Dan Gustafson, Representative
Michigan House of Representatives

Clark A. Harder, Representative
Michigan House of Representatives

Lynne Martinez, Representative
Michigan House of Representatives

Tony Benavides, Council President
Lansing City Council

Mark Meadows, Mayor
City of East Lansing

Joe Drolett, Supervisor
Delta Charter Township

Bruce A. Little, Supervisor
Meridian Charter Township

John Daher, Supervisor
Lansing Charter Township

Leonard Peters, Chair
Eaton County Board of Commissioners

Richard Hawks, Chairman
Clinton County Board of Commissioners

Linda Sims, Chair
Ingham County Board of Commissioners

Sharon C. Peters, President
Lansing Board of Education

Dr. John Tomlanovich, Superintendent
Eaton Intermediate School District

Jann Jencka, Superintendent
Ingham Intermediate School District

David L. Brown, Mayor
City of Charlotte

Harry R. Ammon, Township Supervisor
Delhi Charter Township

Michael Towns, Mayor
City of DeWitt

Donald C. Colestock, Mayor
City of Eaton Rapids

Brett Bernard, Mayor
City of Grand Ledge

Russell W. Whipple, Mayor
City of Mason

Richard Starck

Richard Starck, Mayor
St. Johns City Commission

James DeForest

James DeForest, Mayor
City of Williamston

Mary R. Stid

Mary R. Stid, Chair
Tri-County Regional Planning Commission

Michael D Chappell

Michael D. Chappell, Chair
Dimondale Village Council

Abel B. Sykes Jr.

Abel B. Sykes, Jr., President
Lansing Community College

Peter McPherson

Peter McPherson, President
Michigan State University

Membership List: *Lansing Works! Keep GM! Regional Resolution*

Contact	Company	Job Title
David L. Brown	City of Charlotte	Mayor
Michael Towns	City of DeWitt	Mayor
Mark Meadows	City of East Lansing	Mayor
Donald C. Colestock	City of Eaton Rapids	Mayor
Brett Bernard	City of Grand Ledge	Mayor
David Hollister	City of Lansing	Mayor
Russell Whipple	City of Mason	Mayor
Richard Starck	City of St. Johns	Mayor
James DeForest	City of Williamston	Mayor
Richard Hawks	Clinton County Board of Commissioners	Chairman
Harry R. Ammon	Delhi Charter Township	Supervisor
Joe Drolett	Delta Charter Township	Supervisor
Leonard Peters	Eaton County Board of Commissioners	Chairman
John Tomlanovich	Eaton Intermediate School District	Superintendent
Linda Sims	Ingham County Board of Commissioners	Chair
Jann Jancka	Ingham Intermediate School District	Superintendent
John Daher	Lansing Charter Township	Supervisor
Tony Benavides	Lansing City Council	Chairman
Abel Sykes	Lansing Community College	President
Sharon Peters	Lansing School District	President
Bruce Little	Meridian Charter Township	Supervisor
Laura L. Baird	Michigan House of Representatives	Representative
Lingg Brewer	Michigan House of Representatives	Representative
Alan L. Cropsey	Michigan House of Representatives	Representative
Frank M. Fitzgerald	Michigan House of Representatives	Representative
Terry Geiger	Michigan House of Representatives	Representative
Dan Gustafson	Michigan House of Representatives	Representative
Clark A. Harder	Michigan House of Representatives	Representative
Lynne Martinez	Michigan House of Representatives	Representative
Dianne Byrum	Michigan Senate	Senator
Michael J. Rogers	Michigan Senate	Senator
John J. H. Schwarz	Michigan Senate	Senator
Peter McPherson	Michigan State University	President
John M. Engler	State of Michigan	Governor
Mary Stid	Tri-County Regional Planning Commission	Chair
Nick Smith	United States House of Representatives	Congressman
Debbie Stabenow	United States House of Representatives	Congresswoman
Spencer Abraham	United States Senate	U.S. Senator
Carl Levin	United States Senate	U.S. Senator
Michael D. Chappell	Village of Dimondale	Chairman

INDEX

ABOUT THE AUTHORS

David Hollister served as Mayor of Lansing, Michigan from 1994 to 2003, until he became Director of the Michigan Department of Labor and Economic Growth in then Michigan Governor Jennifer Granholm's administration. During his tenure as Lansing Mayor, Hollister championed the movement to keep GM in the Lansing area; GM building the Grand River Assembly Plant; and GM replacing the Lansing Car Assembly Plant which dated back to 1903.

Ray Tadgerson is former CEO and President of C2AE, Project Director of the Blue Ribbon Committee to Retain GM, Coordinator of the Mayor's Quick Response Team, and Senior Advisor to Mayor David Hollister for the "Lansing Works! Keep GM!" campaign.

David Closs is Professor, McConnell Endowed Chair, and Chairperson of the Department of Supply Chain Management in the Eli Broad College of Business at Michigan State University. He serves on the State of Michigan's Commission for Logistics and Supply Chain Collaboration and regularly works with the State of Michigan on economic development. Dr. Closs is one of the world's leading authorities on logistics, supply chain management, and value chains.

Tomas Hult is Professor, Byington Endowed Chair, and Director of the International Business Center in the Eli Broad College of Business at Michigan State University. He is also Executive Director of the Academy of International Business, President of the Sheth Foundation, and serves on the U.S. District Export Council, Lansing Regional Sister Cities Commission, Lansing Economic Club, and the Global Business Club of Mid-Michigan. He regularly works with the State of Michigan on economic development and making Michigan companies globally competitive. Dr. Hult is one of the world's leading authorities on global strategy, global supply chain management, and marketing management.